NESLISHAH

NESLISHAH

THE LAST OTTOMAN PRINCESS

MURAT BARDAKÇI

The American University in Cairo Press
Cairo   New York

This paperback edition published in 2019 by
The American University in Cairo Press
113 Sharia Kasr el Aini, Cairo, Egypt
200 Park Ave., Suite 1700, New York, NY 10166
www.aucpress.com

Dar el Kutub No. 26169/18
ISBN 978 977 416 929 8

Dar el Kutub Cataloging-in-Publication Data

Bardakçı, Murat
        Neslishah: The Last Ottoman Princess / Murat Bardakçı.—Cairo: The American
University in Cairo Press, 2018.
        p.   cm
        ISBN: 978 977 416 929 8
        1.   Neslishah, Fatma, 1921–2012
        2.   Princesses—Turkey
        3.   Turkey—History—1960
        923.1

1 2 3 4 5   23 22 21 20 19

Designed by Adam el-Sehemy
Printed in the United States of America

Contents

Turkish Spelling and Pronunciation

Turkish names of places and persons in this book are spelled in the Turkish manner, except for Neslishah (Neslişah) and Istanbul (İstanbul).

Approximate pronunciation of special characters in the Turkish alphabet:

c   as *j* in *jacket*

ç   as *ch* in *chair*

ş   as *s* in *sugar*

ı/I   as *a* in *about*

i/İ   as *ee* as in *feet*

ö   as in German *König*

ü   as *u* in French *tu*

ğ   lengthens a preceding vowel

Ottoman Titles

An Ottoman emperor had the title *Sultan*, which preceded his given name, as in Sultan Vahideddin. He would be addressed as *Efendimiz*.

The sons of the emperor were called *Şehzade* (Imperial Prince), while the daughters used the title *Sultan* (Imperial Princess) following the given name, as in Neslishah Sultan.

In addressing a şehzade, his first name was followed by the word *Efendi*, as in Faruk Efendi. The imperial princesses were addressed as *Sultan Efendi*.

The sons of the şehzades retained the title of their fathers, the daughters used the title *Sultan*, while the sons of the imperial princesses were known as *Beyzade* or *Sultanzade* and their daughters as *Hanımsultan*—they were princes and princesses, but of a lower status than a şehzade or a female sultan.

Ottoman dynastic law was patrilineal, whereby the affiliation to the dynasty was passed from father to son and continued through the male line. All şehzades and female sultans were members of the imperial dynasty, while the children of the hanımsultans and the sultanzades were not members of the dynasty but only part of the Ottoman family. The same was true of the wives of the sultans, who used the title *Kadınefendi*.

At the beginning of the Ottoman Empire, the succession to the throne was based on the system of primogeniture, whereby the first born son of the sultan became the ruler of the empire. Later, senior-ity prevailed and the oldest male member of the dynasty inherited this position.

Neslishah's Family Tree

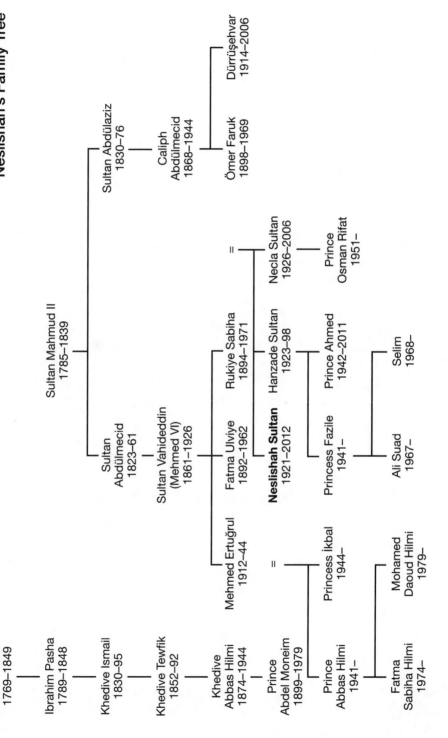

Who's Who

Abbas Hilmi II (Alexandria 14 July 1874 – Geneva 20 December 1944): The son of Khedive Tewfik Pasha and the father of Prince Mohamed Abdel Moneim. Egypt's last khedive and Neslishah Sultan's father-in-law. Deposed by the British in 1914 for his unfaltering allegiance to the Ottoman Empire. He died in exile.

Abdülmecid Efendi (Istanbul 30 May 1868 – Paris 23 August 1944): The son of Sultan Abdülaziz, the cousin of Sultan Vahideddin, and the last Ottoman caliph. The father of Prince Ömer Faruk Efendi and Princess Dürrüşehvar. The father-in-law of Sabiha Sultan, daughter of Sultan Vahideddin. The grandfather of the princesses Neslishah, Hanzade, and Necla, as well as the princes Barakat Jah and Karamat Jah.

Ali Haydar Bey Germiyanoğlu (Istanbul 20 September 1889 – Istanbul 1968): Sultan Vahideddin's son-in-law through his marriage to the sultan's eldest daughter Princess Ulviye. Ali Haydar was her second husband.

Amr Ibrahim (Cairo 18 April 1903 – Montreux 1977): Egyptian prince. The husband of Necla Heybetullah Sultan, Neslishah Sultan's youngest sister and Prince Osman Rifaat Ibrahim's father.

Dürrüşehvar Sultan (Istanbul 26 January 1914 – London 7 February 2006): Ottoman imperial princess, daughter of the Ottoman caliph Abdülmecid Efendi and sister of Prince Ömer Faruk Efendi, who became the son-in-law of Sultan Vahideddin. Princess Dürrüşehvar was Neslishah's aunt and married Azam Jah, son of the nizam of Hyderabad, Osman Khan.

Emine Nazikeda Kadınefendi (Sohum 9 October 1866 – Cairo 1944): Sultan Vahideddin's first wife and last *baş kadın efendi* (title given to the first wife of the sultan) of the Ottoman Empire. The mother of Ulviye Sultan and Sabiha Sultan.

Farouk (Cairo 11 February 1920 – Rome 18 March 1965): The son of King Fuad and second king of Egypt. He ascended the throne at the age of sixteen upon his father's death. Some members of the Egyptian royal family thought it suitable that he should marry Neslishah Sultan. After the Free Officers' revolution of 23 July 1952 he was exiled to Europe and died in Rome while having a meal in a restaurant.

Faisal (Baghdad 2 February 1935 – Baghdad 14 July 1958): The third and last king of Iraq. While engaged to Princess Fazile Ibrahim, the daughter of Neslishah Sultan's sister, Hanzade Sultan, he was murdered during the revolution in Iraq together with other members of his family.

Fuad (Cairo 26 March 1868 – Cairo 28 April 1936): The son of Khedive Ismail, the brother of Hussein Kamel, who was appointed sultan of Egypt by the British in 1914, and the father of King Farouk. Fuad was the first king of Egypt: on the death of Sultan Hussein Kamel in 1917 he succeeded him to the throne, and in 1922 changed the title of *sultan* to *king*.

Gamal Abd al-Nasser (Alexandria 15 January 1918 – Cairo 28 September 1970): An Egyptian army officer who with the Free Officers ended the Egyptian monarchy with a military coup on 23 July 1952. After the coup, he became the head of the Revolutionary Council as well as the Prime Minister, and from 1956 until his death, he was the president of Egypt, influencing the entire Arab world with his radical politics. In 1956, he nationalized the Suez Canal, but in 1967 during the Six-Day War, he was bitterly defeated and had to relinquish the Sinai peninsula.

Hanzade Sultan (Zehra Hanzade İbrahim Osmanoğlu; Istanbul 19 September 1923 – Paris 19 March 1998): Imperial princess, the granddaughter of the last sultan Vahideddin and the last caliph Abdülmecid Efendi, the second daughter of Sabiha Sultan and Prince Ömer Faruk Efendi, and the sister of Neslishah Sultan and Necla Sultan. Married to Prince Mohamed Ali of the Egyptian royal family. The mother of Princess Fazile Ibrahim and Prince Ahmed Rifaat Ibrahim.

Hümeyra Hanımsultan (Suade Hümeyra Özbaş; Istanbul 4 June 1917 – Kuşadası 17 May 2000): The only daughter of Ulviye Sultan, daughter of Sultan Vahideddin, and his first granddaughter. Married to Halil Özbaş, who came from a well-known family of Söke (Izmir). She was the mother of Hanzade and Halim Özbaş.

Mahmud Namık Efendi (Istanbul 23 December 1913 – Cairo 13 November 1963): Imperial prince, the grandson of Sultan Reşad and the son of Şehzade Ömer Hilmi Efendi. In 1959 he was accused of taking part in a conspiracy against President Gamal Abd al-Nasser of Egypt and was condemned to fifteen years in prison with hard labor. He died in the famous Tora Prison in Cairo.

Mohamed Ali Ibrahim (Cairo 29 April – Paris 2 July 1977): Egyptian prince, the husband of Hanzade Sultan, Neslishah's sister. The father of Princess Fazile Ibrahim and Prince Ahmed Rifaat Ibrahim.

Mohamed Ali Tewfik (Cairo 9 November 1875 – Lausanne 18 March 1955): The son of Khedive Tewfik, brother of Abbas Hilmi II, the last khedive of Egypt, and uncle of Prince Abdel Moneim, Neslishah's husband.

Mehmed Ertuğrul Efendi (Istanbul 5 November 1912 – Cairo 2 July 1944): Imperial prince, Sultan Vahideddin's only son from his second kadınefendi Şadiye Meveddet Hanım. When the sultan went into exile, he took only Ertuğrul Efendi with him. Ertuğrul Efendi fell sick during a tennis match and died a few hours later.

Mohamed Abdel Moneim (Alexandria 20 February 1899 – Istanbul 29 December 1979): Egyptian prince. The son of the last khedive of Egypt, Abbas Hilmi II. After the 1952 military coup in Egypt, he was appointed regent. Neslishah Sultan's husband, and the father of Prince Abbas Hilmi and Princess İkbal Moneim Savich

Necla Sultan (Necla Heybetullah Amr Osmanoğlu; Nice 6 May 1926 – Lisbon 6 October 2006): Imperial princess, the granddaughter of the last sultan Vahideddin and the last caliph Abdülmecid Efendi. The youngest daughter of Sabiha Sultan and Şehzade Ömer Faruk Efendi. The sister of Neslishah Sultan and Hanzade Sultan. She was married to Prince Amr Ibrahim and mother of Prince Osman Rifaat Ibrahim.

Neslishah Sultan (Fatma Neslişah Osmanoğlu; Istanbul 4 February 1921– Istanbul 2 April 2012): Imperial princess, the granddaughter of the last sultan Vahideddin and the last caliph Abdülmecid Efendi. The oldest daughter of Sabiha Sultan and Şehzade Ömer Faruk Efendi. She married the last regent of Egypt, Prince Abdel Moneim, who was the son of Abbas Hilmi II, the last khedive. She is the mother of Prince Abbas Hilmi and Princess İkbal Moneim Savich.

Ömer Faruk Efendi (Istanbul 27 February 1898 – Cairo 28 March 1969): Imperial prince, son of the caliph Abdülmecid Efendi and older brother of Dürrüşehvar Sultan. In 1920, he married Sabiha Sultan, Sultan Vahideddin's daughter; they divorced in 1948. He was the father of the princesses Neslishah, Hanzade, and Necla. He died in exile in Egypt, but in March 1977 his remains were moved to Istanbul and buried in the tomb of Sultan Mahmud.

Osman Khan (Hyderabad 6 April 1886 – 24 February 1967): In 1949 India annexed the state of Hyderabad, where Osman Khan of the Asaf Jah dynasty had ruled for thirty-seven years as the last nizam of the realm. He was the father-in-law of Dürrüşehvar Sultan and Nilüfer Hanımsultan.

Sabiha Sultan (Rukiye Sabiha Osmanoğlu; Istanbul 2 April 1894 – Istanbul 26 August 1971): Imperial princess, the youngest daughter of Sultan Vahideddin. Married and divorced Prince Ömer Faruk Efendi, the son of the caliph Abdülmecid Efendi. Sabiha Sultan was the mother of the princesses Neslishah, Hanzade, and Necla.

Ulviye Sultan (Fatma Ulviye Germiyanoğlu; Istanbul 11 September 1892 – Izmir 25 January 1967): Imperial princess, the oldest daughter of Sultan Vahideddin. She married and divorced the son of the grand vizier Tevfik Paşa, İsmail Hakkı Bey. Her second husband was Ali Haydar Bey, a member of the Germiyanoğlu family. Ulviye Sultan was the mother of Hümeyra Hanımsultan.

Vahideddin (Mehmed VI Vahideddin; Istanbul 2 February 1861 – San Remo 16 May 1926): The last Ottoman sultan. The father of Ulviye Sultan, Sabiha Sultan, and Ertuğrul Efendi. The father-in-law of Prince Ömer Faruk Efendi and the grandfather of Neslishah Sultan, Hanzade Sultan, Necla Sultan, and Hümeyra Hanımsultan.

Zeki Bey (Adapazari 188? – Nice 1930s): The brother of İnşirah Hanım, who was married to Sultan Vahideddin for four years, until he divorced her in 1909. Zeki Bey accompanied the sultan in exile, and there managed to spend all of the sultan's money to the last penny. In 1926 he was accused of murdering the chief physician Reşad Paşa. He was arrested in Italy and then released. In Turkey, he was judged in absentia and condemned to death. He committed suicide in Nice, while living in the house of Ömer Faruk Efendi, Sultan Vahideddin's son-in-law.

Preface

Princess Neslishah Osmanoğlu, the granddaughter of the last Ottoman sultan Vahideddin and the last caliph Abdülmecid Efendi, was the last Ottoman princess to be given the official title of *Sultan* before the fall of the Ottoman Empire, which had lasted for six centuries. Born on 4 February 1921, her name was recorded in the Register of the Ottoman Dynasty, and a golden commemorative coin was issued in her honor.

After Neslishah, no other female sultan or şehzade would ever be documented in the Register, as the empire had come to an end and the Ottoman Dynasty would now become just a family.

The biography of Neslishah, the subject of this book, is based on documents as well as on her recollections. It is not only one of the first detailed biographies of a member of an imperial ruling family whose empire has been terminated but it also illuminates the history of the Middle East, and in particular of the Egyptian royal family. And it is the story of the last Ottoman sultan, the last caliph, and their families, and in a way the sequel to my book *Şahbaba*, first published in 1998.

The Great War began in 1914 and lasted four years. Millions of people lost their lives, while millions of others witnessed unprecedented hardship and destruction. The war saw the downfall of empires as well as the end of their dynasties. The defeated Kaiser Wilhelm of Germany and Emperor Charles of Austria, together with their families, the Hohenzollerns and the Habsburgs, were forced to live in exile for many years. The Romanov rulers of Russia had a more tragic fate, the last Czar Nicholas and his family—men, women, and children—being executed by a Bolshevik firing squad.

The Ottomans were also among those who lost their throne. On the morning of 17 November 1922, the last sultan, Mehmed Vahideddin, left Istanbul on the British warship *Malaya*, and sixteen months later, in March 1924, all other members of the Ottoman dynasty were expelled, for a period that would last twenty-eight years for the women of the family and fifty years for the men.

Neslishah, then three years old, was among those who were exiled. Twenty-three years later, as a princess of another country, she was able to visit Turkey again, but she had to wait a further seventeen years before she was able to settle down to live in the country of her birth.

When in exile, though she had her moments of glory and some years of luxury, Neslishah led a difficult life: she often faced financial problems, political turmoil, and troubles that even included being taken from her palatial residence to a military tribunal. But the hardest part for her to endure were all those years away from her native land.

The reader, while savoring Neslishah's eventful life, will encounter another distinctive feature of her character—the strong, deeply-rooted feeling of identity provided by her family. She was brought up with the values of an Ottoman imperial princess and never relinquished those values, whatever the circumstances.

In addition to Neslishah Sultan's story, there are snapshots here of other lives that were often eventful and at times miserable. The imperial prince Ömer Faruk Efendi, the imperial princess Sabiha Sultan, other Ottoman princes, Prince Abdel Moneim and the Egyptian princes and princesses, and even attendants like Mrs. Burdukoff are some of the characters described in this book.

The keystones of this book are the live recordings of the long conversations with Neslishah Osmanoğlu that I had throughout the years. In this book, the princess's own words are introduced by the phrase: "Neslishah recalled." On rare occasions when I thought a phrase was disconnected, or an event was in need of clarification, I have made some amendments, but all in all, I have given special care to retain the original wording, exactly as it was spoken.

The hardships that Sultanefendi, as we used to call Neslishah Sultan, endured during her long and eventful life did not lessen her energy or prevent her from providing me with her unyielding help and support while preparing this biography. Month after month, with no sign of fatigue or boredom, she made available documents and photographs from her family archive, which she had graciously allowed me to consult years before. My gratitude toward her is endless. By the same token, I would like to extend my heartfelt gratitude and thanks to her daughter Princess İkbal Moneim, who was always present during our long working sessions.

Neslishah's mother, Sabiha Sultan, in her unpublished memoirs, wrote in reference to the historical role played by the Ottoman dynasty: "Today is the day of the foundation of the republic. Our family has done its duty and passed on. . . . The empire was a different era, but it belonged to the Turks just as today's republic belongs to the Turks."

Prologue

"I miss my toys! Let's go back home! I want to go home!"

A three-year-old girl, choking herself to tears while trying to hide behind the curtains in the stationmaster's room at Çatalca train station, was shouting, "Let's go home!" It was as if she sensed that something was wrong, as if she knew that her parents were in deep trouble.

A few ladies moved toward her, as her mother said, "We are going in a little while, my child. Look, the train is waiting for us." Then the Swiss nurse picked her up in her arms and with a strong German accent whispered in French, "Ne criez pas ma cherie, ne criez pas!"—Don't cry my darling, don't cry! Eventually, her weeping gave way to a tranquil doze in her nurse's lap.

The little girl was not the only one crying in the stationmaster's room. Some ladies timidly perched on the edge of the chairs were silently drying their tears with exquisitely embroidered handkerchiefs in their trembling hands, trying hard to stifle their sobs.

There were others who managed to refrain from crying. The little girl's mother was one of them. A few days before traveling, she had locked herself in one of the many rooms of her *yalı*—a mansion on the shore of the Bosphorus—in Rumelihisarı, where she cried constantly, thinking about what the future would hold for her and her family. The more she thought about it, the more frightened she was and the more she wept. Then she told herself, "On the day of our departure I have to

1

be strong. Crying is unseemly, and I don't want people to rejoice while watching my tears."

She put her decision into action with an unbending will; from the station in Çatalca where she boarded the train until she heard the whistle blowing and the sleeper in motion, not one tear ran down her cheeks.

Hours later, when the little girl woke up in the arms of her nanny, the train that was carrying them into exile had already reached Bulgaria. She had not seen the soldiers surrounding the Çatalca station saluting her, saluting her mother, or the other passengers for the last time.

As soon as she woke, the child looked for her mother and found her sitting just in front of her. Her mother was smiling, but there were tears in her eyes. Again she thought that something was just terribly wrong, but her childish mind prevented her from reasoning any further.

"Come on darling," said her mother. "Miss Brunner will give you dinner and then you may play with your cousins. Hümeyra and Osman are both here with us."

Once she finished her meal she went into another compartment with her nanny, and then together with her cousins she ran along the narrow corridors of the train, until the three of them were utterly exhausted.

Finally, she slept again. When she woke up this time, even Bulgaria was well behind them.

All this happened on the evening of 10 March 1924. Neslishah Sultan was three years old when together with her mother Sabiha Sultan, her younger sister Hanzade Sultan, and other relatives and members of the Ottoman family she had to leave Turkey. That child lived to the age of ninety-one, and lived a life of splendor and opulence equal to none, yet trouble, sorrow, distress, and tribulation never left her side.

Part One

Turkey

A Cold Night in March

1
Waiting for Oğuz Osman

On 3 July 1918 Sultan Mehmed V Reşad passed away after nine years and two months as ruler of the Ottoman Empire, having ascended to the throne on 27 April 1909. He was succeeded by his only living brother, Mehmed Vahideddin, seventeen years his junior, who ascended the throne with the name of Sultan Mehmed VI.

The fifty-seven-year-old new sultan was to be the last sovereign of the Ottoman Empire, which had lasted six centuries, and for years to come Mehmed VI's role and place in history would be the subject of contentious debates.

Throughout his childhood, his youth, and even during his middle age, Sultan Vahideddin had financial difficulties and worries. He was less than six months old when he lost his father Sultan Abdülmecid and four years old when his mother Gülistu passed away. He grew up with nannies, female servants, and tutors. During the thirty-three years of his brother Sultan Abdülhamid's reign he lived under the Palace's close scrutiny, like the rest of the Ottoman Dynastic family. Every step he took, every move he made was strictly monitored.

Although he was no spender, there were times when his allowance was insufficient and he would be obliged to ask his older brother the sultan for help.

Şehzade Vahideddin was Sultan Abdülmecid's forty-second and last son. At his father's death, he was tenth in line of succession to the

Ottoman throne. It was therefore unthinkable that he would one day rule the empire.

According to the traditions of the seraglio, upon the sultan's death his children, his wives, and all the women of his *harem* were immediately removed from the palace and sent to other mansions and manors. After Sultan Abdülmecid's death on 25 June 1861 rule passed to his brother Abdülaziz, so all the former sultan's wives and children left Dolmabahçe Palace and moved elsewhere.

One of Sultan Abdülmecid's wives who had to leave the palace was Gülistu Kadın, who with her two children, five-year-old daughter Mediha and five-and-a-half month-old Vahideddin, took up residence in a palace on the waterfront of Eyüp, where she died four years later in an outbreak of cholera. Şehzade Vahideddin Efendi and his sister Mediha were now left without a mother, a father, or a home.[1]

The children were entrusted to two of the wives of Sultan Abdülmecid: Mediha Sultan was given to Kemaleddin Efendi's mother Verdicenan and Vahideddin Efendi to Şayeste Hanım. The little prince had a rough time with his overbearing stepmother, and at the age of sixteen, he left his stepmother's mansions with the three attendants who had been serving him since childhood. He moved into one of the apartments of the Feriye Palace in Ortaköy, built to lodge members of the Ottoman family who did not have a mansion or a home of their own.

As an orphan, Vahideddin Efendi had to educate himself. He took private lessons, he read a great deal, and he was interested in various subjects, including the arts, which was a tradition of the Ottoman family. He took courses in calligraphy and music and learned how to write in the *naskh* script and to play the *kanun* (a kind of zither). Then he became interested in Sufism, and unknown to the Palace he followed courses at the madrasa of Fatih on Islamic jurisprudence, Islamic theology, interpretation of the Qur'an, and the Hadiths, as well as in Arabic and Persian. He attended the dervish lodge of Ahmed Ziyaüddin Gümüşhanevi, located not far from the Sublime Porte, where Ömer Ziyaüddin of Dagestan was the spiritual leader, and he became a disciple of the Naqshbandi sect.

During his youth his closest friend was Şehzade Abdülmecid Efendi, the son of his uncle, Sultan Abdülaziz. But sadly in the years to come the two cousins became unyielding rivals.

Before moving to the Feriye Palace the prince had lived briefly in the mansion in Çengelköy owned by Kemaleddin Efendi, a son of Sultan Abdülmecid. Sultan Abdülhamid then bought this eighteenth-century estate in the silent hills of the Bosphorus for Vahideddin—his younger brother—and registered the deed of the property in his name.

During the reign of Sultan Abdülhamid, Vahideddin Efendi was considered to be the sultan's closest brother. In the years to come, when the young prince ascended to the throne, this closeness would greatly influence his political attitudes, such as his intense dislike of the Young Turks and the Union and Progress Party, and his sympathy for the British. Likewise, when faced with situations where conditions were conflicting, his general attitude of wait-and-see, rather than making hasty decisions, was also due to the influence of his older brother. Even during the War of Independence, when he was accused of being a "supporter of the English," his overall outlook was based on Sultan Abdülhamid's political legacy.

On the Çengelköy estate given to him by his brother, Vahideddin Efendi had another house built for Şayeste Kadın, with whom he had spent his childhood: even though he had not got along well with his stepmother in the past, he could not forget the struggle she had gone through while bringing him up. He drew the plan of the house himself and had it built by a craftsman named Süleyman. Then he had his own house pulled down and he commissioned the well-known Levantine architect Alexander Vallaury to design the new one, where the internal apartments of the house were planned by him. Due to financial difficulties he was unable to finish the construction himself, but eventually with the help of his brother Sultan Abdülhamid he managed to complete the building, though not its furnishing.

Vahideddin Efendi resided in Çengelköy with his family and servants until he became the sultan. Away from the city and from its inhabitants, he lived a solitary life. In the beginning, during the winter months he would move to the Feriye Palace, returning home for the summer, but eventually he stayed in Çengelköy all year round, going to town once or twice a year on special occasions or on official duties. Even when he became heir apparent to the throne, he declined to move to Dolmabahçe Palace, or to any other palace, but continued to live on his Çengelköy estate, where in various pavilions of the garden he bred rare and exotic fish in large aquariums. He also kept monkeys in the garden and maintained a farm adjacent to the forest behind the property.

One day in his twenties, visiting his older sister Cemile Sultan (1843–1915) at her palace in Kandilli, Vahideddin Efendi saw a young girl whose eyes were the color of honey and whose long auburn hair flowed softly down to her slender waist. Her name was Emine Marshan, an Abkhazian princess born in Sukhumi in 1866, the daughter of Prince Hasan Bey Marshan. She had been brought to Istanbul as a young child, where her father entrusted her to the seraglio together with her wet-nurse. She was then sent to the palace in Kandilli of Cemile Sultan, where her Caucasian name, according to the custom at the Ottoman court, was changed to Emine Nazikeda.

Cemile Sultan's youngest daughter Fatma Hanımsultan had tuber-culosis, and Emine Nazikeda became her closest companion: Cemile raised the girls together as if both were her own. Nazikeda's Caucasian nanny remained with Emine even as she grew up, although she had been told that she could return to Caucasia if she wished. Her reply was clear: "Hasan Bey would ask me why I had abandoned his daughter and would raise hell and even kill me should I do such a thing," and she stayed on at the palace, remaining with Emine Nazikeda until she died.

Vahideddin Efendi fell deeply in love with this barely seventeen-year-old Abkhazian girl. According to the rumors, it was love at first sight. The young şehzade asked his sister to give him the girl in marriage, but Cemile Sultan flatly refused. She did not want her sick daughter Fatma Hanımsultan to be deprived of a companion, and at the same time she was afraid that her brother would eventually take a second wife after Nazikeda, whom she considered as her own daughter. "I shall not give my girl to an imperial prince. Not to you, and not to anyone else," she said.

However, after more than a year of the şehzade's pleading Cemile Sultan eventually acceded to her brother's demand, but on one condition: Vahideddin had to swear that he would not take a second wife. The young prince took the oath requested by his sister, and on 8 June 1885 celebrated his marriage to Nazikeda in one of the palaces of Ortaköy. The groom was twenty-four while the bride was nineteen years old.

After the wedding, the young couple went to live in one of the palaces of Feriye, where they spent several years in a three-story wooden mansion. One night, a fire started—no one knows how—and spread into Vahideddin Efendi's apartments. The young şehzade, still in his nightgown, watched with sorrow as all his belongings turn to ashes. The only things he could save were a tortoise-shell tray with gold handles, a sunstone hookah, and an inkstand in solid gold, which he had been using since childhood, made to order for his grandfather Sultan Mahmud and used by him as well as by Sultan Abdülmecid.

Now there was only one place they could go: the mansion in Çengelköy, where work was still unfinished due to lack of funds. But that is where they moved, and where they spent their days riding for hours in the vast premises behind their house. In the evenings, in the privacy of his apartments, the şehzade would engage in religious conversations with the ulema (Muslim scholars) or be entertained by a *fasil* concert (a form of classical Ottoman music) given by his music-loving servants or by famous musicians of the time who would come to his mansion to play.

All these activities, however, were under the strict surveillance of the Palace at Yıldız, that is to say of his older brother, Sultan Abdülhamid. The informers waiting outside Vahideddin's residence in Çengelköy notified the Palace of the identity of all visitors, using the post office in Üsküdar. There are several of these reports in the Ottoman archives.[2]

The couple's first daughter, Fenire, was born in 1888 but sadly lived only a few weeks. She was followed by Fatma Ulviye, born on 11 September

1892, and two years later, on 19 March 1894, by Rukiye Sabiha. The doctors told Nazikeda that she would not be able to bear other children after this third birth.

In the years to come, Vahideddin would wed other women, but all his marriages would be made with the consent of his first love, Nazikeda. Even though at the time her husband's succession to the throne was unlikely, Nazikeda knew very well that a şehzade had to have a male heir and therefore each time accepted his wish to remarry. By doing so, of course, Vahideddin broke the vow he had made to his sister Cemile Sultan.[3] None the less, upon his ascension to the throne he gave Nazikeda the title of Başkadınefendi (head wife), and his respect toward her never failed. Nazikeda would always be the "last empress," and even during Vahideddin's years of exile in San Remo, his daily routine was to visit the room of his first wife, which was on the same floor as his apartment, to drink his morning coffee with her.

Years later, on 5 October 1912, Vahideddin Efendi had his first and only son, Şehzade Mehmed Ertuğrul, whose mother Meveddet Hanım then took the title of *ikinci kadınefendi* (second wife). The young şehzade's fate was to be no brighter than his father's: in 1944, at the age of thirty-two, after an unidentified illness that lasted only one day, he passed away in Cairo.

During the reign of Abdülhamid II, between 1876 and 1909, it would have been sheer fantasy to imagine that one day Şehzade Vahideddin Efendi would ascend to the throne. His older brother Murad V, who had been deposed in 1876, had first been imprisoned at the Çırağan Palace. When Ali Suavi raided the palace in an attempt to reinstate the dethroned sultan, Murad was transferred to the Feriye Palace, where he lived as a prisoner together with his family. Sultan Abdülhamid's other brothers Reşad Efendi, Kemaleddin Efendi, and Süleyman Efendi, all older than Vahideddin, as well as Yusuf İzzeddin Efendi, his uncle Sultan Abdülaziz's oldest son, all came before him in the line of succession to the Ottoman throne.

Then these şehzades, with the exception of Reşad Efendi, died one after the other. The first to go was Kemaleddin Efendi in 1905, while

Abdülhamid still reigned. In 1909 Abdülhamid himself was deposed, and replaced by Sultan Reşad. A few months later Süleyman Efendi passed away.

Now there was only one heir in line before Vahideddin: Yusuf İzzeddin Efendi. And on 1 February 1916, he died. Was it suicide, or was he murdered? His death is a much disputed matter even today. As a result, Vahideddin Efendi became the crown prince of the Ottoman Empire when he was least expecting it.

By now Vahideddin and Nazikeda's daughters had grown and reached the age of marriage. The eldest, Ulviye, was the first to marry: the groom was İsmail Hakkı Bey, the son of the last grand vizier of the Ottoman Empire, Ahmed Tevfik Paşa.[4] The wedding took place in a *yalı* in Kuruçeşme on 10 August 1916, while Vahideddin Efendi was still the crown prince.

Vahideddin often said that he did not want to become sultan, and to his inner circle he even declared that he was ascending "not a throne but a latrine." But on 4 June 1918 he was indeed invested as the thirty-sixth sultan of the Ottoman Empire. His youngest daughter, Sabiha Sultan, was still unmarried at this time, but had several admirers. Those who knew her always said that she was not like the other women of the Ottoman family: "Sabiha Sultan was different," said the Turkish poet Yahya Kemal. She was beautiful and intelligent, and she was her father's confidante.

Her first suitor was believed to be Rauf Orbay, known then as the hero of the Hamidiye Cavalry. He was followed by Mahmud Kemal Paşa, the undersecretary of the Ministry of Defense, who made an official request to the Palace for her hand. After investigation, however, it appeared that Mahmud Kemal Paşa's father had at some point been a stableboy, and so the marriage proposal was refused. Among the other suitors was Fuad Bey, of the Babanzade clan, who was thought to be "too fat" and therefore was not approved. Many more hoped to become the sultan's son-in-law. Captain Savfet Arıkan, Lieutenant Suphi Bey from Damascus, and several others were at the door of the Palace, but none of them were accepted.

*

A deposed Muslim ruler, the shah of Iran Mohamed Ali Qajar, lived in exile in Istanbul at the time, having been forced to abdicate in 1909. He had been born in 1872, and in 1907 upon the death of his father Mozafaredin Shah, ascended the throne. During the two years of his reign, he had to struggle against revolts and insurgencies and fight against Russia's interference as well as Britain's imperial ambitions in Iran. The Qajar dynasty, which had ruled in Iran since 1796, was losing its grip. The monarchy had practically lost all power. The opposition demanded serious reforms and a stronger parliament. The reformists' demands for civil rights persistently increased, and eventually in June 1908 Mohamed Ali declared martial law in Tehran, appointing a Russian colonel as its commander. The prominent leaders of the opposition were either killed or arrested. But the situation became so unmanageable that on 23 June 1908 the shah gave the order to bomb the parliament building, then four days later he dissolved parliament and suspended the constitution.

In Istanbul, after thirty-two years of absence, the Ottoman parliament was restored in July 1908 and the people were celebrating the establishment of the Second Constitutional Era, while in Iran the wind was blowing in the opposite direction. The severe measures taken by Mohamed Ali Shah had the adverse effect, and in less than a year turmoil spread to the whole country, while the troops sent to crush the insurgents were defeated everywhere. The Bakhtiari tribe conquered Isfahan, and on 12 July 1909 opposition forces occupied Tehran. The powerless shah took refuge at the Russian Embassy, and on 16 July he abdicated in favor of his son Ahmed Mirza, who was then eleven years old. On 9 September the Russians took the shah to Odessa.

In exile, however, the former shah was restless. The Russians were already uneasy about the expansion of British influence in Iran, and to regain their dominant position of the past they decided to make use of him. He marched into Iran with an army backed by the Russians, but his soldiers were defeated by the government's troops. Once more he was obliged to take refuge with the Russians, and had to abandon his country forever. He finally realized that he had to give up his dream of claiming his throne again, so he arrived in Istanbul with a crowded entourage and settled in a rented mansion on Büyükada, the largest of the Princes' Islands in the Sea of Marmara.

The deposed shah remained in contact with his son, to whom he had handed his throne, frequently giving him political advice. The young shah, however, was not in a position to implement any of the suggestions that reached him via his father's attendants, who traveled back and forth between Istanbul and Tehran, since he no longer held any sway in the government of his country: Ahmed Shah was merely a symbolic figurehead.

When Mohamed Ali settled in Istanbul he took with him his daughters and his grandchildren. At one point he even went into business and earned a substantial amount of money, so much so that on the abolition of the sultanate in September 1923 there was debate over whether he should be paying taxes.[5] In 1924 Mohamed Ali and his family left Istanbul for France, then moved to San Remo in Italy, where he rented a villa and lived until his death on 5 April 1925. In 1921, after the ousted shah's son Ahmed signed an agreement accepting a British protectorate, the Russians invaded Iran. Reza Khan, a brigadier commander of the Persian Cossack Brigade, defeated the invaders. The upheaval that followed forced Ahmed Shah to designate his younger brother and heir apparent, Mohamed Hassan Mirza, as his regent and leave the country for Europe in 1923. Finally, in 1925 Ahmed Shah was deposed by parliament and replaced by Reza Khan. After ruling for 129 years, the Qajar dynasty surrendered the Persian throne to the Pahlavis. In turn, the son of Reza, Mohamed Reza Pahlavi, the last shah of Iran, had to abruptly leave the throne in 1979 with the advent of the Islamic Revolution.

From his exile in Büyükada, Mohamed Ali Qajar was unable to enforce the instructions he was giving his son Ahmed Shah. But he was still the father and had a say in the family matters, where there was no reason for others to interfere. In 1919, Ahmed Shah was twenty-one years old, and his father wanted to see him married and went searching for a bride worthy of his family. The girl of his choice should not only have beauty and poise but should also belong to an old and noble lineage like his.

Furthermore, if the marriage were to serve the purpose of opening up the doors of politics, so much the better.

After pondering and investigating at length, and seeking advice from his close entourage and exchanging ideas with Mahmoud Khan, the Iranian ambassador to the Sublime Porte, Mohamed Ali Qajar finally decided on the suitable bride for his son: Sabiha Sultan, the youngest daughter of Sultan Vahideddin, the ruler of the country that had given him asylum. Mahmoud Khan's wife had previously visited the *harem*, where she was introduced to Sabiha and for whom she immediately felt a deep admiration. On several occasions, she had told her husband, who was looking for a spouse for the young shah in Tehran, "The sultan's daughter is an ideal choice."

Thus at the beginning of spring 1919, the Iranian ambassador to the Sublime Porte Mahmoud Khan invited İsmail Hakkı Bey, Princess Ulviye's husband and Sultan Vahideddin's son-in-law, to the residence of his embassy.

İsmail Hakkı Bey was a professional soldier, a graduate of the Prussian Military Academy, who had been part of Kaiser Wilhelm's Cavalry Brigade. He was a member of the Yıldız Palace special commission, established to keep the sultan informed on military issues. The ambassador greeted the sultan's son-in-law with the respect due to a person of his rank, welcoming him into the drawing room, where all the embassy's high officials were present.

Showing him a box containing a shining medal on a small table, the ambassador said, "This is Iran's most important decoration. It is His Majesty the Shah's will that I should bestow it upon you." Then in accordance with protocol, he removed the medal from the box and hung the ribbon over İsmail Hakkı Bey's neck. Once the ceremony was over, the embassy's dignitaries bade farewell to the ambassador and his guest, leaving Mahmoud Khan and İsmail Hakkı Bey alone.

As they sat facing each other, the ambassador spoke seriously. "As you well know, the Ottoman Empire and Iran are two powerful Muslim states. His Majesty the Shah feels that our relations should be much closer and that we would become even more powerful if we were to be related by family ties. He thinks that the best way to secure this objective would be by uniting in matrimony Her Imperial Highness Sabiha with the Shah of Iran." Then he stood up and with a thrill of excitement in his voice said, "His Majesty believes that you are the only one who can secure this marriage. He is convinced that only you can persuade His Imperial Highness the Sultan."

İsmail Hakkı Bey was so taken aback by what the ambassador had told him that he forgot to stand up when Mahmoud Khan did, and from the depth of his armchair he was just able to mumble in astonishment, "I shall submit your request to His Imperial Majesty the Sultan immediately." It was now clear why Ahmed Shah had bestowed İsmail Hakkı Bey with Iran's most prestigious decoration.

The Iranians saw off the sultan's son-in-law with the same pomp as when he arrived at their embassy, and İsmail Hakkı Bey went immediately from Cağaloğlu to the Yıldız Palace, where he reported to the sultan the conversation he had had with the ambassador.

Sultan Vahideddin was even more surprised than his son-in-law. After listening to İsmail Hakkı Bey, he did what he usually did when pondering a subject: he closed his eyes, leaned his head slightly backward, and stayed motionless for a short while. Then slowly lifting his eyelids he declared, "Impossible, totally out of the question. I am both the head of the Ottoman Empire and the caliph of all the Sunni Muslims. How can I give my daughter to a Shia ruler? It is out of the question!" Having said that, he quietly advised İsmail Hakkı Bey, "Make sure you don't meet the ambassador. In fact, lie low for a while, let time pass and things cool down. I think this would be the most gentle way to show our refusal."

Despite his feelings, he thought he should let his daughter know about the request. Sabiha Sultan was also extremely surprised, but she shared her father's opinion.

Sultan Vahideddin expected that Mohamed Ali would understand in time that such a marriage was not possible, but the deposed shah did not seem to give up so easily. A few days later, the Iranian Embassy requested an audience from the Yıldız Palace: the former shah living in Büyükada wished to pay a visit to the sultan. Vahideddin understood then that Mohamed Ali was persisting in his pursuit of the marriage. To refuse an appointment would be considered a diplomatic discourtesy. He was obliged to agree, but what next? The sultan summoned his son-in-law to discuss what had to be done. The deposed shah would be granted the audience and would be greeted as a king. His demand would be heard, but the assessment of his request would come subsequently, as they were determined to draw things out.

On the appointed day, one of the sultan's yachts was sent to Büyükada to collect the former shah. Ambassador Mahmoud Khan was by his side. They were then driven from the Dolmabahçe pier to the Palace of Yıldız, where Mohamed Ali was welcomed with the honors due to a head of state. But when they met in the reception room of the ground floor of the palace, they were two fathers rather than two sovereigns. After the usual ceremonial exchange of courtesies, the former shah presented his case. He praised his son at length, describing how much effort and sacrifice he had made to raise him properly. "He is now twenty-one years old, but until this day he has neither touched nor looked at a girl or a woman. Furthermore, as a result of his upbringing he has become such a good monarch that my subjects no longer ask for me." He then openly asked the sultan's consent to take Sabiha Sultan to the palace in Tehran, as the bride for his son.

Vahideddin's reply was diplomatic. He explained how much he admired Iran's young shah, and repeatedly declared how delighted he was with this visit. He even mentioned how the marriage of the shah to a lady suitable to his rank would make him happy, but with regard to Mohamed Ali's request he said neither Yea nor Nay; he pretended not to have heard it. Then in a manner worthy of his rank, he bid the former shah farewell.

The sultan's intention was again to leave the Iranians without a reply, hoping that the whole affair would eventually be forgotten, but the shah and his father were not ready to give up. This time, it was the young shah himself who came to ask for Sabiha Sultan's hand. On 19 August 1919, Ahmed Shah stopped in Istanbul for a few days on his way home from England. He first went to Büyükada to see his father and then settled in at the Splendid Palace Hotel. This was not an official visit, so there were no official greetings, just a welcoming delegation as required by protocol. But of course a head of state arriving in another country, even unofficially, must pay a courtesy visit to the sovereign of that country. Before the visit, planned for 21 August at the Yıldız Palace, both parties were agitated. Ahmed Shah dreamed of becoming engaged by the time he left Istanbul, while the sultan and his entourage were trying to find ways and means of getting rid of this embarrassing situation.

Ahmed Shah went to the palace with his retinue, where he was welcomed with a ceremony worthy of his crown. He spent two hours with Sultan Vahideddin and his heir to the throne Abdülmecid Efendi. He was then taken from Yıldız to Dolmabahçe Palace, and in the afternoon Sultan Vahideddin went to Dolmabahçe to reciprocate the visit. On the same day the shah and Abdülmecid Efendi also visited one another. Throughout all these encounters marriage was never mentioned, but at the same time there was no hint in the sultan's behavior to make the young shah understand that this marriage would never take place.

When rulers meet on official visits, they customarily give each other medals and exchange the highest decorations of their respective countries. Ahmed Shah gave Sultan Vahideddin the Royal Medal of the first degree, and to Abdülmecid Efendi, the heir to the throne, he gave the same but of the second degree. Meanwhile the sultan thought it sufficient to give the young shah the Murassa İmtiyaz Nişanı (the Medal of Distinction) and not the highest decoration, which was the Order of the Ottoman Dynasty. The shah and his entourage did not understand that the sultan, even if indirectly, was trying to tell them, "Do not ask for the hand of my daughter, I shall not give her to you."

Then the shah came to Istanbul with his uncle Nasru's-Saltana, who requested an audience from Sultan Vahideddin, which was granted on 26 August. Without beating around the bush, Nasru's-Saltana officially asked for the hand of the sultan's daughter for his nephew. The sultan then did what he should have done months before: he spoke openly, though not quite truthfully. "You have greatly honored us by wishing to create a family bond between us, but my daughter is engaged. Therefore this marriage is not possible." Sabiha Sultan, of course, was not engaged at all.

Ahmed Shah was waiting in Büyükada at the Splendid Palace Hotel for his uncle to bring him the good news, but when the old prince arrived he said, "Forget this marriage. He is not giving you his daughter."

The shah was incensed and took revenge on Mahmoud Khan, the Iranian ambassador, since he had been the first to suggest this match: he discharged him from his post, took back the jeweled medal he had previously bestowed, and even—knowing that the marriage had been the idea of the ambassador's wife—ordered him to divorce her, saying, "Since I am deprived of marrying the princess, you will be deprived of your wife."

The young shah stayed four more days in Istanbul, leaving on 30 August for Iran. His dreams of marriage were so shattered that he did not even go to say goodbye to his father, who lived just a few minutes away from his hotel. Furthermore, simply ignoring the rules of protocol, instead of paying a personal farewell visit to the sultan, he sent his minister of foreign affairs to the palace, along with the ambassador he had just dismissed. These two conveyed to the sultan's head chamberlain that, "The shah regrets to be unable to bid the sultan farewell personally, because he is unwell." The Palace, on the other hand, was pleased that this never-ending marriage saga was finally resolved.

Many years later on the Mediterranean shores of Italy, history played a strange trick.

The deposed shah Mohamed Ali Qajar had left Istanbul and moved to San Remo. And after leaving Turkey on 17 November 1922, Sultan Vahideddin lived in Malta for a short time, then in Egypt and Arabia, before settling permanently in San Remo. (When Mohamed Ali Shah passed away, Sultan Vahideddin was already in San Remo and attended the funeral. The sultan's last photograph was taken during this funeral.) Meanwhile, Ahmed Shah left Iran in 1923 to live in France. On one occasion when he visited his father in San Remo, he became friends with Neslishah Sultan's father Ömer Faruk Efendi, that is to say, with the husband of Sabiha Sultan, the princess he had wished to marry. The two men even went hunting together several times.

Ahmed Shah married five times and had three daughters and one son. He died in 1930 at the age of thirty-two in Neuilly-sur-Seine, a suburb of Paris.

As keen as the Iranians had been to acquire an Ottoman princess as a bride, the Palace of Yıldız was also eager to find a groom, and it seemed that they had, in Mehmed Ali Bey, the son of Shevki Paşa and the nephew of Gazi Ahmed Muhtar Paşa, who was working at the embassy in London. The engagement of the couple was announced, and the young diplomat was requested to come to Istanbul for the wedding arrangements. However, Mehmed Ali Bey was taken ill with a disease he could not disclose to others, and was unable to accept the invitation. In fact, he did not even reply to the request, and his suit fell through.

While those waiting at the doors of the palace hoping to become sons-in-law to the sultan fantasized about a life full of Arabian Nights riches, Sabiha Sultan turned her dresses inside-out and wore them over again, since her father, even as sultan, had never been wealthy. Her cousin Naciye Sultan, who was married to Enver Paşa, ordered her dresses in Vienna and rolled in jewels, even during the most brutal days of the Great War, while Sabiha was obliged to wear her old clothes. Even after her father had ascended the throne, nothing much in her life changed.

The quest for a bridegroom and the requests of the suitors continued, as a love story developed at the palace, unnoticed by the rest of the family: Sabiha Sultan and Şehzade Ömer Faruk Efendi, the son of Abdülmecid Efendi, Sultan Vahideddin's heir, were in love. Meanwhile, another suitor came forward, a famous soldier in those days: Mustafa Kemal Paşa. With his marriage proposal, Mustafa Kemal Paşa—later to become better known as Atatürk—possibly wanted to repeat what his long-standing rival, Enver Paşa, had done years before: to become a bridegroom to the Palace. Perhaps he was a genuine admirer of Sabiha Sultan, or perhaps he had some other idea. We shall never know. But even this marriage did not take place. The Palace did not accept his proposal. Years later Sabiha Sultan confirmed the proposal to her close friends: "I saw him once and liked him. He was very handsome. He had fiery eyes, but I could not have married him, as I saw first-hand what Enver Paşa was capable of doing, and I was afraid that Mustafa Kemal Paşa might do even more. I did not want to be part of it. And I loved somebody else." The "somebody else" was her cousin Şehzade Ömer Faruk Efendi, the son of Abdülmecid Efendi, who later became caliph.

Only one document remains to confirm this marriage proposal: a few lines dictated by Sabiha Sultan forty years later, to Suat Hayri Ürgüplü, who was a prime minister of Turkey. In these memoirs, which were written in the form of an interview, Suat Hayri Ürgüplü asked Sabiha Sultan: "Is it true that Mustafa Kemal Paşa proposed to you, but your father did not accept?" To which Sabiha Sultan replied, "Yes, he proposed. He did not speak to me, but I was afraid, and I refused. The lives of Enver Paşa and Naciye Sultan were a bad example for me. What's more, he was famous. . . . I did not believe that I could have had a family life with a military commander."[6]

Vahideddin's heir to the throne was Şehzade Abdülmecid Efendi, the son of his uncle Sultan Abdülaziz. He was born in 1868 and was seven years younger than the sultan. He spoke several languages and painted and composed music. He was one of the founders of the Ottoman Artists' Association, and was considered to be one of the first modern Turkish painters. His mansion in Çamlıca was a meeting place of intellectuals, and an informal academy. The music he composed was in the western classical style—chamber music and piano concerti, which were played by his friends or by a group of ladies living in his mansion. He exhibited his oil paintings both in Turkey and abroad and sponsored other Turkish artists to take part in these exhibitions. Foreign ambassadors in Istanbul reported that "when he is not wearing a fez, he looks like a well-bred Frenchman."

When they were young, Vahideddin and Abdülmecid were close. They would go hunting together in the woods behind the hills of the Bosphorus, join literary or musical gatherings, and listen to the music each had composed. Vahideddin's music was in the Ottoman style, while Abdülmecid's was in the European style. Later this friendship turned sour, and, more than rivals, they became enemies. The reasons behind their falling out were political. When Vahideddin was still a şehzade, he was very loyal to his older brother, Sultan Abdülhamid. Abdülmecid Efendi, on the other hand, hated his cousin the sultan, and would even tell his close friends, "I wish I had the opportunity and a very sharp knife to chop up Abdülhamid." Even the European countries the two cousins favored were different: Sultan Vahideddin's policy was "friendship with the English and closeness to the French," which he said was a legacy from his father and his older brother Sultan Abdülhamid, and throughout his reign he sided with the British.[7] For Abdülmecid Efendi, the future of his country was only with France.

But destiny, through the marriage of their children, bound these two cousins who hated each other into even closer family ties. Abdülmecid Efendi had two children from two different wives: Şehzade Ömer Faruk Efendi from Şehsuvar Kadın and Dürrüşehvar Sultan, sixteen years younger than her brother, from Mehisti Kadın.[8]

Faruk Efendi was born in 1898. He was four years younger than Sabiha Sultan and was considered very handsome. He was first sent to the Galatasaray Lycée—Abdülmecid Efendi spoke French and he had a connection with the school through a close friend, Tevfik Fikret, who was the school's headmaster. Ömer Faruk Efendi's application to the lycée was prepared by Salih Keramet Bey, son of the Ottoman poet Nigar Hamim and assistant to Tevfik Fikret. Salih Keramet Bey had earlier given private lessons to the şehzade, and later he became private secretary to Caliph Abdülmecid Efendi. When the caliph was sent into exile, he initially accompanied him. Many years later, Salih Keramet Bey undertook a long legal struggle to bring the remains of the caliph back to Turkey, but to no avail. He died in Istanbul on 7 March 1987, at the age of 103.

Ömer Faruk Efendi attended the Galatasaray Lycée for a few years, until it was decided that he should have a more serious vocational training, and at the age of eleven he was sent to Europe. He was to have a military education, and, as was common practice with princes at the time, he attended the school created by the Empress Maria-Theresa in Vienna in 1751, the Theresianum Military Academy.

After a visit to the Hırka-ı Saadet, the Chamber of the Blessed Mantle in the Topkapı Palace, where lengthy prayers were said, he made his way to Vienna. Salih Keramet Bey accompanied him and settled him into the academy. He spent several years there, undergoing military training that also included extracurricular courses in basket-weaving, carpentry, masonry, construction works, metalworking, and other manual skills.

But for a more rigorous, iron-fisted, and disciplined training, Ömer Faruk Efendi was transferred from Vienna to the Potsdam Military Academy in Prussia. This transfer was probably the idea of Enver Paşa, the most powerful man in the empire, both war minister and imperial son-in-law. Enver Paşa had realized that most imperial princes did not attend school but were given private tutoring at home, thus growing up in a world of their own, far removed from the conditions and the latest developments of modern life. He therefore decided that the young şehzades should receive a military education, and for this purpose he allocated the Palace of Ihlamur as the Şehzadegan Mektebi (the Princes' School). It became compulsory for all şehzades below the age of fifteen to attend this school. Here besides their military training they were taught literature, history, religion, mathematics, and geometry.

The two older imperial princes, Ömer Faruk and Abdülmecid's grandson Sherafeddin (the brother of Naciye Sultan, Enver's wife), were already in Vienna. Enver Paşa thought they should not be trained in the land of the waltz as "ballroom officers," but instead should proceed to Potsdam, where they would receive a Prussian education and become strong, reliable officers. So they were transferred to Germany, and the Ministry of War issued a Decree on Education just for these two şehzades.

A rumor spread among the members of the Ottoman family about the transfer, to the effect that Enver Paşa was thinking of overthrowing the sultan after the war, to replace him with a young şehzade. The prospective ruler would naturally be Ömer Faruk Efendi, who had a serious

military education and who knew Europe well. Even when he came back
to Istanbul from Germany on holiday, as recorded in the formal letters addressed to the prince at the residence of his father Abdülmecid
Efendi in Çamlıca, Enver Paşa requested him to take part in daily military exercises.

Ömer Faruk Efendi graduated from the Prussian Military Academy
in Potsdam as a professional Prussian officer. His demeanor reflected
his strict German education, and until his death he remained a severe
soldier—but only in appearance, as deep down he was a romantic at
heart, and he never gave up some of his Turkish habits, such as his passion for trotter soup with garlic or *tirid* (leftovers of meat or soup with
stale bread). During his exile in Europe and Egypt he had to be served
trotters at least once a week!

The Germans did not want to send the young graduate straight
to the war front, presumably because they were afraid that something
might happen to this young member of the Ottoman reigning family,
their ally. But Ömer Faruk Efendi did gain familiarity with the front
line when he came to Istanbul on holiday: when Enver Paşa went to
the front in Çanakkale, he took the şehzade with him. Many years
later, the prince described his experience: "Enver Paşa placed us in
a trench and said, 'Don't move from here, the enemy will be firing
soon,' then left. As it was getting dark, the English began to shoot, just
like he said. The bullets were whizzing overhead around the trench.
We were scared stiff. This is where we learned what a battle meant.
We were truly terrified, asking ourselves why on earth we had come
here. . . . A little while later Enver Paşa appeared during a break in the
shelling. He was walking by the trenches in front of the line of fire.
He stopped in front of our trench, pulled his cigarette case from his
pocket, and lit a cigarette. Then he moved from one side of the firing
line to the other, not giving a damn about the fact that his glowing
cigarette might encourage the opposing side to open fire. He seemed
to be engrossed in his thoughts while just looking at the ground, taking
several deep puffs from his cigarette. . . . Seeing the paşa behaving in
this manner, we all felt as strong as lions and forgot our fears."

Once back in Germany, the şehzade wished to be sent to the front, but the Germans refused again. Ömer Faruk Efendi then bombarded his tutor Salih Keramet Bey with letters: "Intercede with the Germans so that they send me to the front." Eventually, his request was granted, and on 13 November 1917, he sent a postcard to Salih Keramet Bey, who was then in Vienna:

> My Dear Friend Keramet Bey,
> We have been posted to the Russian front for the past three weeks. We are presently busy visiting the combat zone. I firmly hope that I shall finally be sent to the front line as a Troop Commander, though my destination has not yet been established. Write to me now and then.
>
> Respectfully yours,
> Şehzade Ömer Faruk

The şehzade was sent to Galicia, and from there to Verdun, where he was assigned to the battlefield and where the battles with the French were quite bloody. He fought like a professional soldier, and Kaiser Wilhelm II granted him first the Red Eagle medal, then the Iron Cross of the First Degree. The Kaiser sent a golden cigarette case, as well as a signed photograph of himself together with the medal.

The Romanian officers of Galicia amazed Ömer Faruk, with his strict Prussian military background: "They did not give a damn about the battle. All they cared about was looking elegant at the front line. . . . Imagine, they even wore a girdle under their uniforms. As if this was not enough, they powdered their faces. . . . I was astonished when I first saw them, and asked myself, 'What kind of soldiers are these?'"

When the Germans lost the battle at Verdun, Ömer Faruk Efendi returned to Potsdam, where he was appointed to the German emperor's First Foot Guards Regiment. The two requirements for enrolment in this regiment were that one must belong to one of the most aristocratic families in Germany and be taller than 1.9 meters. Every Prussian prince was registered as an officer in this regiment from the age of ten, but those short in height would not take part in the parades. The şehzade was accepted into the regiment despite being only 1.85 meters tall. He was the shortest among his colleagues, yet he took part in all the parades in front of the kaiser.

Two questions bothered the mind of Ömer Faruk until the end of his life: Firstly, although he was an imperial prince, he had only recently graduated from the Military Academy and he was just a young officer of low rank. So how was it that he had been awarded the Iron Cross, first class, usually granted to high-ranking officers and war heroes? And secondly, how was it that he had been accepted into the First Foot Guards even though he was not as tall as he should have been? Was this good fortune, or was it the result of certain contacts between Kaiser Wilhelm and Enver Paşa? Though he thought about this for years, he never found the answer.

Time passed and the Great War was finally over. Germany was defeated, together with its ally the Ottoman Empire, and the political situation in both nations became chaotic. In the Ottoman Empire, the Committee of Union and Progress, which for the last ten years had been running the empire, withdrew from the government. On 30 October 1918 the Ottoman Empire was forced to sign the ominous Armistice of Mudros, while Kaiser Wilhelm II fled Germany and found asylum in Holland.

In Istanbul, a change of government meant that some diplomats and bureaucrats appointed by the Unionists lost their positions. One of these diplomats was the ambassador to Berlin, Mahmud Muhtar Paşa. As he and his wife Nimetullah, an Egyptian princess, and their children were about to leave Berlin, he received a telegram from his friend Abdülmecid Efendi, the heir to the Ottoman throne: "Should you be leaving Germany for a safer place, please take my son with you and look after him." So it was that Ömer Faruk Efendi left for Switzerland with Mahmud Muhtar and his family.

On 12 February 1919 Abdülmecid Efendi sent a letter to his son through an American diplomat, in which he wrote that the future of the country was not at all heartwarming:

> I am sure that you are concerned about our situation. I do not know if
> you read the papers. Obviously, since the newspapers there are subsidized

by our enemies, they always write against us. Nevertheless, as things drag on, we become vulnerable. Perhaps the past blast of violence is quietening down. Unfortunately, our domestic affairs are the same as usual. On the other hand, it is quite obvious that we cannot change things with these narrow-minded people. The policies of Sultan Hamid are [illegible] a little, but in a less skilful manner, with less acumen, worse than the politics of the Unionists and even more incompetent. In other words, may God show us the right path, as our expectations are fading away one after the other. Our only hope lies in the young ones. If they also come to nothing, then there is no future for the Ottomans, or for Islam. History will curse this generation and us in particular.

Meanwhile in Switzerland, a prospective bride was proposed for Ömer Faruk Efendi: Emine Hanım, the daughter of Mahmud Muhtar Paşa.[9] One evening, while the paşa was conversing with the young şehzade, the subject came to marriage. The paşa remarked that one should marry young, pointing out to the prince that he was still a bachelor, and then very candidly said, "Your Highness, you have reached the age of matrimony. We should find you a bride worthy of you, like my daughter Emine for instance, who comes from a good family. . . . Would you not consider marrying Emine?"

Many years later recalling that evening, Ömer Faruk Efendi would describe his utter surprise at the proposal: "The paşa's daughter had a beautiful figure, but her face did not appeal to me. Besides, all I could think of was Sabiha. I still don't know how those words came out of my mouth, but I said: 'I am engaged. . . . I am to marry my cousin Sabiha.'"

There was no mention of an engagement at that time. In fact, Faruk Efendi and Sabiha Sultan had not made the slightest insinuation of the subject, but faced with the suggestion by Muhtar Paşa, the şehzade came out with the name he had on his mind.

Months went by, the fighting in Europe had finally ceased, and Ömer Faruk Efendi went back to Istanbul, to his father Abdülmecid Efendi's mansion in Çamlıca.[10] The attraction that the şehzade felt toward his cousin Sabiha Sultan went back several years, and on his return from

Europe they were together on several occasions, and the attraction turned to love. One day the young prince mentioned the matter to his father Abdülmecid Efendi quite openly, and without further ado said, "I love Sabiha. Please talk to His Imperial Majesty and ask for Sabiha's hand for me." Abdülmecid Efendi was probably never as dumbfounded as he was that day: his only son had fallen in love with the daughter of his rival—if not enemy—Sultan Vahideddin. He first tried to dissuade his son: "In our family, marriages between relatives are not welcome. This has never happened before. Besides, Sabiha is four years older than you." Faruk Efendi's reply was such that Abdülmecid Efendi could do nothing more. The young şehzade said, "If I cannot marry Sabiha, or if she is promised to someone else, I shall commit suicide."

In the autumn of 1919, the heir to the throne requested an audience with Sultan Vahideddin.

After the terrible defeat of the Great War, as Turkey lived with the burden of the armistice, Abdülmecid Efendi frequently wrote to the sultan, and occasionally visited him. The message of his letters and his visits was always the same: "You are making a mistake," or "Because of your policies, I find myself in an awkward position." When Sultan Vahideddin was informed of the crown prince's request he thought, "He is probably coming to give us his usual advice," and unwillingly agreed to see him.

In a small living room of the Yıldız Palace they sat facing each other. Abdülmecid Efendi had come to ask for something, but Vahideddin could never have guessed what this might be: he reported what his son had said and asked the sovereign for the hand of his daughter Sabiha, for Ömer Faruk.

The sultan was certainly surprised by this request from a man who never failed to criticize him and his government at every opportunity. Conscious of the dispute between the children of Sultan Abdülmecid and those of Sultan Abdülaziz, which had been ongoing for years, he responded, "My daughter is engaged. Furthermore, in our family there is no such thing as a marriage between cousins." Abdülmecid Efendi replied, "If you do not allow this marriage to take place, Faruk will kill himself. My son's life is in your hands. Faruk is my only son and as a father I demand this from you." He said nothing further, bowed to the sultan and left.

After this first approach the women became involved: Faruk's mother Şehsuvar Hanım called on Sabiha's mother Emine Nazikeda Kadın at the Palace of Yıldız. "Please don't allow my only son to kill himself," she implored and sobbed until she finally convinced the soft-hearted kadınefendi.

Vahideddin and his wife did not decide on the matter: they asked their daughter's opinion. They then realized that this love was not one-sided, but that Sabiha Sultan was also in love with her cousin Ömer Faruk Efendi. Whenever he came from Germany the şehzade would visit his cousin Sabiha without fail, and pay his respects to Emine Nazikeda. The kadınefendi liked this handsome young man; and from now on when he came to visit his cousin, Sabiha Sultan did not feel the need to hide her joy.

Years later, Sabiha Sultan recalled:

> I was engaged before marrying Faruk. My fiancé was a diplomat and at the time he was probably a secretary at the embassy in London. He was about to come back for our wedding.
>
> Meanwhile, Şehzade Ömer Faruk returned from Germany. We knew each other and used to meet at the palace. His father asked my father whether I could marry his son. My father was surprised. "How is it possible? She is engaged to be married very soon!" he replied. Upon the insistence of Abdülmecid Efendi he said, "Well then it is for her to decide," and they asked for my opinion.
>
> At first, I wanted to wait for my fiancé, but then a mutual friend told me that my fiancé thought that our country was in a precarious situation, that he did not want to put himself in danger, and so on. . . .
>
> As soon as I heard about it, I went to my father and told him that I would marry Faruk. He was surprised, but when he understood the reason, he accepted and we were married.[11]

As soon as news of the proposal spread, gossip began in the seraglio. The family members of the Abdülaziz branch protested, "How could they marry off a girl to the grandson of Sultan Mecid? How can we forget that the Mecid branch was involved in the deposition and murder of His Imperial Highness Sultan Abdülaziz?" The ladies of the *harem* were baffled: "This is not a good omen. Şehzades do not wed imperial princesses. We do not have such strange customs. If they do marry, terrible things will happen." But both Sultan Vahideddin and Abdülmecid Efendi ignored what was being said and announced the engagement of Ömer Faruk Efendi to Sabiha Sultan.

While they were engaged, a new rumor spread in the palace: the şehzade had gone, at what was considered to be a late hour of the night, to the *harem* of the palace and spent a long time with his fiancée and her ladies-in-waiting, conversing, . . . and even laughing.

The next day at the Palace of Yıldız, there was consternation. Some of the ladies were scandalized, "My God, what is the world coming to! Seeing the face of the bride before the wedding? Visiting her and staying by her side for hours? It is scandalous! Something dreadful will happen." Others took Sabiha Sultan's side: "What's wrong with that? Not only are they engaged, but they are also cousins, just like brother and sister. Can't two cousins get together and talk? The imperial prince did not come to visit his bride, but his cousin. Furthermore, they were not alone; we were all there together."

In spite of all the unpleasantness in the palace, destiny took its course and Sultan Vahideddin's daughter Sabiha married Şehzade Ömer Faruk, son of the heir to the throne Abdülmecid Efendi.

The ceremony took place on 5 December 1919, after the afternoon prayer, in the Chamber of the Blessed Mantle at the Topkapı Palace, and the Shaykh al-Islam Haydarizade İbrahim blessed the marriage. The dowry was of one thousand and one pouches of gold. The representative of Faruk Efendi was the chief chamberlain Ömer Yaver Paşa, while Sabiha Sultan's was the first secretary Ali Fuad Bey. Sultan Vahideddin's other son-in-law İsmail Hakkı Bey and the son-in-law of the aide-de-camp Naci Paşa were the groom's witnesses, while the keeper of the Privy Purse Refik Bey and the chief eunuch Cevher were the bride's witnesses. The illiterate eunuch used his seal to sign the marriage certificate.

For centuries, it had been a tradition of the Ottoman family to give the right of divorce, known as *ismet hakkı*, to women and not to men. This practice was applied to this marriage as well, even though the groom was a member of the family: the right of divorce was given to Sabiha Sultan.

The wedding reception took place four months later, on 29 April 1920, at the Yıldız Palace. Efforts were made to keep things simple, since the country was at war (the War of Independence). Besides, the sultan did not have the means for a sumptuous wedding. For the wedding dress, however, no expenses were spared; Kalivrusi, the dressmaker most in demand at the time, made the gown.

While Sabiha Sultan and Ömer Faruk Efendi were getting married, Mustafa Kemal Paşa was in Sivas. No one knows what he felt when he heard the news. Had things been different, had Sultan Vahideddin or Sabiha Sultan accepted Mustafa Kemal Paşa's proposal, who knows how history would have differed!

Sabiha Sultan's *yalı* in Rumelihisarı was made of stone and had been built at the end of the nineteenth century by the French architect Alexander Vallaury, for the famous field marshal Zeki Paşa. The paşa had been eager to see his building completed, but sadly he was never to live in it. According to rumors of the time, when construction began and large stone walls were built, Palace informers reported to Sultan Abdülhamid: "Zeki Paşa is making a *yalı* on the Bosphorus, a *yalı* like a fortress, and there God knows what he will be plotting against Your Highness."

Abdülhamid, fearing the worst, did not allow Zeki Paşa to live in the house, although he was a devoted subject. When the building was completed, Zeki Paşa implored the sultan for permission to spend at least one night in his new property. The permission was granted after much pleading, and Zeki Paşa spent that single night in the *yalı*, sitting on a chair and freezing in the winter cold in his thin fur coat. At sunrise, he left the premises in tears, never to return. In 1908, after the declaration of the Second Constitution, Zeki Paşa was demoted and exiled. He died in Büyükada in 1914.

The *yalı* remained empty for years, until Sultan Vahideddin bought it from Zeki Paşa's successors as a wedding present for his daughter

Sabiha. There was practically no furniture in the property, so the sultan gave orders to his private treasury to furnish the house. This was done between the marriage and the wedding reception, and during the first week of May 1920, ten days after their wedding, Sabiha Sultan and Ömer Faruk Efendi moved to the *yalı* in Rumelihisarı.

In October of the same year, Sultan Vahideddin bought two houses for his daughters in Nişantaşı, for thirty-five thousand Turkish liras. The mansions were known as the Twin Palaces and belonged to the charitable foundation of Bayezid II, whence they were acquired by the sultan's private purse. Vahideddin gave one house to his oldest daughter Ulviye, the other to Sabiha, registering the deeds of the properties in their names. Sabiha Sultan and Ömer Faruk Efendi decided to live in Nişantaşı during the winter and in Rumelihisarı in the summer. But they were able to use these two properties for only a few short years, before being sent into exile.

At the time, the *yalı* was considered to be somewhat out of town. Ömer Faruk Efendi loved it and at first did not want to move to the mansion in Nişantaşı, which had been prepared for the winter months. "I am fed up with the city. Here it's like being in paradise," he used to say. But once the weather turned colder and it became difficult for friends to reach Rumelihisarı, they went back to the city.

Their first child was born in the Nişantaşı mansion on 4 February 1921. Ömer Faruk Efendi wanted his first child—indeed all his children—to be male. And he had already decided on the name of his firstborn: Oğuz Osman, a name inspired by a fashion that had started toward the end of the reign of Abdülhamid. As independence movements among the non-Turkish population of the empire intensified, many territories were surrendered to other nations, while the Union and Progress Party rose to power. To boost the morale of the people, reference was repeatedly made to the past, especially to the foundation of the country. So the names of ancient heroes and early rulers, such as Ertuğrul, the father of Osman Ghazi, who had given his name to the Ottoman Dynasty, and Osman's son Orhan, and even Oğuz, the legendary founder of the Turkish people, were in fashion again, having been forgotten for centuries. Newly born şehzades were named Ertuğrul and Osman and Orhan. And so Ömer Faruk Efendi wanted to name his first child—which he firmly believed would be a boy—Oğuz Osman.

But his first child was a girl. And she was named by her two grandfathers: Sultan Vahideddin chose the name Fatma and Abdülmecid Efendi chose Neslishah. The first child of Ömer Faruk Efendi and Sabiha Sultan was Fatma Neslishah.

2

Last Entry in the Register

O n 31 March 1921 a letter signed by Rifat Bey, Sultan Vahideddin's first secretary, was sent to the government, which was then
located at the Sublime Porte, stating that on 4 February a baby
girl named Neslishah had been born to Şehzade Ömer Faruk Efendi and
Sabiha Sultan and that the sultan had ordered that the birth certificate of
the child be sent to the Sublime Porte, where the required procedure was
to be initiated. The birth certificate was signed by three former grand
viziers, Salih Hulusi, Ahmet Izzet, and Ali Riza Paşa.

The "required procedure" was that the name of the newborn child
was to be recorded in the Register of the Ottoman Dynasty. The use
of the Register had begun during the reign of Sultan Reşad in 1913. In
earlier times the imperial princes were not allowed to marry and have
children, but the restriction was lifted under Abdülmecid I around 1840,
after which the now permitted marriages increased the number of members of the family. So on 16 November 1913 Sultan Reşad ordered a
Family Register of the members of the Ottoman family,[12] describing
their status and position, as well as recording their birth certificates,
weddings, divorces, even their debit and credit status, and all other deal-
ings that might be of interest to the state.

On 31 March 1921 the last entry in this Register—recorded on row
thirty-one of page fifty-one—was Neslishah, the daughter of Şehzade
Ömer Faruk Efendi and Sabiha Sultan. She was the last member of the

Ottoman family to be born in Turkey during the period of the Ottoman Empire.

Istanbul at the time was under military occupation. In Anatolia an armed struggle was going on, so it was out of the question to celebrate the birth of the sovereign's granddaughter: only congratulations from family members were accepted. Tea parties were given, reciprocated calls were made, and in the mansion in Nişantaşı prayers were recited on several occasions. The sultan, however, wanted to commemorate the birth of his granddaughter in some manner, so a few gold coins were issued and distributed to close members of the family, as well as to his attendants. Sultan Vahideddin even ordered the firing of 121 cannonballs. And Faruk Nafiz Bey Çamlıbel, a young poet of the time, composed a chronogram to commemorate the date of her birth.

Sabiha Sultan's child was delivered by the most famous gynecologist of the 1920s, Professor Asaf Derviş Paşa, a descendant of the grand vizier Halil Hamid Paşa, who had been executed in April 1785 upon the orders of Abdülhamid I. In 1909 Derviş Paşa opened the first gynecological clinic at the Military Hospital of Gülhane, and in the years to come he would become known as the founder of gynecology in Turkey.

It was an easy birth, but Neslishah's health was soon in danger. It was standard practice at that time to give newborns two vaccinations on the thigh. Asaf Derviş Paşa must have thought, "This is no ordinary child, but the grandchild of the sultan, so for good measure . . . ." And when she was forty days old he injected her with six different vaccines at once, including smallpox. All six were effective, and the baby's temperature shot up to over forty degrees Celsius. It was thought the child was dying, and several doctors were called, who with great difficulty managed to lower the fever. Neslishah kept the marks of these vaccinations on her leg until the age of seventy, when they unexpectedly disappeared. Until then, every time she looked at the shiny marks on her leg she thought of Asaf Derviş Paşa.

Once the baby had recovered and Sabiha Sultan had recuperated from the fatigue of childbirth, the family moved to Rumelihisarı. Upon

Ömer Faruk's insistence they did not return to the mansion in town at Nişantaşı. Instead, they spent both winters and summers in Rumelihisarı, which became Neslishah's home. In later life the only memories that Neslishah had of the *yalı* were the large, tall windows, and the dolphins playing in the cool waters of the Bosphorus. She would climb on a chair to look at the sea for hours, clapping her hands with pleasure whenever she caught sight of the dolphins.

There were several head servants in the house, but it was Miss Brunner who took care of Neslishah. Miss Brunner was from Zurich, and she was both a governess and a nurse. She always wore a uniform, and always stayed with the child. When Neslishah started to walk, they would go to the garden behind the *yalı* or onto the quay in front of the house. In winter, they would make snowmen or play snowballs, while in spring they would spend time in the boathouse, which was covered with blue wisteria. The quay was large, and the trolley line from Bebek crossed it, in front of the *yalı*. Sometimes Neslishah would walk along the quay with Miss Brunner to a small soap factory. She liked to spend time there playing with the colored soaps, and would return with her arms full of blue, pink, and yellow soap ribbons that the Greek owner had given her.

Her meals were taken with Miss Brunner, who called her Nesli, Nashdi, or Schatzi (German for 'darling'), and though her mother tongue was German, she otherwise addressed the little girl only in French: this was at least partly the reason that Neslishah's French was as good as her Turkish.

The Ottoman Empire had a number of state medals, but the Hanedan-ı Saltanat Nişanı, the Order of the Ottoman Dynasty, was reserved for the members of the imperial family. This decoration was created by Sultan Abdülhamid II in 1893 and was given only to the imperial princes and princesses, that is, to the direct descendants of the sultans on the male side, while the beyzades and the hanımsultans, on the female side, could not receive or wear this distinction. Besides members of the family, the sultans could also give this decoration to foreign heads of states or to the khedives of Egypt if they wished.

Sultan Vahideddin, the last Ottoman sultan, gave the Order of the Ottoman Dynasty to his one-year-old granddaughter Neslishah. One day in Rumelihisarı, Neslishah was playing with the daughter of her aunt Ulviye Sultan, Hümeyra Hanımsultan,[13] four years her senior. Hümeyra saw the decoration Neslishah was wearing and said in tears, "I want one too!" She was calmed down with great difficulty.

Soon after this, when Hümeyra was taken to see her grandfather Sultan Vahideddin in Yıldız, she suddenly remembered Neslishah's decoration and began to cry again. This time, it was the sultan who quietened her down, by putting around her neck the last Hanedan-ı Saltanat Nişanı he had left. However, the decoration given to Hümeyra was no more than a present from a grandfather to his granddaughter and had no official value. Neslishah was given hers because she was an imperial princess, thus her decoration was the last Order of the Ottoman Dynasty given during the Ottoman Empire.

In the spring of 1919 the War of Independence began, and the Palace had to be part of the struggle. If a member of the Ottoman family joined the fight in Anatolia, it was thought this would boost the morale of the Anatolian population, who were fed up with wars that had been going on for years and initially not very supportive of the national struggle against the occupying powers.

So the heir to the throne Abdülmecid Efendi received three letters of invitation, from Mustafa Kemal Paşa, Cami Bey, and Hamdullah Suphi Bey, delivered by Abdülmecid's former aide-de-camp, Yümni Uresin Bey, who was later to become one of the first generals of the Turkish republic, as well as the Minister of Transport and Communications. To persuade the prince, the National Assembly also appointed another former aide-de-camp, Hüseyin Nakib Bey, who would later become Abdülmecid Efendi's private secretary during his years in exile.

Abdülmecid Efendi said he wished to think about the invitation for a few days. He replied two days later saying that although he wanted to go to Anatolia, he preferred to wait and consider whether it would be useful for the people, as well as for the country. The message, though not explicit, was understood, and Ankara's decision in 1924 to send the imperial family into exile was certainly influenced by Abdülmecid's refusal to join the national struggle.

The intelligence officers of the Allied powers occupying Istanbul were well aware of all these contacts and kept Abdülmecid Efendi under close scrutiny.

Although Abdülmecid Efendi did not agree to go to Anatolia, there was someone very close to him who was eager to do so: his son Ömer Faruk Efendi. Faruk had graduated as a professional soldier from the famous Prussian Military Academy in Potsdam. And he believed it was crucial for the future of the country, as well as for the future of the Ottoman dynasty, that a member of the family should join the fight in Anatolia.

His marriage had coincided with his father's failure to join the movement in Ankara. He first waited a little to settle his new family life, and then he learned that he was to become a father, so he was obliged to delay his Anatolian adventure until after the birth of his child. But in 1921, when Neslishah was two months old, he decided it was time to go.

Contacts were made with the organization in Anatolia, while the prince's secret departure from Istanbul was planned to the smallest details. He wrote five letters to be distributed after his departure, addressed to his father-in-law Sultan Vahideddin, his mother-in-law Emine Nazikeda Kadınefendi, his sister-in-law Ulviye Sultan, his brother-in-law İsmail Hakkı Bey, and Ali Nuri Bey, Hakkı Bey's brother. Sabiha Sultan was to deliver them personally. In the letter to his in-laws, he apologized for leaving without warning, asking for their blessings. Sabiha Sultan was reluctant to take the letter to her father herself, so she had it delivered, adding a note starting: "My Darling Father, My Benefactor."

On the night before his departure, Ömer Faruk Efendi organized a party in Rumelihisarı, as cover. It lasted until the early hours of the morning of 26 April 1921, and at sunrise he took leave from Sabiha Sultan: "Once I reach Anatolia, I shall send for you. You will bring Neslishah and join me," he said, and after changing his clothes he left for Karaköy. According to the plan, he first embarked on a cargo ship, where he had trouble hiding in a cabin, and after an arduous journey he reached İnebolu on the Black Sea coast. But after all this planning Ankara would not accept him in the cause, and he was sent back to Istanbul on another vessel.

Thirty years later, while in exile, Ömer Faruk Efendi related his Anatolian adventures to a journalist, in an interview published in 1952:

> They were going to load the vessel until five o'clock in the morning. They told me to wait and locked me in the cabin. I was imprisoned, and this had a terrible effect on me. I was chain smoking. Eventually, they came back. It was seven in the morning. I was sitting on a wooden chair. One of the guys said, "Get up quickly!" and took me to the dining saloon that was just at the bow of the ship. There he opened an iron door to a small cubbyhole.
>
> While I was thinking how on earth I would fit in there, he pushed me, locking me in. It was as dark as a dungeon; there was neither light nor air except what penetrated from the keyhole. Hours passed by, but no one came. There was less and less air. I had difficulty in breathing, and I was in agony. Finally, around ten o'clock the vessel set sail. From where I was, I could hear the chain drawing the anchor.
>
> We sailed for about twenty minutes, and I sighed with relief. Then guess what happened? The vessel stopped again, dropping the anchor with a terrible clamor. My spirit fell into the sea together with the anchor. "Oh no," I said. "They have heard, have been informed, they will find me here." I took the gun in my hand. I thought of killing those who were after me. I would kill them first, then myself.
>
> After a long wait, I heard English being spoken. These must have been English officers searching the vessel. It was past twelve when the ship set sail again, and ten past two when the fellow opened the cupboard door to let me out. I had been imprisoned in a cubbyhole no bigger than a matchbox for exactly seven hours and ten minutes.
>
> I came out from my hiding place with great difficulty and collapsed on a chair. The lack of air, the lack of light, and the tension had exhausted me. I lit a cigarette, as I could not smoke in the cubbyhole. A little while later the officer came. "Sorry to hear what you went through,

sir," he said. "We were also in trouble, as seventeen motorboats of the Allied troops were searching the vessel. There must have been a tip-off for them to be so suspicious."

I went up to the deck and had something to eat, with civilian clothes of course and bareheaded. Everyone on the ship was looking at me, pointing at me and saying to each other, "Ah . . . look who's on board."

The following day we reached İnebolu. The officer came and asked me, "I am going ashore, do you need anything?" Upon which I asked him to send a cable to Mustafa Kemal Paşa, the head of the Grand National Assembly, informing him that I had arrived to serve the country and fulfill my military duty.

We had lunch all together in the house of a notable of the area. After their departure, I went down to the garden. A recruit came, saluted, and handed me a telegram. It was from Mustafa Kemal Paşa personally.

When I opened it and read it, I was shocked. [It read: "It is preferable for the Ottoman family to remain in Istanbul until the time their services will be required."]

I then wrote a second telegram, stating that I had come to serve my country as a soldier, and that I had no political aspirations. If they wished they could send me straight to the front line; if they did not find it appropriate they could have me interned wherever they thought it suitable, but I made it clear that I would not go back to Istanbul, and if this was also not accepted I requested permission to be sent to Europe. I never received a reply.

I was extremely disappointed. At the time, I was twenty-three years old, totally inexperienced and deeply distressed. Like it or not, the only thing left for me to do was to return home. Back in Istanbul I could be arrested by the English, imprisoned at the Croker Hotel [headquarters of the British occupation forces], exiled to Malta, or even murdered. I was also thinking about the attitude of the Palace, and how Vahideddin might want to take revenge on me.

Three days later we set sail in a small Yugoslavian ship. We entered Istanbul from the Bosphorus. As we approached the port, I was trembling with fear and with excitement. I remained in my cabin during the health

inspection. The vessel docked on the quay of Sirkeci. I gave my belongings to a porter and went straight to Sabiha Sultan's house. Luckily my
fears were unfounded."[14]

Ömer Faruk Efendi had left for Anatolia with high hopes, and was
forced to return to Istanbul just three days later, deeply disappointed.
Ankara did not want the şehzade to take part in the War of Independence. The meaning behind Mustafa Kemal Paşa's telegram was clear:
Your family did not come when we invited them, now we do not need
you, don't come.[15]

From Sirkeci the şehzade went straight to Rumelihisarı, and once in
the *yalı* he burst into tears, crying for hours. When Sabiha Sultan went
to see her father at the Yıldız Palace after all that had happened, the
sultan told her, "How childish can you be? Did you really think I was
not aware of what was happening? Right from the beginning, I knew
that Faruk would be going and would be sent right back. Now we have
to find a way of preventing the English from harming him—this is presently the main issue."

The şehzade's Anatolian adventure caused him considerable distress,
not the least of which was that, due to having been locked in a cupboard
for seven hours and ten minutes, he developed claustrophobia, which
remained with him for the rest of his life.

Mustafa Kemal Paşa's telegram to Ömer Faruk Efendi became a
source of pride for the şehzade: during his exile he had it framed and
hung on the main wall in his study, and even had copies made of it that
he distributed to his friends, saying, "You would make me very happy if
you could hang this picture in a visible place in your house."

While the adults worried, Neslishah spent her time making snowmen,
playing games in the boathouse, and taking trips to the soap factory.
Eventually, the War of Independence ended in victory for the Nationalists and defeat for the Allies. Neslishah was not even two years old, so she
could not be aware of her parents' apprehension, as all ties between Sultan
Vahideddin and the Nationalist government in Ankara were now severed.

The predictable end arrived on the first day of November 1922. The Allied powers, feeling the need for a peace treaty, invited the governments of Istanbul and Ankara to a peace conference separately. But the last curtain came down with an exchange of telegrams between Ankara and the grand vizier Tevfik Paşa, the father-in-law of the sultan's eldest daughter. On 29 October, in the last telegram that Tevfik Paşa sent to Ankara, he wrote: "If the Sublime Porte does not attend the Peace Conference, it will mean that the six-century-old historical identity of the Ottoman State has been crushed," and he suggested that Istanbul and Ankara should act together.

Ankara's reaction was much stronger than expected: they abolished the sultanate. On 1 November 1922, the Grand National Assembly in Ankara passed a decree, by which it terminated the reign of the Ottoman Empire, even backdating the decision by declaring that it had been taken two years earlier, on 16 March 1920, when Istanbul was still occupied by the foreign powers.[16]

The sultanate had been abolished, but the caliphate was still untouched. Refet Paşa, the representative of the government in Ankara, conveyed the decision of the parliament to Vahideddin. Until the day before, Vahideddin had still been the sultan, and though Refet Paşa did not show any lack of respect in his presence, he did not address the former ruler as "Your Illustrious Highness" or "Supreme Sultan," as had been customary. Instead, he used the title "Your Excellency the Caliph," upon which Vahideddin said, "A caliphate without a sultanate is unacceptable, even to the most incapable member of our family."

After the parliament's decision in Ankara, Vahideddin received his second blow from Tevfik Paşa, his daughter's father-in-law. On 21 October 1920, Tevfik Paşa had been appointed grand vizier for the third time; but on 4 November 1922 he announced his resignation not to the former sultan but to the government in Ankara, and locked himself up in his mansion in Gümüşsuyu, which was later to become the famous Park Hotel, leaving Ankara to take over the administration in Istanbul.

Many things changed in Turkey on 17 November 1922, as Neslishah's "Şahbaba" (as she called her maternal grandfather) went into exile and settled initially in Malta. While in exile, the former sultan's contact in Istanbul was his youngest daughter Sabiha Sultan, with whom he corresponded until March 1924, when together with the other members of the family she was also sent into exile. Vahideddin often ended his letters with phrases like "Kiss Neslishah for me" or "Kiss Neslishah's lovely eyes and beautiful face."

With the abolition of the sultanate, Vahideddin lost his empire and his throne. He did not challenge the decision, but he did not give up the title of caliph. Years later when in San Remo, his permanent residence in exile on the Italian Riviera, while dictating his memoirs to Avni Paşa, his chief aide-de-camp, on the subject of his departure from Istanbul he said, "We did not run away. We took the Hijra of the Prophet as an example, when he moved from Mecca to Medina, and we left with the intention to return." He went on:

> It is public knowledge that after the victory, Refet came to Istanbul in all his pompous glory. The great Tevfik Paşa did not hesitate to hand over to that little man both the government and his position of grand vizier. Finding no one to stop him, Refet talked and complained until he had no voice left. Even you might have heard what he was saying. The newspapers wrote about it. Everybody heard him, everyone from here to China. What was the objective of this performance, of these speeches?
>
> As you know, the *Kanun-i Esasi*—the constitution that stemmed from the authority of the sultan—was replaced by the *Teşkilat-i Esasiye*—the constitution where the sovereignty belongs to the people—and the constitutional monarchy was substituted by the republic. Meanwhile the caliphate and the sultanate, which the government of Tevfik Paşa left pending in the air, were waiting to know their fate.
>
> Then one day Refet contacted the Palace requesting to meet us. We fixed the date and the time and he came. He expressed his opinion. We listened. This tiny little man, hiding behind grand ambitions and concealing his true intentions, told us that if we gave up the constitutional monarchy, which we had sworn to protect, and accepted a restricted caliphate,

as if the original one did not exist, we would save both our position and ourselves. Furthermore, if we recognized the new constitution as well as the government in Ankara, by sending a telegram, he would be able to convince Mustafa Kemal. We replied merely that this proposal had to be discussed, as greater thought had to be given on the subject.

The following day, when we read in the newspapers Mustafa Kemal's harsh words against us and our family, I knew it was time for us to take a decision. The dreadful situation that followed the decree of 1 November abolishing the sultanate became evident. This treacherous ruling separated the indivisible sultanate and the caliphate from the state and its government, reducing the cornerstone of the Islamic world to a meaningless word, thus putting the very heart of the caliphate in danger.

We were therefore obliged to accept or reject a powerless caliphate, refute the attacks from Anatolia, and find ourselves pitted against Mustafa Kemal. Blindness and ingratitude were everywhere. We were exasperated by the greed and the radical changes surrounding us. We could not see the possibility of either opposing or complying with this kind of caliphate. Thus we decided to leave this treacherous region, until public opinion calmed down and the general situation reached some clarity.

We requested the mediation of the English general Harrington, because he was the commander-in-chief of the Allied Forces of Occupation, to allow us to go to the Holy Land, and as a stopover and a lesser evil we finally accepted to go to Malta.

By doing so, as a representative of the Blessed Prophet following in his footsteps, we walked away from those who acted against our religion and the Islamic sultanate, and even though we migrated we never renounced our lawful rights as sultan and as caliph, rights that we have inherited from our forefathers and which we shall never surrender."[17]

Parliament had abolished the sultanate but not the caliphate, and even after his departure Vahideddin was still officially the caliph. Once Ankara heard that the deposed sultan had left Turkey, though, the Grand National Assembly confirmed a fatwa (an Islamic religious edict), made on 18 November by Vehbi Efendi, a member of parliament for Konya and the representative for religious affairs, which dismissed Vahideddin from the caliphate. The election of the new caliph took place the following day: Abdülmecid Efendi was chosen to fill that position by 148 votes against five.

Abdülmecid Efendi did not listen to his friends or those members of the family who thought he should refuse the caliphate. He accepted the decision of the parliament without objection, and on 24 November he officially became the caliph, after the ceremony of allegiance in the Chamber of the Blessed Mantle at the Topkapı Palace. He thanked the parliament for electing him, wishing the Islamic world joy and prosperity.[18]

A few days later he made a speech, in which he attacked Vahideddin: "My father was his uncle. He did not even remember it. How painful it is to have to mention it. Now he has been discarded not only from his position, but also from the family. Let us forget this affair and look ahead to the future. May God bless the future of our country and our religion."[19]

In Malta Vahideddin heard that he had been replaced as caliph by Abdülmecid Efendi. His first reaction was, "Only our Glorious Leader [the Prophet Muhammad] can depose us." Later, however, he said, "Mecid Efendi has attained his goal. It is easy to sit on Murad's emerald throne, but Mecid is not even worthy enough to reach this hero's boots. Poor man, they sent him an imam's coat, and pretending still not to notice he strives to drag his robe to the throne."[20]

Mustafa Sabri Efendi, the chief religious official of the empire, who had also left Turkey, declared: "This caliphate is beyond reason. Abdülmecid Efendi cannot represent our beloved Prophet; he cannot even be the devil's representative, as even the devil would not accept such foolishness."[21]

Only seventeen days after Vahideddin had told Refet Paşa in the Yıldız Palace that "a caliphate without a sultanate is unacceptable even to the most incapable member of our family," a member of that family, his first cousin Abdülmecid Efendi, accepted the caliphate without question. The relationship between "Şahbaba" and Neslishah's other grandfather was forever damaged. But Neslishah was still the granddaughter of the caliph.

*

The first time Neslishah went to Dolmabahçe Palace, her grandfather the caliph Abdülmecid Efendi's official residence, she was around two years old. She later recalled:

> I vaguely remember my first visit. . . . It was a day of Bayram (a religious festivity) that by chance occurred in summer. They made me a very elaborate dress; the top was in white tulle and the skirt was light pink. There were embossments on the tulle that looked like cotton flakes. Several fittings were required before the dress was ready.
>
> That morning they dressed me, but I distinctly remember not wearing my Ottoman decoration. As the sultanate was over, we could not wear our decorations. Furthermore, my parents were trying to raise me in the simplest way possible, so they would not have approved of me wearing such adornments.
>
> A boat came alongside our quay in Rumelihisarı and sailed us all to my grandfather in Dolmabahçe. For a child of my age, it was such a wonderful treat to go on a boat. That is why I well remember this journey on the water.
>
> That morning there was the *Muayede* ceremony, the traditional event for a religious celebration when the caliph receives greetings on the occasion of these festivities. The boat docked at the quay of the palace, and we went to the ceremonial hall. Our arrival coincided with the end of the ceremony: everyone had left, and only family members remained. My grandfather was sitting on a large throne like an armchair. When we came in he immediately embraced and kissed me. My parents kissed his hand; then it was the turn of the other princesses and princes, who also kissed my grandfather's hand and offered their greetings.
>
> The palace mesmerized me—everything was glittering, and the crystals, the enormous chandelier above my head, the furniture, the dimensions of the room, all filled me with admiration.

At the beginning of 1923, Sabiha Sultan was pregnant with her second child. The elder members of the family were informed, and Sabiha

Sultan's husband, Şehzade Ömer Faruk Efendi, went to Dolmabahçe Palace to give his father the caliph Abdülmecid Efendi the news that another grandchild was to be born in the fall.

"Sabiha should not give birth in Rumelihisarı or Nişantaşı, she should give birth here," said Abdülmecid Efendi. "They say there is no sultanate, but I am the caliph. Now come immediately to Dolmabahçe, let the child be born in the palace. All facilities will be available, and my grandchild will be born in the proper place." So in the spring Sabiha Sultan, Ömer Faruk Efendi, Neslishah, and the family's attendants moved from Rumelihisarı to the Palace of Dolmabahçe. Abdülmecid Efendi assigned his son and daughter-in-law one of the apartments in the *harem*.

Neslishah recalled:

> The sultanate had been abolished, but my grandfather still wanted his grandchild to be born somewhere "official," in the palace. For this reason he asked us to move to the Palace and have my mother give birth in Dolmabahçe. We all moved together from Rumelihisarı to the *harem* of the palace.
>
> I was three years old and not fully aware of what was happening, but I remember bits and pieces. For example, I saw the tray carriers: the food for the palace was cooked in the kitchens on the other side of the street and then it was carried to the *harem* on large trays. Later on, these buildings were given to the army; I think they became a military barracks or something. I was playing with one of the young servants in the garden of the *harem* when a eunuch entered the garden and yelled "Make way, make way!" When the women heard the eunuch shouting in this manner, they had to rush indoors. The servant girl said, "Come, sweetie, we have to go now, we have to go inside." "Why?" I asked, and she told me that the tray carriers were bringing food, so we were not supposed to stay outside. "But I want to look," I insisted, while the poor girl repeated, "You can't, my darling. If we stay they will get angry with us."
>
> I was just a child, and I ran away from her and hid. There was a place there like a small bamboo wood, where I concealed myself behind the bamboo shoots. The poor girl, who could not possibly leave me behind, had to hide beside me. We watched the tray carriers from there.

There was one eunuch in front, and others were walking on each side of the tray carriers and at the back. There were about twelve carriers with enormous trays, wrapped with quilted cotton to keep the food warm. The food was placed in shallow pans with a lid on, then into the quilted trays that also had quilted caps. And finally, to prevent insects from contaminating the food, the whole thing was tied up.

When the Palace discovered that we had stayed outside, there was a bit of a commotion. The servant girl was scolded, but I had seen the tray carriers.

We also had an adventure with a peacock. In the courtyard of the *harem*, there were peacocks of all colors. My aunt Dürrüşehvar was ten years old at the time. One day while we were playing, we thought of catching a blue peacock and bring him inside the *harem*. There was a narrow staircase leading to my parents' apartment. We climbed the stairs with difficulty, carrying the bird in our arms. At the end of the sitting room there was a kind of washroom, and just then my father was shaving in there—his face was covered with white foam. When he saw my aunt and me with the peacock in our arms, taken by surprise he shouted at the top of his voice, scolding us. Frightened by the sound of his voice, we stepped backward toward the stairs and rolled all the way down. Imagine the scene: a man with a face full of soap, two children tumbling down the staircase, my mother at the top of the stairs, tongue tied with fear on seeing us falling, while a blue bird shrieking his head off was scattering his feathers all over the place. Fortunately, when we reached the bottom of the staircase, we were not hurt.

On 19 September 1923 Sabiha Sultan gave birth to her second child at the Dolmabahçe Palace. It was a girl again, and as with Neslishah, each grandfather gave a name to the newborn. The caliph Abdülmecid Efendi named her Hanzade. Vahideddin, now in San Remo and informed by telegram of the birth and the good health condition of the mother and child, replied, "May the name of the newborn be Zehra."

So the last princess to be born in the Dolmabahçe Palace was named Zehra Hanzade. But since the sultanate had been abolished ten months before her birth, she was not recorded in the Register of the Ottoman Dynasty—Neslishah's name remained the last entry in that register of a dynasty that had lasted for six centuries.

Neslishah recalled the night of her sister's birth:

> One night I was in my room with my nanny, when suddenly there was a commotion in the palace. Someone came to fetch the nanny, leaving me in the room all alone. Apparently my mother was going through a painful labor. Then the lights went off. It was pitch black everywhere. They had turned on all the lights in the palace and used all the sockets for various equipment, and so the fuses had blown. I was petrified.
>
> The next day I was told that my sister had arrived, and my grandfather was calling me to show her to me. I was taken to a small sitting room. The door opened, and I saw my grandfather standing by a tiled stove. Hanzade was in his arms. "Look my darling, your sister has arrived and she has brought you presents. Now come and kiss her." Looking around I saw that the room was full of toys. They had literally brought a toyshop to the palace. I was very happy of course, and I did what my grandfather bid me: I embraced my sister.

Almost a year had passed since the abolition of the sultanate on 1 November 1922, and there was still no proper government. The administration was in the hands of the Grand National Assembly in Ankara. The uncertainty with regards to the form of governance ended on 29 October 1923, when the republic was declared, and Mustafa Kemal was elected president. The caliphate was to coexist with the republic for another four months.

Shortly after Abdülmecid Efendi was elected caliph, Ankara had sent him a set of guidelines with instructions on what he could and could not do, requesting him not cross those limits. Abdülmecid Efendi never failed to send a telegram to Ankara when necessary: when Mustafa Kemal Paşa's mother passed away, he sent a message of condolences, when the paşa married Latife Hanım he sent a message of congratulations, and even when the republic was declared he expressed his felicitations. However, he had no intention of abiding by the given guidelines. For instance, he took part in the Friday procession to the mosque, as the sultan–caliph had done under the sultanate, he did not hesitate to request an increase of his allowance, and he held meetings with political figures. Furthermore, disobeying Ankara's instructions requesting him to wear only a frock coat, at times he would wear a turban, and pictures of the caliph with a turban were sold on the market.

After the announcement of the birth of the republic, there were sad days at the *yalı* of Rumelihisarı. Ömer Faruk Efendi and Sabiha Sultan were in the sitting room of the *yalı* when a servant brought in an envelope on a small tray and presented it to the şehzade. Faruk Efendi took the envelope, opened it, and began to read. As he read the letter he flinched, turned pale, and without uttering a word to his bewildered wife wobbled off toward his bedroom. Sabiha Sultan followed him, but the door was closed. She stopped for a moment, surprised. Then she knocked on the door a few times, and called out to her husband, but there was no reply. She was disturbed and anxious.

She knocked again, called again, but still no reply, so timidly she turned the handle of the door, and realizing that it was not locked, she gently pushed it and entered the room. Her husband was perched on the edge of the bed, his head between his hands, sobbing. On the bed were his impeccably ironed uniform, a kalpak, medals, a whip, a pistol, and the envelope with the letter that had arrived a few minutes ago.

Sabiha Sultan was so dumbfounded that not only did she not try to understand, she did not even think of asking what was happening. She stared at her husband and then sat beside him drying his tears. Ömer Faruk Efendi, silently handed her the letter. It was from the Ministry of Defence in Ankara, formally notifying the şehzade that his position in the army had been terminated.

"It's over," he sobbed. "I had a profession, I had a job, I was a soldier! Now everything is over! I cannot make a living any more. I am worthless!"

For the rest of his life the şehzade remained upset at being discharged from the army that he loved so much, and whenever he remembered November 1923, when he received the notification, his eyes would fill with tears.

It was a difficult task to keep the republic and the caliphate together, and most people were aware that Ankara was just waiting for the appropriate time to abolish the caliphate. This came earlier than expected, partly because Abdülmecid Efendi did not comply with Ankara's instructions, but also because a dispute had arisen between the military and the parliament as to whether it was the caliphate or the parliament that held the higher authority.

And then shortly after the declaration of the republic, a new row erupted. The Aga Khan and the Emir Ali, who considered themselves the leaders of the Muslims in India, wrote a letter to the Turkish prime minister İsmet Paşa (İnönü) on 5 December 1923, which was published in the Turkish newspapers *Tanin* and *Ikdam* even before the prime minister had received it, then again the following day in the daily *Tevhid-i Efkar*. The import of the letter was that the abolition of the caliphate would cause discord in the Islamic world, stressing that the power of the caliph should not be any less than the power of the pope. It suggested that far from the caliphate being abolished, its influence should be increased.

Ankara considered this letter an interference in the internal affairs of Turkey and a provocation, especially since it was given to the press well before İsmet Paşa could read it. Furthermore, the Aga Khan, who was living a comfortable life thanks to the political support he was receiving from England, had nothing to do with the caliphate, which was a Sunni religious institution; he was not a Sunni, but the spiritual leader of the Ismailis, a Shia sect. When Sultan Reşad gave his fatwa on war at the beginning of the First World War, the Aga Khan reacted strongly against it, going so far as to declare the fatwa unlawful, and saying, "Indians should remain loyal to England, not to the Ottomans."

The journalists who published the letter were sent to the independence tribunals, while a heated debate began in the press and political circles about the future of the caliphate. Abdülmecid Efendi's chamberlain Hikmet Bey told the press that the caliph was waiting dispassionately for any possible developments. If, however, the decision included the removal of the caliphate from Turkey, then Abdülmecid Efendi would rather go to an Islamic country, preferably Egypt, than to Europe as Vahideddin had done.

As days went by, rumors of the abolition of the caliphate and the exile of the Ottoman family spread, and such stories began to appear in the press. The family was perturbed by the news they were hearing. On 1 March 1924 Caliph Abdülmecid sent a cable to the Grand National Assembly of Turkey, in which he wrote that the abolition of the caliphate would mean that Turkey was parting from the rest of the Islamic world, and that this would have a negative impact on the Muslim consciousness. Such a decision, he said, would be a sorrowful and a deplorable event.[22]

In the meantime, the imperial family, though aware that something was about to happen, did not remotely consider the possibility that they could be sent away never to return. They mostly thought along the lines: "Our forefathers conquered this land, our family established this six-century-old empire. The Turks cannot do this to us. Without us they are nothing." And even if they were to be exiled for some time, perhaps for a few months, they believed that the people would certainly call them back. Many of the older members of the family remained in denial even after they went into exile, waiting through all the difficult years abroad to be called back.

Other members of the family, however, such as Neslishah's mother Sabiha Sultan, were more realistic and knew that a return from exile would not be possible and that the years ahead would be hard for all of them.

On 28 February 1924, four days before the dissolution of the caliphate, Sabiha Sultan wrote to her father, who by that time had settled in San Remo, about the alarming news in Istanbul:

What we feared has finally happened. We have been told that the caliph and the whole family will be expelled from Istanbul. Our family is faced with more difficulties than anyone else. I, of course, together with the children, will follow Faruk. My sister is trying to rent her house and will live off that. My mother, if the women of the family are to be allowed to stay on, will stay with my sister. If not, I shall find another solution. There is not much time left to think. Assuming that the women will stay on, they will still have to leave Feriye.

My mother is selling all her furniture, keeping just some essential things. The rest of the family is waiting for your instructions. What should we do with your furniture and the rest of your belongings? I still do not know where I shall be going. Faruk will follow his father. As for me, if they allow me to remain for a little while longer to settle my affairs, I shall stay in Istanbul and join them later."[23]

3
The Muddy Roads of Çatalca

O n 3 March 1924 the fears and the anxieties of the Ottoman
family became reality, when the Grand National Assembly abolished the caliphate by enacting Law 431, which also
allowed the confiscation of imperial possessions, condemning all members of the family to live outside Turkey forever and giving them no
more than ten days to leave the country.

The deliberations of parliament on the law had lasted more than
seven hours. During the debates, one young man was even more
exhausted than the members of parliament: he was the clerk transcrib-
ing the proceedings. He sat just below the presidential chair, charged
with recording in writing all the inflamed speeches given by the
members of parliament, as well as the animated discussions they held
among themselves. Trying not to miss a word of the deliberations, he
sweated away under his fez as he recorded the minutes of the session
for posterity. Once the law was passed the deputies left the room saying, "Let's hope for the best." The young man's hand was numb from
writing so much. The room was emptied, the young man put the minutes he had written in order, and handing them over to the chair of the
parliament he went home.

Although tasked with recording the minutes of the meeting, he was
not a regular civil servant. He was a shop owner who was called into
parliament at times to record the debates. These were difficult days in

Ankara, during the establishment of the new state, and finding civil servants who could read and write was not easy. So anyone literate, whether soldier, accountant, teacher, or merchant, could be summoned to work in the parliament.

The clerk, Ahmed Vehbi Efendi, was twenty-three years old at the time. As the young nation and the young man grew older, he became one of Turkey's best known businessmen and the founder of modern Turkish industry—Vehbi Koç. But the records of the parliamentary discussion on the abolition of the caliphate, one of the most important events in Turkish and Islamic history, and which the young Koç had so diligently transcribed, remained unknown.

Years ago, when I first heard that Vehbi Koç had been the recording clerk in the session of the parliament that abolished the caliphate, I had not been able to confirm this. And there was another matter that I was keen to discover: the prime minister, İsmet Paşa, had accepted all the clauses of the resolution, but there were rumors that Mustafa Kemal Paşa was against some of the articles of the decree, such as the exile of the women of the Ottoman family. No one, however, knew the truth. But in February 1996, two months before the death of Vehbi Koç, I learned the details from his daughter, Sevgi Gönül. In her written reply to my questions, she confirmed that her father was indeed the clerk who had recorded the minutes of the secret session in parliament, that Mustafa Kemal and İsmet Paşa had voted together, and that they did not differ on either the abolition of the caliphate or the exile of the Ottoman family.

Years later, the minutes of the parliament's secret session of 3 March 1924 were finally published, thanks to the records transcribed by the then twenty-three-year-old Vehbi Koç.

Following the approval of the resolution, Ankara gave orders for the immediate expulsion of Caliph Abdülmecid Efendi.

The governor of Istanbul, Haydar Bey, and the chief of the police, Sadeddin Bey, went to Dolmabahçe Palace to announce the decision. Police and the soldiers had surrounded the palace, the telephones had been disconnected, and there was no way for those inside the palace to communicate with the outside world. Abdülmecid Efendi was in the library with his brother-in-law Damad Şerif Paşa.[24] The caliph's first reaction to Ankara's decision was: "I am not a traitor. Under no circumstance will I go. How can they make me leave the land that was conquered by Fatih, my ancestor?" And turning to Şerif Paşa he said, "Paşa, Paşa, we have to do something! You do something too!"

Şerif Paşa's reply was unexpected: "My ship is leaving, sir." It was as if the paşa was not aware of what was going on, as if he did not hear what Abdülmecid Efendi had said. He bowed, left the room, and left the palace. But strangely, during Abdülmecid's years of exile, Şerif Paşa, who had abandoned him in his most difficult moments, became his best friend. He battled on behalf of Abdülmecid Efendi in the claim of the Ottoman assets, and he even founded the "Family Council" to take care of the family matters. Ömer Faruk Efendi was with his father when the caliph was told he had to leave the country, and he witnessed Şerif Paşa's response and departure from the palace: he would never forget the paşa's actions, and during the years in exile he made a point to keep well away from him.

When Abdülmecid Efendi heard Haydar Bey and Sadeddin Bey declare: "If you do not comply with the will of the people, we may have to make you leave the palace by force," he realized that the order was definitely going to be executed, and he had no choice but to accept the decision of parliament.

The preparation for the journey lasted an hour and a half. The caliph's three wives, Şehsuvar, Hayrünisa, and Mehisti, accompanied him together with his son Şehzade Ömer Faruk Efendi and his ten-year-old daughter Dürrüşehvar Sultan. They were all driven from the palace to Çatalca, where they boarded the Orient Express for Europe, on which several sleeping cars had been reserved for him and his party.

Before he got into the car parked in front of the palace, Abdülmecid Efendi addressed Haydar Bey, saying, "Since you are working for the welfare of the people and the country, may God bring you success." Then he turned to Sadeddin Bey and said, "I shall continue to pray for this nation, for the welfare and the happiness of its people. And be sure, even dead in my grave, my bones will carry on praying."

The soldiers and police surrounding the palace saluted the departing group for the last time, and the journey to Çatalca began. The Orient Express departed from Istanbul's Sirkeci Station in the evening of the day after 3 March, the date when Abdülmecid Efendi was removed from Dolmabahçe Palace, collecting the caliph and his entourage in Çatalca to the west of Istanbul, on its way to Europe. The reason he had been sent to Çatalca and had to wait there was because Ankara wanted his departure to be immediate and discreet, to avoid any incident that could have occurred once the abolition of the caliphate became official.

On the night of 3 February, when Caliph Abdülmecid Efendi was talking with the governor of Istanbul in the library of Dolmabahçe Palace, two little girls were playing in a room not far away, totally unaware of what was going on. They were the ten-year-old daughter of the caliph, Dürrüşehvar Sultan, and his three-year-old granddaughter Neslishah. Dürrüşehvar was Neslishah's aunt but was only seven years older than her. At first, the girls were perturbed by the strangers who were going in and out of the living room, then when the discussions became more animated and the volume of the voices increased, they were scared and ran to their nanny for comfort.

A few hours later the caliph came to the children and said to Dürrüşehvar, "Come my darling, we are going. Say goodbye to your niece. You will be together again very soon." Dürrüşehvar noticed that her father's eyes were slightly red, but did not understand what was happening. She did as she was told, kissed Neslishah, and left the room holding her nanny's hand.

Neslishah was oblivious to what was going on. She could not understand why the caliph had come into the room, why then her father kissed her and held her tight, or why her mother Sabiha Sultan followed, saying tearfully, "We are going home now, my dear." Likewise, she could not understand why in the middle of the night all of them—that is, her mother, her sister Hanzade, her nanny, and a few other people in their service—had to leave the palace and go all the way to Rumelihisarı, or why her father was not with them.

After the departure of the caliph and his family, the Dolmabahçe Palace was vacated. Those who did not live there permanently and who would have to leave the country during the following days were sent home. The fifty older ladies who had lived in the palace since the days of Sultan Abdülaziz were moved to the Hospice of Darülaceze, after which the palace was sealed.

The caliph's chamberlain Hüseyin Nakib Bey, his secretary Salih Keramet Bey, and his doctor Selahaddin Bey followed him into exile. In 1964, after forty years in exile, Salih Keramet Bey published a diary of the exile of the caliph, in which he recalls how a Jewish stationmaster bade farewell to Abdülmecid Efendi on his departure from Turkey:

> *4 March 1924:* The preparations for the journey were completed at
> the crack of dawn. The caliph's son Ömer Faruk Efendi, his daughter
> Dürrüşehvar Sultan, and his wives were instructed to go to the ground
> floor. To my wife, who was waiting on the stairs, kissing his hand, he said,
> "I am sorry that we cannot take you with us; if there is a possibility in the
> future, I shall summon you." He embraced his aide-de-camp, who saluted
> him for the last time, and before getting into the car he opened his hands
> to pray for the well-being of our country and our people.
>
> Accompanying His Serene Highness was his chamberlain Hüseyin
> Nakib Turhan Bey and his private doctor Selahaddin Bey. There was a
> long convoy of vehicles in front of and behind the cars carrying the family.
> It was early morning by the time we arrived in Edirnekapı.
>
> After Çekmece our journey was quite arduous. The roads were dam-
> aged and the military police gathered large stones on the side of the road
> to place under the wheels of the cars so that they would not become stuck
> in the mud. After two or three stops, we finally reached the train station of
> Çatalca in the afternoon.
>
> The stationmaster was a Jewish compatriot, who, as there was no
> appropriate place for His Serene Highness and his family to rest, offered

these high-ranking and unexpected guests his apartment on the upper
floor of the station. Together with the rest of his family, the stationmaster did his utmost to accommodate them, treating them with honor and
respect. When the caliph thanked him with appreciation for his sincere
hospitality, the stationmaster replied, "The Ottoman family is the benefactor of the Jewish people. When our ancestors were expelled from Spain
and were looking for a place to go, it was the Ottoman family that saved
them from perishing, welcomed them in their land, and gave them the
right to become Ottomans, allowing them to continue to practice their
faith and their language freely. To be able to serve this family during
these difficult times is merely the evidence of our gratitude." These words
brought tears to our eyes.

The Orient Express arrived in Çatalca toward midnight. At the door
of the sleeper, the governor gave His Serene Highness a large envelope,
wishing him a safe journey. The passengers of the other carriages looked
at us with curiosity from the windows in the corridors.

5 March 1924: We learned from the waiter who knocked at our doors
waking us for breakfast that the train had just crossed Bulgaria. We got
ready and waited for His Serene Highness to call us. He first summoned
Dr. Selahaddin for his morning consultation. When the doctor came back,
we were pleased to hear that Abdülmecid Efendi had had a good night. It
was then our turn to inquire about his health. His Serene Highness, may
God be praised, looked well. He asked me to open the envelope that the
governor had given him. From it, I took out our passports and a smaller
envelope containing some British pound notes. The passports were valid
only for our departure, and the Swiss consulate had stamped a visa. This
meant that we had all been hastily sent away, not to return.

The two thousand pounds that came from the envelope as traveling money would be sufficient just for a few weeks. We still did not know
where we would disembark the train in Switzerland. The Orient Express
passed through the southwestern part of the country, and since in this
region the majority of the people spoke French, Prince Faruk suggested
that on our way we should send a cable to reserve rooms at the Grand
Hotel des Alpes in Territet.[25]

Dürrüşehvar Sultan, the daughter of Caliph Abdülmecid, relates in her memoirs published in 1948 what she went through the night she was exiled:

I was walking slowly in the garden of Dolmabahçe Palace, engrossed in my thoughts. The blue waters of the Bosphorus slapped the shores unceasingly, singing their sorrowful song, while the sun above spilled rays of gold on the waves. The islands, like a silver cloud from afar, announced the beginning of the Sea of Marmara. In front of me majestic mosques and gracious minarets, reminders of the glorious past, watched their reflection in the translucent waters, while the palace, hiding centuries of secrets in its forbidding heart, appeared among the dark cypresses.

It had been confirmed that we were to leave the motherland. When my father was the caliph, the newspapers were full of praise, while now they were cursing him. My father, whose family had been ruling for the past seven centuries, had sacrificed his life and his happiness for the people who no longer appreciated him.

I could understand that this disastrous prospect was taking shape as a tragic catastrophe. In my bitter thoughts, a voice hiding in a corner of my heart made me shudder with fear. We might never return to this land so much loved by our ancestors; maybe in a few days' time, the water that separates us from our motherland will separate us forever. As I was reminiscing, my eyes filled with tears.

I leaned toward the flowers to whom I had come to say goodbye, as a few tears fell on them like diamonds, blending with the dew. I sat on the green lawn, watching my beloved friends the birds and the flowers. Today the flower buds that once filled the air with fragrance are of a sad pallor, whereas the lively voices of the flirtatious birds are gloomy and seem to want to tell me something. I moved closer to the roses that were fading like my hopes, whispering, "My Dear Friends." At that moment, above my head, I heard the captivating voice of a nightingale, as if he were trying to give me solace. Without even looking at the little bird, I hid between the green leaves and the wilted flowers, and I cried.

That evening after dinner, we were sitting in the *mabeyn* (the hall or reception room between the *harem* and the men's residential quarter). I asked for the evening papers, which had written against my father and the family. My father did not want me to see the hypocritical side of people, or to read sentences that would break tender hearts like mine. He added that these were incidents of life, which when compared to substantial misfortunes were always irrelevant. Those affectionate words sounded like the comforting part of a dreadful dream, or like a lullaby that you whisper in the ear of a crying baby. For a few moments, it made me forget the pain of those troubled days.

Another day passed before our departure. My father, who was enduring this terrible blow with stoicism and courage, fell ill by Sunday morning from grief. When I went to see him, he still had a smile on his face, and my mother told me that he needed rest, ordering me to go to my room. I had a feeling that spring had faded away from us, that the garden of life where days were like flowers in bloom was now over, while the sun that irradiated happiness was hiding behind dark clouds.

On the Tuesday night, in my sleep I saw houses crumbling down around me, and a voice interrupting my dream said, "Come, get up, we are going." I opened my eyes, looking around groggily. My mother, quite composed, was standing calmly in front of me: "Come on, get up we are leaving!" she repeated.

Ah, these words were not part of my nightmare, but were reality. "Where to?" I asked, as if I did not wish to understand the phrase "We are going," which would open an even deeper wound in my injured heart. Indeed, where to? Toward an unexpected disaster, or days of exile, sorrowful and enduring? This sudden shock shattered all my hopes, turning off the lights of happiness. I got up immediately and dressed quickly. Then I ran up the stairs and, passing my father's apartment, I reached the large hall, but the sight facing me was so terrible that I hid in a dark corner of the room, where with my tears I tried to erase the memories of those frightful days. I understood then how much I loved the land of our ancestors, and I asked God to give me the strength to endure the pain that this departure was causing me.

The echoes from dark corners of the room repeated the heartbreaking moans in that enormous hall, while on the right-hand side a small chandelier diffused a sad light on the old faces with their extinguished hopes. Everybody was crying, everyone wanted to drown his or her sorrow in tears. The moon gave light through the windows with its pale beams, hiding behind clouds as dark as my thoughts, while now and then observing the exiled caliph. My father's old nanny, the housemistress, came to me, her thin body shaken by heavy sobs. "Don't forget me, please," she said, and crushed by the sorrowful events she collapsed in a chair.

Eight people were to travel with my father, including his first wife, his second wife, my mother Mehisti Kadın, Behruze Kalfa, my brother Ömer Faruk, and my father's secretaries Keramet Bey, Hüseyin Bey, and Selahaddin Bey. Keramet Bey and Hüseyin Bey were busy moving our personal belongings, which consisted of a few trunks and suitcases. We were told that the time had come, so we started to walk down the long corridor toward the *mabeyn*. This sumptuous room, witness of a glorious past, was now surrounded by a fearsome silence. From the windows facing the sea, the pallid beams of the moon, interrupted at times by fleeting clouds, illuminated our path and followed us slowly, as if wanting to stress the resilience growing in our hearts. Before leaving my beloved homeland, I wanted to go just once more to Çamlıca, filled with memories of a happy and peaceful past. I wanted to see for the last time the green forest, the hidden mansion, and say goodbye to the pretty room where I spent my childhood. I wanted to bury the memories of my happy life, which had come to an end like a beautiful dream, among the flowers that bend their stem to the wind, and thus fulfill my last duty of respect to the beauty of that lovely place, but alas this too, like all my hopes, was crushed by that appalling decision.

At eleven o'clock Haydar Bey, the governor of Istanbul, informed us that we had to leave immediately. We had been ready for some time now. Every moment brought us closer to the great departure; the sound of the clocks told us of the forthcoming hardships of the unknown, while we responded to it with the sighs of our wounded hearts.

I heard a voice and walked toward the prayer room next to the library. There behind a black cloud, I barely recognized my father's aunt, whom I loved dearly, and two of my aunts. The tears that I was shedding for my beloved motherland blurred my vision. I wanted to be close to them in order to stop the sorrow that made me cry, as I was in need of consolation. I needed a remedy to relieve the pain of this tragedy. Who would comfort me? The ordeal we were going through made us all unaware of the time that was slowly passing, until it was five o'clock. We were told that the cars were ready, so we all went downstairs. The wailing and moaning disrupted the tranquility of the palace; the tears oozing from our wounded hearts were striving to quench the grief-stricken souls, and our past good fortune, which was a source of joy, now shook us with hopelessness.

Before leaving, my father performed his morning prayer in the chamberlain's chamber, where I am sure he prayed for the welfare of the nation and the well-being of its people. Then my father said goodbye to Cevad Paşa, Celal Bey, and Shekib Bey, who were always loyal to him, and embraced Şükrü Bey who was attempting to hold back his tears.

Finally we left the palace, leaving behind us an unattended throne and seven centuries of Ottoman rule that filled Turkish history with glory, while bidding farewell to the beloved homeland of our ancestors.

I was very young at the time, so I do not remember well that sad part of my short life obscured by clouds of despair, but I do know that at the moment of our departure my father prayed aloud for the prosperity of our country and its people. I shall never forget that moment, or the pain that my father felt when parting from his beloved country.

Finally we boarded the cars, and in the dark of the night I thought I saw strange, massive silhouettes, among which an overbearing one seemed to approach us, at which point I could no longer hold back and said, "O prodigious Fatih, look in whose hands your masterpiece has fallen! They do not want your noble family, those who are your rightful descendants and your only defendants! They are banishing your lawful grandchild the caliph from his country. They have refused his services and have crushed his heart filled with love for his fatherland. They have blemished the unsoiled name of the people. They have dismissed the

House of Osman, who brought to light the nobility of the Turkish lineage, from the loving arms of their ancient land."

The sun was rising slowly. The first light of the day on the still dark shores of Istanbul threw a pink shade on the city, while the majestic mosques and palaces slowly appeared as the night drew away. Now the capital of Turkey looked like a gloomy and faded rose. I looked out from the window. The darkness of the night pulled away, while the surroundings were wrapped in crimson beams and on the horizon the rays of the sun shimmered. The graceful minarets stretched toward the sky, which had now turned red, as crimson as our flag. Even the tops of the white domes turned red. The sun drizzled the blue sea with gold, shedding shiny sparkles on the windows of the buildings. I could not tire of watching this beloved land of the Turkish people and of our noble ancestors. We were leaving Istanbul, and I bade farewell to the city, which stood out like a beautiful flower under the shining sun. "At least do not forget us," I said, but in my aching heart there was not even a drop of hope.

As I had been up all night, my father forced me to sleep, so I tried to forget those terrible moments by resting my head on my arm. Sleep, however, did not bring me comfort. While the Turks were gradually waking up in their homes, we were getting further and further from Istanbul. Passing through streets in semidarkness with the new rising sun partially lightening up the buildings, we proceeded toward a future of dismal days. This evening as the sun goes down below the horizon, so will our happiness, while this grievous separation will dry out the last drops of joy from our hearts.

The road to Çatalca was a very rough one. At times, the car would plunge into a pool of mud and at times we could not proceed because of a pitfall in the road, so we would have to wait. The police escorting us would fill the pit with large stones and only then would we be able to drive on. At around eleven o'clock we stopped by the sea at a place whose name I don't remember, where we ate the food we had brought with us.

The crystal clear waves broke over the rocks, a couple of boats traced white lines on the blue water, while the seagulls, as if afraid of our dismal silence, flew off in the distance. Everything was calm and beautiful, an unconcerned sea contradicting our feelings, clear and cloudless skies just like our past. The golden colors of the morning had faded, and the radiance of the sun sprinkled a dark gloss on the blue satin sky.

I picked up a pebble from the ground as the last relic of my country. While I held this tiny piece of my land to my breast I thought that it would be the only thing that would bring me solace during my future miserable days. Who knows, perhaps when I am filled with nostalgia, this marbled pebble will remind me of my beautiful city and of our home, where I spent such a happy childhood. There might be a blissful return after a second interregnum,[26] and even though envisaging the possibility of us Ottomans returning to our land thrilled me, a wind blowing from an unknown place whispered softly in my ear, "I wonder?" bringing me unpleasant news from the shores of exile.

I shall not relate here our painful journey, which lasted eight hours, but I wish to note a small incident that happened before we reached Çatalca, which affected me deeply. We were passing in front of a school. The students were on break and were playing in the garden. They recognized my father and they applauded, cheering us warmly, without knowing they were bidding us farewell. But what a sad departure for the expelled caliph to be saluted one last time by the children of our homeland!

We finally arrived in Çatalca. The trees looked gloomy, the sound of the birds was dull, and the flowers were fading, as if they were all commiserating our grim fate. The leaves that trembled with the wind of spring lightly touched our aching eyes, whispering comforting sounds.

We were taken to the stationmaster's house, a small and old abode. We ended up here, having parted from the magnificent palace of our ancestors the Ottoman sultans, each corner of which was a testimonial of their glorious past. It was as if we had to reach the highest level of happiness before falling down, and now our lives were filled with the thorns of withered roses, but the thorns were such that the unforgettable memories of those beautiful rosebuds were injuries to our hearts.

We spent some gloomy hours there walking around, trying to keep ourselves busy. After a half-hearted and humble meal, my father ordered me to sleep. I was in great need of rest after this long and tiresome day.

As I closed my eyes, I wanted to imagine myself in my beloved room of the Dolmabahçe Palace, but the constant voice in my ear saying "We are leaving" and the voice, as if from my heart's deepest corner, responding "Where to, where?" brought tears to my eyes, reminding me mercilessly that I was on an old sofa in the stationmaster's house.

Finally, around one o'clock I was woken from my restless sleep and informed that the train had arrived. My mother hastily buttoned my cardigan, reminding me softly how at the palace I would not get up to do my homework.

We boarded the train at the station, which was close by. A few minutes later, as we moved away from our beloved country and the sacred land of our ancestors, we felt that the time that drew us toward an uncertain future of dismal days was near, while our happiness was now really very far away.

I think it was the second evening of our sorrowful journey, when we passed through the woods of Serbia. The green trees looked peaceful, while the leaves trembled with a secret excitement and the sun's crimson rays shone on in the sky. The vibrant colors pervading the surroundings brightened even this dark forest, spreading glossy shades on the windows of the train. I could imagine what the evening wind caressing the leaves was trying to say. Can the noble souls of our ancestors, who victoriously crossed this forest several times, see us? Can they hear the sighs coming from our wounded hearts? This is why this region that wept because of our happiness a few centuries ago now laughed at our misfortune. Even the birds were cheerful, the colors of the flowers brighter, and likewise the clouds in the sky moved on unperturbed with stealthy delight, as if they were all exulting, now that the hopes and the happiness of the Ottoman family were finally sinking, like the setting sun.

Amid our bitter thoughts, an unknown voice comforted us, while in the depth of our hearts hope was always alive. Perhaps our beloved people would be happier without us; perhaps the new prevailing forces—the government in Ankara—would know how to make them happier than we ever could. But would they be able to love them as much as we did? This love that had burned through seven centuries, this innocent love of the motherland, which thought only of the welfare of the people. Was it our fault if in the past one or two sultans had preferred the dark and prickly briars, believing them a shortcut, over the sunny and shining path? If a worthy descendant of Çelebi, Fatih, Selim, or Süleyman could follow the noble path of their illustrious ancestors, perhaps the glorious ancient times would not be just a memory, but would come back. However, along with this vague consolation, our homeland like our hopes was becoming ever distant, leaving us to foreign landscapes and to the memories of our past.

One day we passed Lago Maggiore. The golden beams of the sun played with the blue waters of the lake, the birds stimulated by the bright flowers twittered coquettishly, while the conceited flowers diffused color and fragrance in the air. The tranquil stillness of the green forest surrounded the white houses, admiring their reflections in the water. Nevertheless, there was an unforgettable absence in this foreign beauty. As if our eyes, searching for hidden domes among the trees and delicate minarets rising toward the sky, were grieved by their absence. In a corner of my heart, a thin weak voice cried out, "My homeland, my homeland," while a bolder murmur advised me, "Look at the lake as beautiful as the sea, look at the trees as green as emeralds, take pleasure from the twittering birds." Meanwhile, the first voice responded, "The waves are moaning, uttering the word 'exile.' Don't you understand the language of birds? They are crying out that you are in exile. The whispering leaves are also repeating the word. Even the flowers are writing the same thing on the grass." The second voice insisted, "You can't always have what you want," while the first cried out, "Oh, my homeland, my homeland."

It was as if I were torn between being a gentle, sensible person thinking rationally and an emotionally unreasonable child, crying for her broken toy.[27]

Eighty years later, Neslishah Sultan returned to the sitting room in the Palace of Dolmabahçe, used by her grandfather as his library, when on 26 January 2004 she was invited to open the restored library and paintings of Caliph Abdülmecid, which for years had been left to rot in the palace warehouse. At the entrance of the library, a young girl held a small tray with a pair of scissors, which Bülent Arınç, the speaker of the Turkish Assembly, handed to Neslishah to cut the ribbon.

In this very same library eighty years earlier three-year-old Neslishah had played with her toys as her family prepared to leave the palace at short notice and leave their country. Neslishah recalled:

> After the exhibition of paintings we went to the reception room that used to be my grandfather's library. At the entrance they asked me to cut the ribbon. Once inside I felt tired and I sat on an armchair. As soon as I sat down I thought, "I know this armchair!" Then I remembered. It was my grandfather's armchair! He used to sit there, taking my sister and me on his lap and embracing us he would say, "My sweet, pretty girls." You can imagine how I felt. I shed one or two tears in that room from where I was kicked out eighty years ago, but composed myself immediately.

In the days following that last night in Dolmabahçe Palace, the members of the Ottoman family prepared themselves for exile. They did not have a large fortune, as the Palace, fearing that wealth would increase the şehzades' ambition for power, did not allow them to accumulate wealth. Only some of the sultans' daughters, thanks to the generosity of their fathers, were able to have a certain amount, but even then it did not amount to a great deal. Most of the palaces where the imperial princes and princesses lived belonged to the Hazine-i Hassa, the sultan's private treasury; they had to be returned to the throne after death, and could not be inherited by the next generation, who were assigned smaller buildings.

The family was not rich in cash either. Their only income was the monthly allowance from the Hazine-i Hassa. This allowance was never enough, and creditors would wait at their doors or seize their belongings—a frequent occurrence, especially during the last years of the empire.

What remained was furniture, some antiques, and jewelry. As they prepared to leave Turkey, the family first sold their furniture and their antiques, which all went for nearly nothing. Law 431, which confirmed the abolition of the caliphate and the departure of the Ottoman family from Turkey, also specified that the liquidation of real estate should not take more than one year: those who did have properties left them to be sold by their assignees. Some of these representatives were to sell the estates during the following years and sit on the money.

Throughout the years in exile, the Ottoman family had great financial difficulties, not only because they did not have any personal wealth. The women especially, thanks to their sheltered life inside the imperial court, knew little of money, so they were often cheated. They would exchange a precious piece of jewelry, for example, for a fur coat; then when they came to sell the fur coat they would learn that it was worth almost nothing.

Sabiha Sultan was one of the few who was fortunate enough to own three properties, and she had to make sure they were in good hands. These were the mansion in Nişantaşı, the *yalı* in Rumelihisarı, and the estate in Çengelköy that belonged to her father, Sultan Vahideddin, and was used by the republic after his departure to lodge his attendants from Yıldız Palace, such as eunuchs and heads of female servants, who had nowhere else to live.

For Çengelköy, Sabiha and her sister Ulviye found a way to transfer the deeds of the property to the head of the female servants, Zehra Kalfa, whom they believed to be trustworthy. Should they return to Turkey one day, they thought they would be able to take their estate back and pay the *kalfa* a sum of money for her trouble. This is indeed what they did, though with great difficulty. Ulviye Sultan and Sabiha Sultan returned to Turkey in 1952 after the amnesty and became Turkish citizens again. Following lengthy negotiations with the brother of the *kalfa*, they were able to regain their property, but they were not able to sell it during their lifetime. The children of the two princesses finally managed to sell Çengelköy in 1970, though a significant portion of the sale went to the descendants of Zehra Kalfa.

Sabiha asked the family of Refik Bey to keep an eye on the *yalı* in Rumelihisarı. Refik Bey was the son of Mihrifelek Hanım, the second *kalfa* of Sultan Abdülmecid, who for years had been in the service of her father Vahideddin. When Vahideddin was heir apparent to the throne, he had married off Mihrifelek Hanım and allowed her to retire; she gave birth to Refik, but as her husband died unexpectedly she returned to the service of Şehzade Vahideddin, along with her son. The şehzade sent Refik to Darüşşafaka (a school for underprivileged children who had lost a parent), then to Germany to continue his studies. On his return to Turkey he became the teacher of Vahideddin's daughters, and when Vahideddin became sultan, Refik was first appointed attendant to the sultan's treasury, then to the directorate of the royal treasury, and finally the directorate general of land registry.

Sabiha Sultan probably thought that entrusting her *yalı* to someone as close to the family as Refik Bey would prevent her home from being looted, but she was to be disappointed. One month after their departure in April 1924, Refik Bey was included as number 8 on the "List of the 150," the personae non gratae to the republic, who were also sent into exile.

As for the mansion in Nişantaşı, on 1 February 1926 the Civil Court of First Instance annulled Sabiha Sultan's deed of property. So the mansion and the land passed first to the National Estate, then to the Bank of Building and Construction, and was eventually allocated to the Terakki Foundation, who pulled down the mansion and built a school. In recent years a large part of the property has become a shopping mall.

One hundred and fifty-five members of the Ottoman family were forced to leave the country. The imperial princes were given between twenty-four and seventy-two hours, the imperial princesses between a week and ten days, according to their order of importance. By the evening of 7 March 1924 not one şehzade was left in the Republic of Turkey. Some departed on the Orient Express from the Sirkeci railway station, others on a French vessel from the Sirkeci quay. By the middle of March all the descendants of Mehmed the Conqueror and Selim the Grim had left Turkey.

The state gave each of the imperial princes and princesses one thousand pounds sterling and a passport valid for a year, and withdrew their citizenship. They were eventually allowed to return to Turkey, the women of the family after twenty-eight years of exile, the men after fifty.

*

Sabiha Sultan, being the last daughter of the sultan, was considered an important female member of the family, so she was given just a week to leave Turkey with her children, and on 11 March 1924, together with her daughters Neslishah and Hanzade, she took the Orient Express to join her husband and her father-in-law in Switzerland.

They were taken from Rumelihisarı to the station by car. Sabiha Sultan never revealed how she felt when leaving her *yalı*, but Neslishah recalled:

> I do not remember much of the night we were expelled. After all, I was only a three-year-old child. All I know is what my mother told me, and I have a few blurred memories.
>
> My mother gathered what she could of our belongings, but took very few other things with her: some carpets, a few paintings, some porcelain, and books from my father's library, especially the ones in German. He used to have beautiful books, but moving from one place to the other, in France and Egypt, most of the books were lost. After his death, the remaining ones also went missing.
>
> When we settled in France some of our belongings were sent to us, as well as part of my father's library from Dolmabahçe.
>
> Our servants did not wish to come with us. One of the girls said, "I want to go to my mother." None of the *kalfa*s wanted to accompany us. Only my nanny Miss Brunner and my mother's lady-in-waiting, Madame Burdukoff, followed us.
>
> For a child like myself, unaccustomed to going out much, a train journey was a real adventure. Perhaps this is why I only remember that until we reached Çatalca I was running up and down the train's narrow corridors with my aunt's daughter Hümeyra and Ayşe Sultan's son Osman Nami.
>
> Everybody had sullen expressions, but we did not notice it on our mothers' faces, and we went on playing. Besides, no one told us anything.
>
> From Sirkeci to Çatalca we traveled on a Turkish train. In Çatalca we were to board the Orient Express, but we had to wait for the train to

arrive. They took us to a kind of waiting room. That is when I realized that something was wrong, and I started to cry. Hiding behind some curtains, crying my eyes out, I said, "I want to go home." It took some time to calm me down.

I have no recollection of the rest of the journey, nor do I recall our arrival in Switzerland, but I know only too well what happened later on.

Having lived through the Russian Revolution, Madame Burdukoff often told Sabiha Sultan well before the exile, "Princess, I have seen this happen before, similar things will occur in Turkey, you must take precautions." She was proven right.

In the 1960s, Salih Keramet Bey, Abdülmecid Efendi's friend and for some time his secretary, who had left Turkey with the caliph, told Neslishah about the events before the abolition of the caliphate: "The beginning of the end came with your grandfather's appearance wearing a turban [banned by Mustafa Kemal and the Ankara government] at the *Cuma Selâmlığı*," the Friday procession in which the caliph appeared in public on his way to the mosque.

Part Two

Europe
The Difficult Job of a Princess

4

Funeral of a Sultan

On the afternoon of 7 March 1924 the Orient Express, with Caliph Abdülmecid and his suite on board, was stopped by a guard at the Swiss border. The guard told the caliph that even though he had an entry visa for Switzerland, he would not be able to enter the country: "Your Majesty, it would be more appropriate if instead of Switzerland you were to go to France. I can give you a transit visa."

Then other frontier guards approached the train. Fortunately, no one among the Swiss spoke Turkish, as otherwise if they had understood what the passengers were saying they would have arrested them all for insulting officers on duty. The caliph's traveling companions were raising the roof with their screams. The men were calling the Swiss terrible names, shouting at them, and insulting them. Years later Abdülmecid Efendi's private secretary Salih Keramet Bey wrote about the wait at the Swiss border:

> Our journey to the Swiss frontier through the Simplon Tunnel was uneventful until the border station of Brig. There, the officer in charge of passport controls, while examining our documents, decided on his own initiative not to let us out in Switzerland. After World War I the king of Greece and the Austrian emperor took refuge in this neutral country, but because of their political activities Switzerland was severely affected. The officer said that the Swiss Federal Government should have informed him of the arrival of a personality as important as the caliph. Therefore, he would call Bern and ask

75

for instructions. Until then the train had to wait. The other passengers were alarmed by this long stop in the tunnel and tried to learn the reason for the delay. Fortunately, the official reply came quickly; the train was allowed to proceed and we managed to reach our destination.[28]

Salih Keramet Bey does not mention the fact that when Abdülmecid Efendi heard the suggestion that he go to France, he refused categorically, saying, "Out of the question." His intention was to make political contacts over the abolition of the caliphate, but in recent years France had become quite close to Turkey, and it would have been difficult for the deposed caliph to continue his political activities there. Switzerland was a neutral country, therefore more suitable for that sort of undertaking. Besides, none of them had a French visa and it was more than probable that they would have faced the same difficulties at the French border.

They had to wait a few hours while there was an exchange of telegraphs between the federal government in Bern and the customs officials. Eventually, the permission to enter Switzerland was granted, on condition that Abdülmecid Efendi sign a letter vouching that he would abandon all political activities and avoid any political statements. It was already evening when the caliph signed the letter of commitment. When they reached Territet, a suburb of Montreux on Lake Leman, Abdülmecid Efendi and his entourage disembarked; at 9:15 he and his entourage settled in at the Grand Hotel des Alpes de Territet, and the Turkish flag was raised on the flagpole of the hotel. The caliph enjoyed the pleasant air of Territet and the magnificent view overlooking the lake, which he said reminded him of the Bosphorus.

Years later his daughter Dürrüşehvar Sultan, who was only ten at the time, recalled that stressful evening at the frontier:

> We had nearly reached the end of our journey and were about to arrive in Switzerland. We were having dinner earlier than usual, when the bad news reached us. The Swiss authorities had told my father that they would allow his family to enter the country, but not him. This unexpected incident alarmed us all. The railway guard said that they would contact the

government and would make the train wait until they received a response. After lengthy discussions, they allowed us to cross the frontier to Switzerland. We moved on, and an hour later we reached Montreux. The train stopped slowly and we got off at the station, where bright lights illuminated our gloomy faces. The other passengers were chatting and laughing, while we were all utterly disheartened.

When it was time to leave, my father thanked the train guard and gave him a watch, as a token of appreciation for his diligent and respectful treatment. The guard's eyes filled with tears as he received the present, and I noticed that he turned his head away while thanking my father. I have always been very touched by the foreigners' way of expressing their gratitude. . . .

We got into the car and drove through broad and well-lit streets. After a short drive we reached our hotel. The manager and other members of the hotel staff were there to greet us, welcoming my father with the honor and respect due to his rank. The lights were on everywhere, shining through the reception room and the corridors we were passing through, just as in a fairy tale.

Finally we reached the apartment that was reserved for us. As I was exhausted, I asked my father permission to go up to my room. I imagined seeing Dolmabahçe Palace on a large white cloud above the sea, while for a few moments I forgot about the hotel in Switzerland and all the other foreign places, thinking instead of being in my lovely green bedroom, which made me so happy. However, looking around the clean and spacious yet unfamiliar hotel room, I was brought back to reality and to the long four days that separated me from my beloved country.

I spent my first sleepless night in exile thinking about the good old days of my life.[29]

A week later, on 14 March, another group of exiles arrived at the Grand Hotel in Territet: Sabiha Sultan and her daughters Neslishah and Hanzade, along with her Russian lady-in-waiting Madame Burdukoff and her daughters' Swiss nanny Miss Brunner. Her husband Ömer Faruk Efendi, who had left a few days earlier with his father the caliph, was waiting for them at the station.

There were only two things for little Neslishah to do at the Grand Hotel: play, and be photographed with her grandfather. For a good-looking Oriental gentleman with a fez and a long beard and bearing the title of caliph was an interesting and unusual image for Europeans, and photographers were constantly coming to the hotel to take pictures. At times the caliph would pose for a photograph on his own, at times he would be photographed with his son and daughter or his grandchildren, and practically every day these pictures would fill the pages of the newspapers.

Not a day passed without people visiting the caliph. The exiled Ottoman family members, concerned about their future, would pay a visit in the hope of some good news. Delegations from Muslim countries would follow one after the other, to discuss the future of the caliphate. These delegations did not come just to exchange ideas with Abdülmecid Efendi; the Indian Muslims and the Egyptians, especially, brought financial aid from their rulers, to cover the expenses required for arranging future contacts to restore the caliphate and to ensure that the caliph could lead an untroubled life in exile.

Neslishah would play with her nanny on the terrace of the hotel when relatives were not visiting, or when photographs were not being taken. Below the terrace was a private school, and she would watch the students coming and going, then would go back to play again.

But among the entourage of the caliph consternation prevailed. Few thought seriously about the future, asking instead, "Why did this happen? Why did it happen to us?" They hoped that things would settle soon and that they would return to Turkey, saying, "We are the founders of Turkey, do we deserve such treatment? The Turkish people sooner or later will object to our exile." They imagined there would come an apology and they would be asked to return and honor their country again.

Strangely, even Abdülmecid Efendi did not seem to comprehend what had happened, or fully understand the nature of the changes that had taken place. Like the others, he assumed he would soon be going back to Istanbul. His thinking was that Turkey could not exist without the caliphate: Ankara would sooner or later realize what a mistake they had made and would be obliged to recall the caliph.

Thus among the exiles of Territet there was no great concern about the future: somehow or other they would be going back. So no one worried much about their finances. The huge bills of the Grand Hotel were paid immediately, and no one thought of reducing unnecessary expenses. On the contrary, handouts were generously distributed to those coming and going at their command.

Years later the caliph's daughter Dürrüşehvar wrote about the time she spent in Territet:

We had been in Territet for a week, but had not ventured beyond the garden of the hotel. Then the doctor told my father that he had to walk, obliging him to go out, and one evening we went for a walk behind the hotel on the road leading up to the mountains. Switzerland looked like a beautiful garden. The streets were clean, the walls were covered with fragrant flowers, and the trees were full of birds singing. After walking for some time we became tired and sat on a wooden bench. The reflection of the imposing mountains on the blue lake reminded me of the happiness we had left behind, which had now disappeared. Looking around at the quaint hotels, the wide streets, and the elegant houses, I thought about how unfortunate Istanbul was, deprived of this prosperity, and how helpless my country was. My father looked sad; perhaps he was having the same thoughts as I was. It was time to go back. The sun hiding behind the clouds shone on the blue water of the lake, and the snow on the peaks of the mountains blushed pink, as we slowly and sadly walked back.

A few days later we went out again. We hired a small rowing boat to take us out on the lake, hoping to forget our sorrows, but it was not possible to heal the wounds in our hearts. We were all depressed, and didn't exchange a word. I envied this joyful country, wishing that Turkey were as happy. Suddenly it was as if all the palaces of the Bosphorus were parading in front of me. I was irritated and asked myself, "Why am I still thinking about the palaces, and especially about my country, when like a mother ignoring her duties she has tossed her children away? Why does this disappointment in such an indifferent mother still burn in my heart?"

I remembered a phrase that I had heard since childhood: "This country is our mother and deserves our greatest respect." But what if she had disregarded her obligations toward her children?

A loving hand touched my shoulder, pulling me away from my thoughts. My father was pointing out the sunset. Once again my beloved city came back to my mind. How many times on board the Söğüdlü[30] had I watched the setting of the sun while cruising on the Bosphorus?

In the evenings, we would often go out for a walk. In the morning, my father would be busy with his books, while we would write letters or read, but we were constantly thinking about our past. Each day was like the previous one, and each passing day left us dispirited.[31]

The only person in Territet who was anxious about the future was Neslishah's mother, Sabiha Sultan. She was worried about the mounting expenses, which were bound to lead to financial difficulties, and she was concerned about the future of her properties. She was afraid that the cash they had would come to an end, while in the event her houses sold for little more than nothing, her future and the future of her children would be in danger.

According to Article 7 of Law 431 (the law that enacted the exile of the Ottoman family), all imperial princes and princesses had to dispose of their properties within a year. Failing to do so, they would be sold by the government, who would thereafter send the payment to the owners. The deeds of the mansions in Çengelköy had been transferred to a faithful *kalfa*, on the condition that the properties would be given back upon the return of the family. But the palace in Nişantaşı and the *yalı* in Rumelihisarı could be sold cheaply at any moment. Sabiha Sultan wrote a letter to Faik Bey, her husband's aide-de-camp in Istanbul and a good friend of hers, to be delivered by hand:

Faik Bey,
I am enclosing this note to my previous letter. My situation is becoming more and more difficult each day. I am writing to you in full secrecy. I am certain of your discretion and I know that you will keep this note secure.

So far I have not been able to write on this subject. It was not safe to post it.

All those that are here with us live as always with high hopes. They do nothing all day. There is no possibility of getting out of this outstanding and critical situation, with such pathetic and inefficient attempts.

What happened in Russia? Those helpless people were thrown out just like us and they are still hoping. But the moment of truth is appearing quite rapidly. Five or six years have passed since the Russian Revolution and what has changed?

The expenses amounting at the hotel are beyond limits. Do not think that money was squandered or spent on amusement. It was spent only on rooms and meals.

Switzerland today is one of the most expensive countries, and the Grand Hotel is highway robbery. It is true that it is an ideal place for the smart set living in luxury, but for those of us who don't leave their rooms, it is quite unnecessary.

Now they are trying to find a villa to rent here in Switzerland. If the house is big enough, we shall all be living there together. The furniture that I have brought with me is in a warehouse, where I pay a small rent plus the insurance.

If the house is rented, they will ask me to bring my furniture. I can do so. But once they have spent all the money they have, what will they live on? If I had no children, I could give my financial support, but as things are today this is not possible.

Should my father manage to stay in San Remo, he promised to rent a small house and help me with a monthly income. This, of course, would be a lifesaver for me. But at the moment, Faruk cannot leave his father. The poor man is so downhearted that I just cannot bear to see him in this state.

Faruk is the same as always. He is now living a very quiet life, but given the opportunity, you know what he would be up to. I am also in a state where I don't know what I should be doing. Concerning the houses, we have been negotiating with Madame [the realtor]. She came and said this is not how it should be done, suggesting various options, which I thought were rather risky. She seriously does not understand where her benefit rests.

If I were rich today and did not wish to sell off a house, I would make it unlivable, hoping to get it back some day. But is this possible now, when my only assets are these two houses?

You know what Egypt has donated to our family. After distributing it to those in need, how long will the remainder last?

You are perfectly aware of Faruk's opinion with regard to the family and the house, so I shall not dwell on the subject. Which does not mean that I am not afraid of the future. Please ask Cavid Bey [Finance Minister of the Union and Progress Party] again, what his thoughts are concerning the house. I wish to know his opinion. Should we sell or not? Has he any other suggestion? I do not want to hurry, I just want to have an idea. It would be a blessing if I could provide an income to organize my life as much as possible, and may God help me if I lose control this time.

If a large house were rented and we were to live all together, it would not be possible for me to do anything. In other words, I am at a loss, Faik Bey.

I feel very sorry for my father-in-law. If it weren't for him, life would be unbearable. I do not know how much longer I can struggle with my conscience.

I have told them what I thought, but they won't listen. They see everything either too rosy or too dark.

I have shared my thoughts and my feelings with you in all honesty. Will I be able to get a reply from you? Not by post, though!

If you have the time, let me have your opinion on the above. If I were not afraid of upsetting the caliph, I would be able to organize my life. At times, I have the feeling that all I do is sacrifice myself for him. But my children's interest is also at stake.

I seriously need your friendly advice.

Sabiha

On 7 March, at the Swiss border, Abdülmecid Efendi had given the Swiss authorities a written guarantee that while in Switzerland he would not engage in politics, but he did not keep his word. He made his first political statement concerning the abolition of the caliphate on 11 March, and Reuters published the written text. He referred to the Turkish republic as "faithless" and to the abolition of the caliphate by the parliament as a "denial of the Sharia." The caliphate came into existence with the acknowledgment of the Islamic world, and it was up to the Islamic world, not the Turkish parliament, to abolish it, he said. He then invited all authorized representatives of the Muslim communities around the world to take part in a religious meeting on the caliphate.[32] In the days that followed, the "Caliphate Declaration" was published. This stated that Turkey was now a "Faithless Republic" that denied the Sharia.

The government in Ankara was greatly disturbed by the caliph's frequent declarations to the press. The minister for foreign affairs of the young republic contacted the Swiss authorities to prevent Abdülmecid Efendi from making any further political statements. The caliph, however, preferred to ignore the Swiss authorities' admonitions, continuing to speak and release declarations. The more he spoke, the more Ankara pressed the Swiss to stop the caliph from talking, until Abdülmecid Efendi felt it was time to leave Switzerland for somewhere he would be more at ease. Besides, he finally realized that both the hotel and Switzerland were too expensive. They looked for a more reasonable place.

Friends coming to the Grand Hotel often talked about Nice, saying that it was a quiet, pretty town where life was much cheaper than in Switzerland and where the climate was similar to Istanbul's. Abdülmecid Efendi sent his two secretaries, Hüseyin Nakib Bey and Salih Keramet Bey to Nice, to see whether the town would be suitable for him, and if so to rent a house. The secretaries explored the town and found a villa called Xoulces up above Nice, in Cimiez, where the rich lived.

On their return to Switzerland, they secured the approval of the caliph to rent the house in Nice, and on 5 October 1942, after seven months in the Grand Hotel, Abdülmecid Efendi, with his family and entourage, left Territet for Geneva, where they spent the night, moving the following day to Nice and settling in Villa Xoulces.

Dürrüşehvar Sultan wrote:

We left Switzerland and moved to Nice in the south of France, where we resided for a few years. Nice was always sunny, entertaining and pleasing to all. However, I preferred Switzerland. That cheerfulness had not relieved my pain.

When I thought of the hurricane that had suddenly plucked the unequaled vibrant flowers of the oriental garden back home, shedding the ailing petals of the flawless buds, my heart was still full of sorrow. We were so happy in that exquisite rose garden, a legacy of our distinguished forefathers! Our pleasure then was like a never-ending path in spring, covered with magnificent flowers. But the severe storm wilted them all, snapping off their thin stalks, replacing them with the sickly yellow leaves of autumn. Will spring chase this sorrowful time of my life, like it does in nature? And if so, returning to my beloved homeland, will I only find the remains of that unrivaled garden and only the memory of those beautiful flowers?[33]

For the exiled Ottomans there were now two main cities: San Remo, the Italian seaside resort where Sultan Vahideddin lived, and Nice, where the caliph had settled. Nice was a main residence not only of the Ottomans but also of other exiled families of deposed monarchs, including members of the Habsburg dynasty, who were no longer allowed to reside in Austria, and the Qajar royalty expelled from Iran, including the deposed shah. The streets were also full of Russian aristocrats, and it was not unusual to come across generals of the White Russian army. These families were very much interested in who was doing what and who was living where, but besides a few chance encounters and a few courtesy visits, they did not have much contact with each other.

Abdülmecid Efendi lived in Nice until just before the beginning of the Second World War, when he moved to Paris. Neslishah Sultan would live in Nice for fourteen years from her arrival there in the first week of October 1924.

*

Sabiha Sultan had not seen her father Sultan Vahideddin or her mother Emine Nazikeda Kadınefendi for two years, and she missed them a great deal. She was constantly corresponding with her father. Even when the sultan was in Arabia, where communications were difficult, he never stopped writing to his daughter, keeping her informed of how he was and what he was doing. But exchanging letters was not the same as seeing each other, and father and daughter longed to be reunited. So shortly after Sabiha had helped to settle Abdülmecid Efendi at Villa Xoulces in Nice, she traveled to San Remo with her husband Ömer Faruk Efendi and her two daughters Neslishah and Hanzade. The reunion was a sad one. Sabiha Sultan noticed that her father had aged more than she had expected, and he had lost weight, which both surprised and troubled her. Neslishah recalled:

> We grandchildren used to call my grandfather Sultan Vahideddin "Şahbaba." Whenever his name is mentioned today, I immediately think of this rather thin man with a beard and a very low voice, who spoke as if he were whispering and who would take me in his arms to kiss and hug me. I distinctly remember his cigarette holder, which never left his hand, and his chain-smoking.
>
> When we went to San Remo Şahbaba was living in Villa Magnolia with his wives and my aunt Ulviye Sultan and her family. The villa had a large garden, at the bottom of which you could hear the trains go by. When Şahbaba or my grandmother were not cuddling me, I would play in the garden with my cousin Hümeyra, running from one end of the garden to the other.
>
> In front of the villa there were two armed Carabinieri guarding the house. The feathers on their hats amused me so much that I still remember them distinctively even now eighty years later.

After spending a few days in San Remo the family returned to Nice. Among those who had known Sultan Vahideddin, Neslishah would be the one who lived the longest.

In the early hours of 15 May 1926 a new member of the family joined Neslishah in exile: Sabiha Sultan and Şehzade Ömer Efendi had their third daughter, Necla Hibetullah. Sultan Vahideddin was informed of the event by telegraph, and after conveying his blessings and his best wishes he wrote, "May the child be named Necla." The differences between the two grandfathers in their perceptions of the world and in their choice of names were again apparent after the birth of this third granddaughter. Vahideddin, who was all for simplicity, had named his previous two granddaughters Fatma and Zehra. Abdülmecid Efendi, who preferred more pompous names, added the names Neslishah and Hanzade. The same happened when the last granddaughter was born: the sultan chose Necla, while the caliph added Hibetullah, so the new-born baby was named Necla Hibetullah.

While the family rejoiced and celebrated the birth of the baby girl in Nice, in San Remo that same day Sultan Vahideddin, aged only sixty-five, suddenly passed away around midnight in the small sitting room of Villa Magnolia, just hours after the birth of his third granddaughter had been announced. Tarık Mümtaz Göztepe, who had been in the service of the deposed sultan, described his passing:

> That evening after dinner, Sultan Vahideddin gathered all the women in the treasurers' room, engaging in a cheerful conversation until late at night. The main topic of discussion was Istanbul, and the mansion in Çengelköy, and everybody evoked sweet memories of the past.
>
> Sultan Vahideddin interrupted this animated conversation saying, "Say your night prayers, then come back. We shall continue our conversation afterward." The women got up and left the room to pray. Then addressing his last wife, Nevzad Hanım, who was always by his side, he said, "I think I have a problem with my gallbladder. Bring me a bowl, I am going to be sick." The bowl arrived immediately, and after vomiting a small amount of yellow bile fluid, he said, "Take the bowl away before the whole room smells." Nevzad Hanım took the bowl to empty it, and when she came back she found Sultan Vahideddin lifeless on his reclining chair.[34]

The Italian authorities, to avoid the possibility of later rumors, decided on a postmortem examination of the sultan. His doctor, Professor Fava, who had been visiting him during his last months, carried out the autopsy and determined that the cause of death was a heart attack.

A large crowd of people gathered in front of Villa Magnolia. Most of them were locals from San Remo, there out of curiosity, but among those who immediately ran to the villa on hearing the news were the sultan's creditors, for he had died penniless. He had left Istanbul with just twenty thousand pounds sterling, taking nothing with him of any value. When his money came to an end, he withdrew what he had kept in a bank in England for his son Şehzade Ertuğrul Efendi's education, and when that too was spent, nothing was left.

His funds should have been sufficient for him to lead a modest life-style for a long time; the reason they ran out so quickly was not only because there were too many people in his service and in his company but also because he had no one who knew how money should be managed.

There were also some who had been spending the sultan's cash on their own pleasures. The main squanderer was Zeki Bey, the sultan's for-mer brother-in-law. He was the brother of İnşirah Hanım, who married Vahideddin well before he ascended to the throne. The marriage lasted four years, and he divorced her in 1909, after which Zeki Bey remained as an honorary aide-de-camp. Vahideddin did not listen to those who said, "You have parted from his sister, why is he still around?" and kept Zeki Bey in his service, even taking him to Europe in exile. Zeki Bey gambled the little money that was left at the casino in Monte Carlo and was a main cause of Vahideddin's insolvency.

Mediha Sultan, the sultan's oldest sister, who was married to Damad Ferid Paşa, the sultan's grand vizier, lived in France not far from San Remo, on the other side of the Italian frontier. Hearing that her brother had spent all his resources, she sold her large emerald ring in London, the last of her valuable jewels, and sent the cash to her brother. When the sultan passed away, that money had already been spent.

The residents of Villa Magnolia, with no financial resources, had no alternative but to buy on credit from the local merchants. They were under the illusion that money would eventually come from somewhere, and they would be able to repay their debts. No one knew from where or from whom this money would come, but hope has no limits and they continued to delude themselves, increasing their debts.

At the sultan's death the amount owed to the tradesmen was sixty thousand lira, and the creditors rushed to the villa, foremost among them the greengrocer Morini and the grocer Steiner, who had not been paid for months.

As if this were not enough, the debts continued to mount even after the sultan had passed away. The Italian government organized the autopsy, but the bill was sent to the family. Nobody had the money to pay Professor Fava, who was told, "We will pay you later," until Sabiha Sultan sent the 2,200 lira he was owed after selling her earrings.

Following the creditors came the debt enforcement officers. They seized the carpets on the floor that had come from Istanbul, took other objects including all the personal belongings of the household, and sealed the rooms.

Sami Bey, the son of Mediha Sultan, provided for a first-class walnut coffin, made to order by the international undertaker Bertrand & Son in San Remo. On the coffin was an engraved plate bearing the inscription: "The Emperor of the Turks and the Caliph of the Muslims, Sultan Mehmed Vahideddin VI, son of His Illustrious Highness Sultan Mecid Han 1926." When the autopsy was completed, the body was first placed in a sealed lead coffin, which was then installed in the walnut one and brought down to the main reception room of the house. But then something extraordinary happened, which had no precedent in Turkish history: the debt enforcement officer seized the coffin, which remained confiscated in the villa for a whole month, until the debts were paid in full. In the meantime, Italians went every day to the villa to pay their respects to the sultan's mortal remains.

The day following the death of the sultan, the Italian police came to Villa Magnolia. They searched the house thoroughly, confiscated all documents belonging to those living in the villa, and arrested Zeki Bey, who was charged with the murder of Reşad Paşa, the sultan's private doctor—though he was eventually released for lack of evidence. The seized documents were stored and forgotten in the criminal court of

San Remo, where some eighty years later an Italian researcher named Riccardo Mandelli found them. The documents revealed that while in exile, the sultan's closest attendants had constantly deceived him, regularly informing the government in Ankara of every detail of his life.

Before determining a burial place for the sultan, all debts had to be paid and the impounding order lifted. Caliph Abdülmecid Efendi sent one of his attendants, Sakkallı Reşid Bey from Nice to pay a small amount, but it was not sufficient for the release of the body. Eventually, it was Sabiha Sultan who secured the release of the body by selling a jewel and sending the cash to San Remo. Among Sabiha Sultan's papers, a document was found describing where the money from the sale of her jewelry had been spent: "Her Ladyship Sabiha Sultan's payment: to wash and enshroud the body 5,200 lira; service 150 lira; autopsy fee for the doctor 2,200 lira. Payment to Emilia [the maid] 1,000. Total 8,550 Italian lira."

Then the time came to find a Muslim land for the burial. Turkey was out of the question, so another country had to be chosen. This was the difficult part, as at that time the only independent Muslim nation was Turkey—all other countries were either dominated colonies or protectorates of European powers.

Abdülmecid Efendi, now head of the Ottoman family, held several meetings at his residence in Nice. The Italian and the French authorities were consulted, letters were written to various governments, and diplomatic help was requested. The family was keen on Syria. Ahmed Nami Bey, who had married Ayşe Sultan, the daughter of Sultan Abdülhamid, in 1911 and divorced her ten years later, was the head of the Syrian government at the time, which meant that he could be of great help in securing a fitting burial place there. But Syria was a French protectorate, and the French government had to give its consent.

The French discussed among themselves for a month. A large number of reports, memoranda, and instructions went back and forth between the French president, the government, the minister of foreign affairs, the authorities in Nice and San Remo, diplomatic envoys, and the French authorities in Lebanon and Syria. Eventually, France agreed to the body being taken to Syria via Lebanon and buried at the Sultan Selim Mosque in Damascus, but Paris sent instructions to the authorities in Lebanon and Syria that no French soldier was to pay military honors to the body.[35]

Vahideddin's only son was just fourteen at the time, and could not take care of the funeral formalities, so it was Şehzade Ömer Faruk Efendi, the sultan's son-in-law, who accompanied the body to Syria and supervised the burial procedures.

On 15 June 1926 the coffin was removed from Villa Magnolia by a funeral coach belonging to the Green Crescent, the Muslim equivalent of the Red Cross. It was driven to the train station, where it was placed on a wagon and taken to Trieste the following day, then loaded into the lower hold of the *Carniolo*. On the afternoon of 17 June the vessel set sail for Beirut. As Faruk Efendi traveled with the sultan's coffin and passed lands that had once been part of the Ottoman Empire, he wrote to Sabiha Sultan in a letter dated 21 June 1926:

> During these last days, my nerves have been deeply shattered. I would have liked to relax on the ship, but will I be able to? On the one hand, various thoughts occupy my mind; on the other, the difficulty of our situation gives me no peace. It must be the will of God that inflicts upon us so much misery these days. . . .
>
> We are off the shore of Crete, whose coastline we can see in the distance. The vessel is following the coast and will probably continue to do so for several more hours. What a beautiful great island! Crete was a province of the old Ottoman Empire. Only God knows the agony that I feel when I look at what I see. Our unfortunate sovereigns were blind: they did not try to understand their people, nor the spirit of the people. What our rulers did, they did to themselves as well as to the people and the country. Miserable and orphan land!"

A few days after leaving Italy, the coffin was unloaded in Beirut and put on a train to Damascus. By this time, unfortunately, the coffin smelled foul. The body had not been embalmed properly, for lack of money, and as a result the mortal remains of the last sultan of the Ottomans had begun to decompose, emanating an unbearable odor.

Ahmed Nami Bey was at the station in Damascus to receive the coffin with an official military escort. Other members of the Syrian parliament were also present, and soldiers and military police were aligned on both sides of the platform. The coffin was loaded into a car and was accompanied by members of the government, the military, and the common people, who walked to the city center, where the Sultan Selim Mosque was located. The sheikhs of all the religious orders chanted as they led the procession.

Sultan Vahideddin's burial place had not yet been prepared, so in the meantime the coffin remained in the mosque, wrapped in precious shawls, with the Kaaba shroud spread on top, as a Syrian guard of honor watched over it. With the collapse of the empire, as in all other formerly Ottoman provinces, there was a large Turkish community in Damascus, and among them were some Ottoman officers, who donned their old uniforms and guarded the body of the sultan. In a letter that Şehzade Ömer Faruk Efendi sent to Sabiha Sultan, he wrote, "I don't know why, but all these ceremonies in this warm and foreign land make me feel as if I were in my own country. The only reason for my happiness!"

It was decided that the sultan would be buried in one of the rooms of the Sultan Selim Mosque, but the tragic fate that had haunted his life pursued him to his grave: when digging was begun in the room that had been chosen for the burial, water rose out of the ground to flood the whole place. As a last resort, he was buried in the courtyard of the mosque.

After Sultan Vahideddin's death, his oldest daughter Ulviye Sultan, with her husband Ali Haydar Bey and their only child Hümeyra, settled in Monte Carlo, taking her mother Emine Nazikeda Kadınefendi with her. The sultan's attendants left for various destinations. Nice became the exile capital of the Ottoman dynasty. In time, various other members of the family slowly moved to Nice and settled either in the city or in villages around it. They were followed by some of those who were on the "List of the 150," as well as former Ottoman administrators and their families. Suddenly this little town in the south of France had become the refuge of a small Turkish community. And the Ottomans in exile had now one leader: Neslishah's paternal grandfather, the last caliph, Abdülmecid Efendi.

5
The Carpet under the Sacred Sculpture

The caliph led a monotonous life in Nice, having slowly realized that it was no longer possible for him to return to Turkey. He spent his time painting, listening to music, and playing with his grandchildren, while devoting all his efforts to two main issues: the welfare of the Ottoman family (including the arrangement of marriages for the younger members) and the unfinished work of Sultan Vahideddin in reclaiming of at least some of the Ottoman properties held outside Turkey. As the head of a large family, Abdülmecid made contact with each of his relatives requesting a power of attorney, and he held meetings with foreign companies. But in spite of his efforts, which lasted for years, no positive result was ever attained.

Ömer Faruk Efendi was living in his father's house with his wife Sabiha Sultan and their three daughters, but he thought it time to move out of Villa Xoulces and set up his own home. The relationship between Faruk Efendi and Abdülmecid Efendi was not an easy one. The caliph was constantly meddling in his son's decisions, always finding matters that displeased him. There was constant tension between them, and to make matters worse, since the caliph had lost all hope of going back to his country, he blamed his situation on Sultan Vahideddin, even shouting at Sabiha Sultan in front of everybody, "It is your father who is responsible for all our misfortunes!"

When Faruk Efendi told his father that they wanted to live in a separate house, the caliph agreed, offering him a monthly allowance, but on condition that he would see his granddaughters Neslishah, Hanzade, and Necla whenever he wanted, and that they would stay with him two days a week. Once again Sabiha Sultan was obliged to sell some of her jewels, in order to buy a large apartment that they found in the Prince de Galles building in Cimiez, not far from the caliph's house.

Sultan Vahideddin's only son was Şehzade Ertuğrul Efendi, by his second wife, Şadiye Meveddet Kadınefendi, a Circassian born in 1893 in Adapazari, who had married Vahideddin on 25 April 1911 in the mansion of Çengelköy. Ertuğrul was born on 5 October 1912. When the sultan left Turkey on 17 November 1922, the only member of his family he took with him was Ertuğrul; the other members of the family, including Şadiye, joined him later in San Remo.

Vahideddin assigned one floor of his villa in San Remo to Ertuğrul and his mother. But when the sultan died in 1926, Ertuğrul Efendi, who was only fourteen years old at the time, instead of continuing to live with his mother went to live with his older sister Sabiha Sultan in Nice. One of the rooms in the Prince de Galles apartment opening onto a long corridor was given to the young şehzade. Şadiye Meveddet meanwhile went to Egypt, marrying a Turk there, and then, taking advantage of the law allowing the widows of sultans to return to Turkey, moved back to Istanbul and settled in the mansion in Çengelköy, which she jointly owned. She died in this house in 1951 and was buried in the property's private cemetery. Ertuğrul Efendi always refused to accept his mother's second marriage and never saw her again: he lived the rest of his short life with Sabiha Sultan and Faruk Efendi.

When fall came, it was time for Ertuğrul Efendi to continue his education. The search for an appropriate school began and eventually the right one was found. Ertuğrul's best friend Abbas, the eldest son of Celaleddin Vlora Paşa and Princess Atiya (a daughter of the last khedive of Egypt, Abbas Hilmi II), went to a boarding school in Grasse, not far from Nice, so the young şehzade was sent to the same school. To pay the school fees, Sabiha Sultan again had to sell one of the few jewels she was left with. Ertuğrul Efendi studied in Grasse for several years, spending all the holidays with his sister in Cimiez. And when in 1939 Sabiha Sultan, Faruk Efendi, and their daughters moved to Egypt, Ertuğrul Efendi went with them. But in 1944, at just thirty-two years of age, the şehzade passed away, and he was buried in Cairo.

Neslishah recalled her life in Nice:

> Our new home was a large apartment on the sixth floor with a considerable number of rooms. Necla shared her bedroom with her nanny. I shared mine with Hanzade. There was a separate dressing room, a place for the laundry, and so on.
>
> Miss Brunner, my nanny in Turkey, had already left us while we were in Switzerland, so when we moved to Nice we did not have a nanny. My father, who wanted us to be fluent in German, hired a German nanny, but we could not get used to her. Then several other nannies followed, one after the other: a Swiss, then a French, then another Swiss.
>
> We led a simple and quiet life. We had a maid and an Armenian cook. My father disliked vegetables and salads. "Am I a goat to eat weeds?" he would say, always complaining because my mother and we girls liked salads and fruit.
>
> While in exile my family had no problem with regard to languages. They had learned several languages when they were still in Turkey. My grandfather spoke French, German, and English. His French was perfect. My father studied in Austria and Germany when he was still a child, and his German was as good as his Turkish. He also spoke English and French, with a German accent. My mother learned French in Turkey as a young girl.
>
> My father was a very oriental man, even though he was sent to Austria and Germany at a young age. When people met him for the first time, they thought he was a German officer, while in fact he was oriental in every way, like his great-grandfather Sultan Mahmud. Sultan Mahmud carried out many reforms to imitate the Europeans: when his army paraded, the military band always played European music. Once back in the Palace, however, he would wear his *entari* (a long loose robe),

he watched displays of clubs or javelins, and he listened to oriental music. My father was just like that.

Even his eating habits were very oriental. For him, a good dish had to be heavy. He loved *tirid* (leftovers of soup or meat with stale bread and yoghurt), *papara* (a similar dish), and *paca* (trotter soup with garlic). My father forced us to eat trotter soup, which was often cooked at home, claiming it would strengthen our bones. This went on for years. When I married and left home, I never had *paca* again. I feel faint just looking at that soup!

He engaged an Armenian cook so that she would prepare this kind of Turkish food. Desserts had to be very sweet: "The sweetness has to burn my throat," he would say, and he ordered complicated puddings made. If at the end of his life he suffered from all sorts of ailments, it was probably because of his eating habits.

During the day, he would go for a walk, at times with my mother, but often alone. They had many acquaintances whom they visited together, and then they would be back home in the evenings.

We had a large convertible Lancia. My father had a Turkish flag fixed on the front of the car. He drove the car himself, and he loved to speed. My grandfather would get very angry when my father dashed around town in his Lancia: "They will say you are the madman with the flag," he used to say. My father hung Turkish flags everywhere, not only on his car but also in his room, on his jacket, just everywhere.

In Nice my father had many flatterers, and God only knows where he found them. Every night we had guests for dinner and some of them were always at our table. One of them was Celal Bey, whom I did not like. I didn't know why I disliked him so much, or why I never wanted to greet him. Much later I understood the reason for my dislike. When my parents divorced several years later he said to my father, "You did very well, Your Highness," and of course he was one of the main backscratchers.

Apart from one or two French families, the people my parents saw the most were exiled princes and princesses like us, or other people expelled later from Istanbul. Enver Paşa's former wife Naciye Sultan, with her second husband Kamil Bey, lived on the first floor of our building, facing the garden. Sultan Abdülhamid's daughter Refia Sultan rented a house not far from us. My mother often spent time with Naciye Sultan, Refia Sultan, and Levrans Cahid, who was married to Cahid Bey, one of the grandsons of Sultan Abdülhamid.

My mother at times helped with the housework, knitted, sewed, and even mended our dresses.

The house was always full of guests: Lebib Bey, the brother of Şerif Paşa, who was Sultan Abdülaziz's brother-in-law, his sister Aziza Hanım, Refik Bey (Sultan Vahideddin's finance minister of the private treasury), and at times Şerif Paşa the Kurd as well as the poet Yahya Kemal. They would all come for dinner together with my father's flatterers.

Then there was King Kong! This is what we used to call Sultanzade Kemaleddin Bey, the son of Munire Sultan, because he was huge and had especially large hands and feet. As children we loved King Kong! His father, Damad Salih Paşa (damad is the title given to the sons-in-law of the Ottoman family), was the son of Hayreddin Paşa the Tunisian, who was one of Sultan Abdülhamid's grand viziers. After the assassination of the grand vizier Mahmud Şevket Paşa, Damad Salih Paşa was accused of being involved in the murder and was condemned to death. Sultan Reşad signed the death sentence without any objection, and so Damad Salih Paşa was hanged.

King Kong lived in Nice with his mother Munire Sultan, who had very limited financial means. And she was not around much, as she was still mourning the death of her husband. King Kong used to come for dinner, while during the holidays he would come to pick up my sisters and me and together we would go up into the hills of Nice.

In our home, there was no protocol. We called our parents "Anne" [mummy] and "Baba" [daddy]; we did not address them in the respectful third person plural; it was only with my grandfather that we used this formal way of speech, while we called my grandmother "Büyükanne" [granny], and used the singular when talking to her.

My father called his father "Baba" [daddy], while my mother called hers "Pederim" [my father], but both addressed their parents in the third person plural. My mother called her mother-in-law "Validem" [my mother], but with her own mother she would only use the formal way of speech in front of guests.

However, there was a hidden protocol among the imperial princesses. They would not call each other Ayşe, Fatma, or Rukiye; they would just say their title, "Sultan." They would use the familiar first-person singular form of speech, but they would not use their names. Thus they would say, for example, "Sultan, come here," which always puzzled us children.

There was a habit in the family of saying things like "We miss Istanbul so much! God willing, we shall return one of these days," or "We have been told that we will be going back shortly," but in fact no one believed that we would see our country again.

The only one who never lost hope was my grandfather! He believed that he had not been forgotten, as sooner or later he would be called back to be told, "We made a mistake, please forgive us, Your Excellency." Not only did he never go back but even his dead body never reached Turkey.

Most of the imperial princesses had no idea of what was going on in the world. They had spent their whole lives enclosed in palaces and mansions, having no contact with the outside world. My mother, for instance, had never seen unpeeled potatoes before her expulsion from Turkey. The first time she saw a cauliflower in the kitchen she thought it was a flower! Later on, my mother learned quite well what life was all about, but the older princesses were incapable of doing so. And it was not just the princesses, it was the same with the *kalfa*s who accompanied them in exile.

The daughters of Sultan Abdülhamid lived a life of their own. They never left the house, and they never saw anyone except for members of the family or other people belonging to the Palace. Some of them had many servants and *kalfa*s, who had accompanied them when they left Istanbul. In Nice, these princesses went on living in the same manner as when they were in their palaces or mansions back home.

Most of the *kalfa*s who were trained in the Palace were Circassians, originally from Adapazari. In Egypt, it was also the custom to bring over Circassian girls and train them to become *kalfa*s. In the olden days, it was the wives of the princes who had started this tradition. Letters were written to families in Adapazari, requesting young girls who would be trained and coached to perfection.

These Circassian girls continued to come to Cairo until Nasser's military coup in 1952, and they were all very well trained. One of the best teachers of these girls was a woman in the service of Princess Nimet Muhtar. The girls would wear long dresses, and they knew how to greet people in the oriental manner (*temenna*), that is, by bowing the head then bringing the right hand first to the lips and then to the forehead. They knew how to serve, how to do housework. When they were taught what they were supposed to learn, they would appear before Princess Nimet, who would personally check each one of them. "Your *temenna* is not good enough, watch me, this is how you must do it," or "Do this in this manner," she would say, correcting their mistakes.

These girls were very much in demand by the princesses and at the Palace. To have well-trained Circassians at one's service was a sign of refinement, while the best-trained girls were in Princess Nimet Muhtar's house. Even the wife of King Fuad, Queen Nazli, would always complain about the girls working for her and would say to the princess, "Your *kalfa*s are so well trained, how beautifully they do the *temenna*. I was not able to train the ones we have as well as yours. Would you mind teaching them?"

A *kalfa* was a helper to the mistress of the house, but not in the sense the word is used today. She would be in the company of the lady of the house at all times. The maids did the housework. The *kalfa*s would teach them how to do the laundry, how to clean or do other household chores, and they would supervise the maids' work.

Naile Sultan, one of Abdülhamid's daughters, lived in a true oriental manner, à la turca. Both she and her husband, Arif Hikmet Paşa, were wealthy, and in Beirut they had managed to lead the same kind of life they had in their mansion and their *yalı* on the Bosphorus. They lived a very comfortable life in their home, which was divided into a *harem* and a *selamlik*, meaning that men and women lived in separate quarters of the house. The *kalfa*s would meet the guests, greeting them with a small or a large *temenna*, holding their hands on their chest in a sign of respect, and would walk backward when they left a room.

The paşa would use his office as the *selamlik* (men's quarters), where he would welcome his guests. On the other hand, Naile Sultan would not leave the *harem* and would not accept male visitors, not even relatives or sons-in-law. If I am not mistaken, the only man that ever entered the *harem* was the husband of her sister Refia Sultan.

Every time I traveled to Beirut with my husband, I would pay a visit to Naile Sultan. She loved me dearly and thought I looked like Sultan Mehmed the Conqueror. She would call me "My Conqueror." She was curious about my husband, but she would say, "Imperial princesses cannot be in the same room as strangers," meaning men—so she never met him!

When I would go to see her, my husband would sit with Arif Hikmet Paşa, while I would go upstairs to her apartment. I would do the *temenna* at the entrance of the reception room and then kiss her hand. Leaving her I would walk out of the room backward, and she just loved it.

As we would leave the premises, she would go to the window, slightly opening the shutters to see what my husband looked like. But she always saw him from the back and never saw his face. Then on one occasion she said, "Darling, go downstairs and walk in the garden with your husband, so that I may see his face behind the shutters, then come back here again." I did what she requested.

I also well remember Zekiye Sultan, the other daughter of Sultan Abdülhamid. She was very chubby, had lost most of her hair, and hardly ever left the house. She would dress up and wear a blonde wig. She collected the silliest things like miniature animals, goats, flowers, all sorts of foolish objects, and she also ate a lot of sweets.

Among Sultan Abdülhamid's daughters, Refia Sultan[36] was by far the worldliest. She was a very gracious lady, and her husband Damad Fuad Bey was an excellent husband: I had never encountered a *damad* like him before.

One solemn duty that the last caliph's son and daughter-in-law took on while in Nice was to wash the bodies of deceased relatives and acquaintances. Neslishah recalled:

There were no mosques in Nice, and no Muslim cemetery of course. There were not many Muslims living there, just refugees like us. The French had no idea what should be done when a Muslim died, so when a relative or a friend of the family passed away my parents would go to wash the body as their last duty. My mother would do it for the women and my father for the men, and not only for our friends and relatives, but also for the friends and relatives of our friends.

One of the richest men in the world at that time, Osman Khan, the nizam of Hyderabad, provided an annuity to the exiled caliph. Abdül-mecid Efendi then gave part of this money to his son Faruk Efendi, who used it for the domestic expenditures of his family. The expenses were always more than the income he was receiving, and Faruk Efendi would often ask his father for an increase, but the caliph always refused his son's request.

In the fall of 1926 another guest joined the dinner table of Ömer Faruk Efendi: Zeki Bey, Sultan Vahideddin's former brother-in-law, who in the opinion of some was the cause of the sultan's death.

In 1905, when Vahideddin was still a şehzade, he married İnşirah Hanım, divorcing her four years later. Zeki Bey was her brother, and he remained a companion of Şehzade Vahideddin even after the divorce. When he ascended the throne Sultan Vahideddin gave Zeki Bey the title of honorary aide-de-camp. Throughout the years of exile, Zeki Bey was always by the sultan's side. According to prominent members of the Committee of Union and Progress Party, the reason the sultan hated the Unionists so much and was closer to the Party of Freedom and Under-standing was mainly because of Damad Ferid Paşa, but Zeki Bey was also responsible for the sultan's choices.

During the sultan's last days in Istanbul, this former brother-in-law was one of the people he trusted with his private affairs, the most impor-tant of which were the contacts made with the British regarding the sultan's departure from Istanbul. Sertabib (chief physician) Reşad Paşa and Zeki Bey were in charge of the negotiations, and it was Zeki Bey who delivered the famous letter written by the sultan to General Charles Harrington, commander-in-chief of the Allied occupation army, on 16 November 1922, which said, "I wish to find asylum in England."

Those who accompanied Vahideddin to San Remo recalled that the sultan did not have much money with him to start with, and what was left, Zeki Bey lost at the gambling tables of Monte Carlo. He was involved in all kinds of scandals, they remembered: "Sabiha Sultan had given him some of her jewels for safekeeping, which he sold and then gambled away the money. He made pregnant a young Italian girl in the service of the sultan, who then had to pay a small fortune to cover up the scandal. And he broke the nose of Mazar Aga, the sultan's second attendant, with his pistol grip."

Above all, he was accused of and arrested for the murder of Sertabib Reşad Paşa, Sultan Vahideddin's chief physician. Reşad Paşa was one of the closest people to the sultan, whom he joined in exile. On 15 March 1924 he was found dead with a bullet in his head at the Villa Nobel, the house the sultan had rented when he first arrived in San Remo. Those who heard the shot found him with a gun in his trembling hand, barely alive, and he passed away a few moments later.

The death was recorded as suicide, but on 15 May 1926, shortly after the sultan had passed away, the Italian police arrested Zeki Bey for the murder of Reşad Paşa. He was released after twenty-four days for lack of evidence, but a case was opened in the Criminal Court of Istanbul against Zeki Bey for the same murder, and on 1 May 1927 he was found guilty in absentia and condemned to death. Years later it came to light that Zeki Bey, who had been on the "List of 150," was a paid informer for the government in Ankara; via the consulate in Genoa, he had sent information about the sultan to the Turkish Embassy in Rome.

When the Italian police set him free, Zeki Bey stayed in San Remo for a while, then he left for Nice and took shelter in Ömer Faruk Efendi's house. Sabiha Sultan did not refuse him hospitality, since he had nowhere else to go. Two years later on 28 November 1928 Zeki Bey, to everyone's surprise, committed suicide by burning coal in the annexe of Ömer Faruk Efendi's house and asphyxiating himself. No one ever knew whether he killed himself because he could no longer bear the hardship he had endured all his life, or whether he was crushed by the guilt of the deeds he had apparently committed. Neslishah recalled:

Had my father believed what was said about Zeki Bey he would not have given him shelter, which means that he must have thought the rumors were mere slander. And my mother must also have been of the same opinion, because if she had opposed the arrival of Zeki Bey my father could not possibly have let him in.

Next to the apartment where we lived there was a garage that belonged to us, where there was a minute little flat. My father's car was kept in that garage, but the flat was empty. When I say flat, I don't mean a proper one; this one had just a small room with a bathroom.

They settled Zeki Bey in that flat. In the daytime, he would go to town, while in the evening he would come to us for dinner. For nearly two years he was constantly at our dinner table, with all the other guests and bootlickers.

I was seven years old when he committed suicide and I remember that day quite clearly. There was a coal stove in his room, which he used both to heat the room and to make coffee. Apparently he closed the window and the door tightly, lit the coal and went to bed, where he died in his sleep. I don't know how the news of the suicide spread, but that morning there were policemen everywhere. Zeki Bey left two letters by his bedside table: one for his family, the other for the Turkish government, in which he complained about not being allowed to return to Turkey and said that because of this, life for him was not worth living any more. He finished the letter by blaming the Turkish government for his death.

A few days before his suicide, Zeki Bey had asked my father for his gun, but my father had refused. This came out after they had found the body. The police inspector told my father, "You are aware I presume, of how you just missed being in serious trouble. Had you given him your gun and had he used it to kill himself, I would have been obliged to arrest you."

The strange thing was that my father never told us or anyone else about the gun, not even my mother. We all heard it for the first time from the inspector, but how he got to know about that conversation between my father and Zeki Bey is an unsolved mystery. Eighty odd years have gone by, and I still wonder.

Once Ömer Faruk Efendi and his family went to live elsewhere, the caliph also moved from Villa Xoulces to another mansion nearby, thinking the rent of Xoulces too high and the house too big now that his children and grandchildren were no longer with him. The mansion he moved to was the Palais Carabacel, but rather than a palace, as the name implied, it was a large house with a garden and two statues of lions placed at the entrance.

Some years later Ömer Faruk Efendi and his family moved again. The şehzade had financial difficulties: the monthly amount provided by his father was not sufficient. They were obliged to sell their flat at the Prince de Galles and moved to another building, Il Riccardo, farther up from Cimiez. The new flat was smaller than the previous one, and they rented it rather than buying: the money from the sale of the old flat was to be used for the expenses that could not be covered by the income that came from the caliph.

The children's nanny Miss Brunner had left them just after their arrival in Switzerland from Istanbul. Now there was just Madame Burdukoff, Sabiha Sultan's lady-in-waiting, with the family. Neslishah recalled:

> Madame Burdukoff's life was as tragic as a novel. Her Christian name was Katerina, but we used to call her Tiotya Katya ['Auntie Katya' in Russian], while she would call us Dushka. She was born somewhere in Poland, and came from a wealthy and noble family. Polish was spoken at home. Her first nannies were Polish, but then her parents thought she should learn other languages. Hence they engaged first a German nanny, then a French one, so Burdukoff became fluent in both languages.
>
> Growing up, Burdukoff became a beautiful young girl who played the piano exquisitely. Her parents sent her to the Academy of Music in Munich. There she met a German count and they fell in love. But it was impossible for them to marry, as the count was engaged to a girl belonging to one of the oldest families in Europe: the Schleswig-Holstein-Sondenburg-Glücksburgs. The sister of this girl, Princess Marina, married the son of George V of England, thus becoming the Duchess of Kent. She was the mother of the present Duke of Kent.

Engagements at the time were like marriages; a separation was unheard of, even more so if the couple was noble. So the broken-hearted Burdukoff went back to Poland. Her family seeing how upset she was decided to move to Russia. They first settled in Moscow, then in St. Petersburg. There the beautiful and kind-hearted young woman was well accepted by the Russian society. A young officer of the Russian Imperial Guard fell in love with her and wished to marry her, but Burdukoff repeatedly refused, as she was still in love with the German count.

Eventually, her brother took matters into his own hands, saying, "This is a nice boy, he comes from a good family. You might not find another one as nice as this one, so marry him. I promise you that if you don't get along with him, I shall help you to get a divorce."

So they married. They had a happy life and had a daughter. Eventually, the revolution broke out in Russia and in that chaos Mr. Burdukoff was killed. Madame Burdukoff's brother found a way to escape from Russia, while she remained there with her daughter in the middle of the revolution. For a while they lived in terror. She hid her jewelry in the lining of her fur coats and then fearing that her servants might report her to the communists she hid them under the floorboards. When her daughter was sixteen or seventeen years old, she fled from Moscow to Crimea, with her daughter and her jewels, where she lived for a couple of years.

I think they were in Sevastopol, where an English naval fleet was stationed. Her daughter met an Englishman, married him, and had a daughter. Then all together they left Crimea on a British vessel. Her daughter was able to go to England because her husband was English, but Burdukoff did not have an entry visa. Therefore she had to disembark in Istanbul, where the Russians who had fled the revolution helped her.

It was then that they heard that my mother was looking for a lady-in-waiting. At the palace, no one taught my mother how to do housework, or how to run a home. This is why she was looking for someone who would teach her these things and who would be her 'dame de compagnie,' her lady-in-waiting. At the time, my mother was expecting Hanzade. The moment she saw Burdukoff she liked her and because she spoke German fluently, as did my father, they employed her.

Madame Burdukoff first came to Rumelihisarı, where she taught my mother how to run a house. Then when we moved to Dolmabahçe Palace, she came along with us. She was twenty years older than my mother. When Hanzade was born, she loved her as if she were her daughter. It was my nanny Miss Brunner who was in charge of Hanzade, but Burdukoff practically took possession of my sister, and even though she loved me and later on loved Necla as well, Hanzade had a special place in her heart.

When Şahbaba had to leave Turkey, she repeatedly warned my mother, "Princess, I have lived this before in Russia. Things are not good here. Try to send some money abroad and be prepared for the worst." To which my mother would reply, "Madame, the people here love us, nothing will happen. Besides, our family does not have that kind of money."

When we left Istanbul, none of the *kalfa*s wanted to join us, only Miss Brunner and Madame Burdukoff did, and they told my mother, "We shall come with you wherever you may go." Madame Burdukoff was in our service until she died.

She was beautiful and very gracious, and her skin was as soft as velvet. My mother, who had never cooked, became an accomplished cook thanks to Burdukoff. I also learned a great deal from her.

My grandfather, on the other hand, disliked her. She would get on his nerves and he would refer to her as "the wretched communist woman." When she lived in my grandfather's house in Nice, Burdukoff probably understood that she was not wanted, so she left for England to be with her daughter.

But in London she did not get on with her daughter and her son-in-law, so she came back to us in Nice. Meanwhile, my sister Necla was born and we moved to an apartment, which my mother bought with the money she obtained from the sale of some of her jewels. We did not have enough space to take Burdukoff into our flat, so we rented a room for her above a pastry shop close to our home. She spent the whole day taking care of us or escorting us to the cinema, and in the evening she would go back to her room.

My father admired Madame Burdukoff. They would speak in German together and he would address her as Gnädige Frau. This was the way people addressed German ladies of noble blood in the past, meaning something like 'My Gracious Lady.'

She never lost contact with the count who had been the love of her youth. They did not see each other, but they exchanged letters. The count sent her a monthly allowance, which gave her a certain freedom. Strangely enough upon his death, the count's son continued to send her the same allowance, and thanks to this income Burdukoff had no financial difficulties to the end of her life.

She did not get a regular salary from us. We paid for her rent and we did our best to provide for her other needs. We had financial problems of our own, so we did not have enough money to give her, but we had all our meals together and she always traveled with us. We took her along wherever we went; she was part of our family. She would advise my mother on how to organize her cupboards, or store household objects, teaching us all many useful things. When I started school, she helped me with my homework.

When we left Nice for Egypt in 1936, Madame Burdukoff went back to her daughter and son-in-law in London, but once again she could not get along with them, so I took her back to Egypt with me.

During the first years in Nice, Neslishah went regularly from her parents' house to her grandfather's Carabacel villa, where life was very similar to the way they had lived in Dolmabahçe: there were the wives of the caliph, the *kalfa*s, the maids, the secretaries, and just as in Istanbul the caliph would be bathed and dressed by the *kalfa*s. The difference between Carabacel and Dolmabahçe was that instead of separate apartments for men and women, now there were spacious rooms. Abdülmecid Efendi did not find it necessary to separate the women in his household from the men, as was the custom in his family when in Istanbul, which was strictly applied when he was young. Even as an imperial prince, against the conventions of that time, he lived a much more bohemian kind of life, while in Nice he chose to live like a European aristocrat.

The caliph spent most of his life in exile at the Carabacel Palace. Neslishah recalled:

My grandfather lived on the financial support of Muslim rulers. In the
beginning he was unable to make ends meet, but then when the nizam
of Hyderabad sent him a monthly allowance and later when my aunt
Dürrüşehvar married the son of the nizam in 1931, he was much more
comfortable moneywise.

At home the caliph lived in an oriental manner, as he used to when at
the Dolmabahçe Palace. He tried more or less to keep up the traditions
observed at the palace in Istanbul. In public, however, he was a real European. If it hadn't been for the fez he wore, he would have looked like an
accomplished European intellectual.

He had a modern mind, he read a great deal, and both his French
and his German were perfect. He was a very likeable and a warm-hearted
person. He was both serious and at the same time simple and cheerful. He
was not very tall, but had an imposing presence, and he was very handsome. Everybody in Nice liked him and respected him.

When my grandfather first arrived in Nice, he settled at Villa Xoulces, but not for long. The rent there was too high and the house was too
big, which meant that too many servants were needed. He then moved
to Carabacel, a smaller and cheaper place. Carabacel was an old-fashioned palatial house. There were two large lion statues at the entrance
of the garden.

The Italian owner of the villa was a religious man, who had placed
large marble angels in front of the house. My grandfather did not remove
the angels, as it was a rented house, but he planted large magnolia trees
in front of them to conceal them. The trees became so tall that the angels
were completely hidden from sight.

The first thing you saw on entering the house was a large old-fashioned marble stairway, divided into two sections, opening up in the shape
of two wings. At the end of the staircase, there was a stained-glass portrait
of Saint George. They did not cover the picture, but in front of it they
placed two statues of black boys carrying objects on their heads, like the
ones seen in Venice. The statues were pitch black with ivory eyes, and to
make the glass picture even less visible my grandfather also asked for a
large full-length mirror to be placed in front of the statues. I loved that

staircase. The banisters were also in marble and well polished. I would climb on top of the banister and slide all the way down.

The caliph had his wives, the *kalfa*s, the cooks, the kitchen boys, the driver, the secretary, and the French maids, plus Madame Alice, the Swiss housekeeper—my grandmother, Şehsuvar Hanım, was not fluent enough in French at the time to manage the household, so they engaged Madame Alice. The *kalfa*s were part of the family and their main job was to take care of my grandfather. They ran his bath and ironed his clothes. They also taught the cooks how to cook Turkish dishes, and they supervised the maids. An Armenian woman was in charge of my grandfather's study. There were other maids to take care of the laundry, as well as the overall cleaning of the house. Two French girls dressed in black with white aprons were responsible for serving and were present at all times.

The food was cooked in both the Turkish and the French styles but mostly the latter, and it was delicious. The cook was Armenian, her helper French. Now and then, when my grandfather wanted to eat Turkish dishes, he would ask for pilaf rice with tomatoes. The rice was cooked in the manner of the palace, and we would eat it with sugar sprinkled on top.

At one point a cook who had worked at the palace in Vienna was also employed. He would cook delicious meals, and he loved his profession. My grandmother was overjoyed, but my grandfather did not like the food he prepared. One day he made an excellent mille-feuille, and my grandfather told him to make a *börek* with the same dough, which he did, but not to my grandfather's satisfaction. Another time he prepared a succulent meal and my grandfather said, "Tell the man that if he had added this ingredient, if he had cooked it this way, it would have tasted better," at which point the cook came out of the kitchen, opened the door to our dining room, said to my grandfather, "Your Majesty, I cannot work in a house where people don't understand anything about food"—and left! My grandmother was so upset that she nearly fainted. Then they had only the Armenian cook.

My father was not keen on European food, so in our house we always ate the Turkish way. Plus our way of life was a simple one. Our cooks were always Armenian, and on our table nearly every day there was *köfte* (meatballs) with pilaf rice and at least twice a week *paça* (trotters) or *tirid* (bread in broth).

My grandfather and the *kalfa*s would pray five times a day, but I cannot remember whether my grandmother did. My grandfather never missed a prayer. He had embroidered white felt mats that he used as prayer rugs, either in his study or in his bedroom. When it was prayer time, wherever he was in the house, the doors would be shut and he would pray.

My grandfather's second wife, Hayrünisa Hanım, taught me how to pray. My other grandmother Nazikeda Kadınefendi, that is my mother's mother, never missed a prayer. Whenever she visited us at home, if it were prayer time she would say, "Sit there in the corner child, I am going to pray now." During the last years of her life, as she could not kneel down, she would pray on her chair.

My grandfather received many visitors, but we never saw them. We children were not allowed to appear in front of them. These visitors were not only Turks: he knew many artists, writers, and so on in Nice, and often invited them for tea. The women of the house, however, were allowed to be in the same room as the guests, and talk with them.

My grandfather had several secretaries. His private secretary was Hüseyin Nakib Bey, who was also his friend. He lived with my grandfather on the top floor of the house. When my aunt Dürrüşehvar married and moved to India, he went with her. When he came back to Nice, he had an affair with my grandfather's housekeeper, Madame Alice. When my grandfather found out he raised hell: eventually, they married and left Nice.

On the lower floor of the house was another secretary, who was in charge of the correspondence and the business of the household. The first to hold this post was Galip Bey, who had previously worked for Şerif Paşa the Kurd. When the paşa left Nice for Paris, Galip Bey stayed in Nice and came to work for my grandfather. During his years in the service of Şerif Paşa he had tried to come up with a method to make the paşa win at the roulette tables in Monte Carlo. Despite this strange hobby, he was a very intelligent and shrewd man, but we were always afraid of him, as the poor thing looked just like a monkey. Eventually, he died of cancer and was replaced by Enisi Bey, a very polite man who was only interested in books. He read constantly.

He dreamed of building a hut in the middle of a forest, where he wanted
to move with all his books. "When I build my hut, I shall name it Seclusion
Sanctuary, and I shall live there in solitude," he used to say.

When my grandfather moved to Paris, Enisi Bey remained in Nice,
but he ended his life miserably: he became a dishwasher at the Hotel de
Paris in Monte Carlo and worked until the day when while washing dishes
at the hotel, he dropped dead!

My grandfather would wake up early and take the bath that had been
prepared for him by the *kalfa*s. In the bathtub, they would stir a greenish
liquid, slightly pine-scented. The whole room would smell like a forest.
My grandfather would lie in that green water for a long time, while the
*kalfa*s would wash him.

In his room, there was a vanity table with a large silver mirror. After
his bath, he would sit in front of this table wearing a white barber's apron
and trim his beard then comb his hair. The *kalfa*s would dress him and
bring his ties. He would choose one and tie it. Behruze Hanım and Ofelya
Hanım were in charge of these tasks.

After these rituals, he would pick the handkerchief that he would place
in the top pocket of his jacket and then he would go to the cupboard where
he kept his prayer beads: there were several shelves full of them. He dressed
very well but in a simple manner. When the weather was cold, he would tie
a scarf around his neck, put his coat on, and place his fez on his head with
great care. He would get in his car with his secretary Hüseyin Nakib Bey
and drive to the Promenade des Anglais, where he would walk by the seaside.

He had a large Fiat, with a uniformed Austrian chauffeur named
Adolf. The car was green, beautiful, and very comfortable. Inside there
were flowers in crystal vases on each side, and there were small perfume
bottles filled with cologne, rose water, or whatever else was needed: these
details were only found in old cars. Such cars were lovely, but as with most
early models, they did not perform very well, and on two occasions the car
nearly caught fire.

At times, my grandfather would take us along, Hanzade and me, and
we would walk together by the seashore. On Thursdays or Sundays we
would go to the zoo. On one occasion Hanzade went too close to the

monkey's cage, and the monkey grabbed her hair. Hanzade was scream-
ing, my grandfather was shouting, and I was crying. Eventually, the guards
arrived, opened the cage, and released Hanzade's hair from the hands of
the monkey.

Another time, again at the zoo, something odd happened that disturbed us all. I was there with my grandfather and my sister, when one
of the staff told us, "We have opened a new section at the zoo today, you
should see it." They had brought in natives from Africa, and in a corner
of the garden they had made an African village, with straw and grass, and
had settled them there. Men, women, children . . . it was like a real village.
The men and women were wandering around practically naked, and the
French people were staring at them as if they were seeing wild animals,
but enjoying it. I was very disturbed by what we witnessed. My grandfather was also upset. "Look what these civilized French people are doing,
exhibiting humans like animals," he said, and we went back home.

This is how we used to spend our Thursdays and Sundays. There was
no school on those two days, so we followed this same routine throughout
our school years. Friday was my grandfather's doctor day. An old doctor by the name of Colonel Castelli would come to the villa, and after
examining my grandfather he would examine everybody else in the house,
servants included.

After his morning walk my grandfather would come back to the villa
to pray in the large reception room, on the embroidered white felt mat
that was kept near the piano. Once the prayer was over, he would fold the
corner of the mat and get up. The *kalfa*s would then come in, remove the
mat, and place it again next to the piano.

Lunch was always at midday and dinner at seven-thirty. There were
two sittings in the dining room. At the first sitting my grandfather and my
grandmother would sit opposite each other; his secretary Hüseyin Nakib
Bey, my aunt Dürrüşehvar, and I were also at the table. There were always
flowers in the middle of the table; now and then my grandmother, without
my grandfather noticing, would make these bouquets larger and larger,
for the following reason: My grandmother was rather plump and suffered
from diabetes, but her appetite was quite voracious; the doctors would

advise her to eat less and to diet, but she would not listen. She pretended to eat the diet food that was specially prepared for her, because she was afraid of her husband, but, hiding behind the flowers, she also ate what was cooked for us.

When we finished our meal, the table was cleared and set again. Dürrüşehvar's mother Mehisti Hanım, the caliph's second wife Hayrünisa Hanım, the secretaries, Behruze, Ofelya, and the other *kalfa*s would eat at the second sitting.

When Dürrüşehvar married and moved to India, she took her mother with her, but when the family traveled from India to Europe and came to France, Dürrüşehvar and her mother would stay at my grandfather's house. Her husband would go to the Negresco Hotel. It was during these visits that Mehisti Hanım's position changed, as she was allowed to eat at the first sitting.

When other members of the family, important guests, or my parents came the table would be extended for the first sitting. Damad Şerif Paşa, Naciye Sultan, and Kamil Bey would eat at this table.

There was a rather large room next to the dining room. This was the billiard room, but my grandfather did not play snooker. Sometimes we would all sit there after a meal looking at magazines, chatting or having long conversations. When my grandmother went up to her room, we children would play either there or in the garden.

Then everybody would retire to his or her room. My grandfather usually read or wrote. He wrote his memoirs or poetry, or at times composed a piece of music. This is how he would spend his day.

When my sisters and I were in his presence we would always do the *temenna*, a really deep one, starting right from the floor. Then we would kiss his hand and he would caress our cheeks, embracing us several times. Our relationship with him was not a formal one; on the contrary, it was warm and intimate, but we had to do the *temenna* and address him in the second-person plural.

He wanted my sisters and me to know all about the Ottoman history. So he made us learn by heart the names of all the sultans to rule the empire. He would make us sit in front of him saying, "Come now, enumerate your ancestors," and we would start in unison: "Sultan Osman, Sultan Orhan, Sultan Murad, Sultan Bayezid, . . ."

He had a large room in the attic of the house that he transformed into a studio. There he had all sorts of paints, brushes, palettes, and easels. Light came from above through a glass ceiling. I think he picked this room to paint because of the light. Thursdays were the days he painted. At times he would not go out, instead, after his bath, going up to the attic to paint.

On other days, after lunch, he would retire to his study to read or write his memoirs, while we played in the garden. In the evenings, he would play the piano and he would ask us to come and listen to him playing. He was not interested in Turkish music, he only played classical music. At times, he would perform together with his wives and the *kalfa*s, in chamber music concerts. He would be at the piano, my grandmother and Hayrünisa Hanım would play the violin, and Mehisti Hanım the cello. On other occasions, one of the *kalfa*s would play the piano, while he listened.

In the living room, beside the piano, there were two small harmoniums, which my grandfather also played, though he preferred to listen to others playing. The music of these organs was engraved onto cylinders that were changed according to the melody requested and were played by pushing the pedals of the instrument. The rhythm of the music changed according to the way you pushed the pedals. One of these harmoniums was completely mechanical; that is, you could only play the music engraved on the cylinders, while on the other one you could also change the orchestration. Once the cylinder was put in place, you could play the music with different instruments, by pulling small levers on the side of the organ.

My grandfather would make us sit at the organ, put the cylinder in place, and say, "Come now, start playing," and would want us to follow the rhythm to see whether we had any aptitude for music. He loved having us in the music room and he would say, "Stay here as long as you wish." Then he would change the cylinders of the harmonium and listen to music for hours. During those years, thanks to my grandfather, I learned to love and appreciate classical music.

The caliph's coffee ceremony was quite à la Turca. Traditionally, the pot and the coffee cups were served on a round silver tray, suspended on three silver chains. Even if the tray were accidently shaken, the coffee would not spill. This kind of tray was called a *sitil*. My grandfather always wanted his coffee served on this sort of tray, which had to be poured by the *kalfa*. One *kalfa* would carry the *sitil*, while the other would carry another tray with a cup and a glass of water with freshly squeezed orange or lemon flower. The *kalfa* would pour the coffee in his cup and he would add a drop of the flower-scented water. This is the way he liked to drink his coffee.

In the summer we would go to the beach. My grandfather thought that Muslims living in Nice might get strange ideas if they saw the caliph swimming, so he preferred to go to Cagnes-sur-Mer. On the beach, we would have a large umbrella, with towels to sit on in the sand. My grandfather would change with the help of Adolf, the driver, and then go swimming. Sometimes his private secretary Nakib Bey would join him, helping him to dress and undress. At times, my parents would also come along with us.

There were often poets and painters at the beach, as a number of artists lived in that area. Sometimes they gave beach parties, and then my grandfather would invite the ones he knew back home. Men and women artists would come to talk about art.

There was also an English spy at the house of the caliph: Julia Gertrude Richards, Dürrüşehvar's English teacher, who had a room at Carabacel overlooking the garden. Every Tuesday, her day off, she would dress up, put on her cherry hat or another one with flowers, leave the house saying, "I am going to my lawyer," and be back late in the evening.

When she fell and broke her hip while playing badminton with Dürrüşehvar she was unable to visit her solicitor for several months, but as soon as she recovered her Tuesday's visits were on again, only now she had to use a cane, as she had been left with a limp.

Miss Richards was either going to the British Consulate in Nice or meeting up with another agent, to whom she would give her weekly report on what was going on at the Villa Carabacel. Everybody in the

villa was aware of what she was doing, but no one reacted, since there
was nothing to hide—what could she report besides "The caliph painted
a great deal this week, he scolded his driver, yesterday one of the ladies
overate, he continued the lessons with his daughter, he kissed his granddaughters while they sat on his lap"?

Şehzade Mehmed Seyfeddin Efendi, the caliph's younger brother by six
years, moved to Cimiez with his two wives and four children, to reside in
a villa not far from the Villa Carabacel.[37] Seyfeddin Efendi was born in
1874 at the Dolmabahçe Palace. His father, Sultan Abdülaziz, died when
he was two years old and he was brought up by women and *lala*s (imperial tutors). All his life he struggled with financial problems: Although he
was the son of a sultan, while still in Istanbul he had debts up to his neck.
Creditors were knocking at his door, and at times the State Treasury had
to pay his debts.[38]

Art was both a tradition in Seyfeddin Efendi's family and a daily
occupation. His father Sultan Abdülaziz had been a painter, his brother
the caliph was both a painter and a composer, considered one of the
leading artists of Turkish painting, and another brother, Şehzade
Şevket Efendi, was a pianist. Seyfeddin Efendi was one of the leading
artists of Istanbul. He painted and sculpted, but his real talent was as
a first-class composer of Ottoman music. In his flat in Feriye or his
mansion in Çamlıca, he often organized musical evenings with well-
known artists, where they played classical Ottoman music and music
he had composed himself. He was a follower of a Sufi order, so he
became interested in religious music and composed a large number
of Islamic hymns. He composed two *peshrevs* (instrumental scores of
Turkish classical music) inspired by the *maqam*s of the famous com-
posers Hüzzam and Bayati, as well as numerous religious hymns that
are still played today.

Beside his interest in art and music, Şehzade Seyfeddin Efendi was
also an accomplished *mahya* craftsman: During the nights of Ramadan,
the month of fasting for Muslims, the mosques were embellished with
illuminated inscriptions made with small oil lamps strung on a rope or

wire between two minarets. This craft was known as *mahya*, and was a painstaking undertaking. Today electric bulbs have replaced the oil lamps. The distance between the letters of these inscriptions and the distance between the minarets were meticulously calculated and then the oil lamps were carefully attached to the wire. When it was time to break the fast, the craftsmen would climb onto the balconies of the minarets to tighten the wire of the *mahya*, from where they would light the oil lamps one by one. Refilling the lamps with oil and renewing the wicks was also a very arduous task.

These illuminated inscriptions were displayed only on the imperial mosques built with funds bestowed by the sultans. His Imperial Highness, the Imperial Prince Mehmed Seyfeddin Efendi was the most important *mahya* craftsman of his time. Neslishah recalled:

Seyfeddin Efendi was my great-uncle. I remember him well: he was as fat as a whale. Even in Nice, they would talk about his talent as a *mahya* master. Apparently every Ramadan the imams of the great mosques would go to Çamlıca to ask him to prepare their *mahya*. I always wondered how a man of his size could climb up onto the narrow balconies of the minarets.

He was born to a different mother, but for my grandfather he was just like a true brother. He had rented a large villa with a garden in Cimiez, farther up from us, just before the tramway line ended, opposite to the Tennis Club. He lived there with his wives and children.

Seyfeddin Efendi would visit my grandfather very often and together they would spend hours talking about music and painting. My great-uncle played the *kanun* [a type of zither] and at times he would bring his instrument with him to play to his brother the songs he had recently composed. Then my grandfather would go to the piano and play his own latest compositions. I don't think they understood much about each other's kind of music, but they took pleasure in listening to one another.

My uncle died suddenly three years after he had moved to Nice. They said it was a heart attack. With great difficulty his body was sent to Damascus, where he was buried in the tomb of my Şahbaba, in the courtyard of the Sultan Selim Mosque.

His wives and children were devastated and left penniless, with nowhere to go. They sold their furniture for practically nothing and for a while the wives tried to live on this small amount of money.

Neslishah did not have many friends in Nice. She spent her days with her sisters, or with the children of relatives, but she was not allowed to see other children. She recalled:

Unfortunately, I had no friends. My father was old-fashioned and very oriental, but because he had studied in Prussia, he also had a Prussian mentality: he was very strict with us. As in Germany, he expected the fathers of the children to come and see him. If he approved of the parent, I would then be allowed to go to their home. I was of course embarrassed to ask such a thing of my school friends. So none of my friends ever came home.

After moving to the Prince de Galles, my parents befriended a French family called Doreau, who lived in the same building. We became friends with their children, but those were the only foreign friends we had. We sisters grew up mainly together.

Up in the hills of Nice, near the Roman ruins, there was a huge building known as Garin de Cocconato, which later on became the Musée Matisse. Now and then I would go up there to play with the caretakers' children. They were my age, but they did not speak French; they spoke Niçois, a dialect used only in Nice, which was a mixture of French and Italian. We were told that this was an ancient dialect that had originated in Liguria. In those days, this was the language that was spoken by the locals. At first, we did not understand one another, but in time I learned to speak Niçois, and I was able to communicate with the other children. When they realized at home that I spoke in dialect, they said, "You are a princess, princesses do not speak that kind of language, it is not suitable. You have to speak proper French." My school was a French school anyway, so in time, I forgot the Niçois dialect completely.

At home we were forbidden to speak French; my parents spoke to each other in Turkish and would tell us about Turkey as if they were describing Paradise—where Turkish was the language spoken. It was therefore crucial that we should speak Turkish. My parents would raise hell when at times they heard us sisters use French words among ourselves. Speaking French with my grandfather was also totally out of the question: we could only use Turkish with him. Years later I understood that we could not have spoken Turkish so fluently if they had not been so strict about it.

Members of other royal dynasties lived in the south of France: if a group of exiles were known to be happy with their new place of residence, others would automatically follow. There were many Russian aristocrats who had fled the revolution of 1917 and some princes and princesses of the Qajar dynasty as well as the former empress. Neslishah recalled:

My grandfather was not in contact with the exiled royalties, but now and then my parents would see the Qajars.

In 1925, Reza Pahlavi had overthrown Ahmed Shah, the last Qajar ruler, and taken his place. The former shah's mother, Empress Melike Cihan, had a house near the port in the old part of Nice. Ahmed Shah had at one time wanted to marry my mother, but she had refused, as had Şahbaba, who had said, "The daughter of the caliph of the Sunnis cannot marry a Shia ruler." Later, in Europe, my father befriended Ahmed Shah, who liked to spend a few months of the year in France when he was still ruler of his country. My father would tell him, "Go back to Iran: if you stay here you will lose your throne." But the shah did not follow his advice, and eventually he was deposed, and he moved to Paris, while his mother lived in Nice.

One day my parents took me with them when they went for lunch to the empress's house. I was nine or ten years old. I had forgotten that one of my grandfathers was a sultan and the other a caliph. "What am I going to do in the presence of an empress?" I thought, and was very nervous. When we arrived a prince, very short in stature, welcomed us. I was even more nervous. I was so afraid of meeting the empress that I nearly peed in my pants.

Then we were taken to the reception room where the empress was expecting us. I was not very tall at the time—I could even have been considered rather short—and what did I see? The empress was even shorter than I was; I was nearly a head taller than her! All my fears disappeared in an instant, and I relaxed.

One of the most unfortunate ladies of the family, Seniha Sultan, the daughter of Sultan Abdülmecid, joined the caliph's household in the Villa Carabacel. She had been born in 1851 in the old Çırağan Palace and was over seventy years old when she arrived in Nice. She had lost both her parents as a child, and at the age of twenty-five she married a man two years her junior who had a promising future: he was Mahmud Celaleddin Paşa, the son of Halil Rifat Paşa. In 1878, Seniha Sultan gave birth to her first son Sabahaddin and a year later to her second son Lutfullah.

Ayşe Sultan, the daughter of Seniha Sultan's brother Sultan Abdül-hamid, wrote of her aunt in her memoirs: "She wore a crown and had beautiful clothes, with long dresses, as was the fashion in Europe, with the tail flowing at the back. She looked very imperial and had a beautiful face. Her hair was always cut short like a boy's, and she never wore it otherwise. She was a free spirit. She used to let out great peals of laughter, and spoke quickly in a husky voice. Seniha Sultan was not much liked at the palace, as at times her behavior was rather eccentric."[39]

In the years to come, the life of this princess, so different from the other members of the family, would be filled with tragedy. Her husband was very critical of Sultan Abdülhamid's governance, never missing an occasion to speak out. Eventually he had enough of being followed and spied on, so in 1899 he took his two sons and fled to Europe, where four years later he died in Belgium and was buried in Paris. His sons were able to return to Istanbul only in 1908, after the declaration of the Second Constitution.

Seniha Sultan's older son was in favor of 'decentralization' and tried to have this idea implemented in the country. His passionate but dissident political involvement made him well known during the last years of the empire, when he was known as "Prince Sabahaddin," and he is remembered as such in the history of the Ottoman Empire, even though, as the son of a princess he was not a şehzade, but a beyzade, and so was not entitled to be addressed as Prince. Nevertheless, he never objected to being called Prince, and according to the rumors of the time, he never refuted the fact that he had aspired to the Ottoman throne.

Seniha Sultan was left on her own after the departure of her husband and her two sons, whose opposition to Sultan Abdülhamid, her older brother, left her in an awkward position. Worse was to come, when in March 1924 she was exiled from Turkey along with the rest of the Ottoman family, at the age of seventy-three. She had no money of her own, and her children were too busy with their affairs to take care of her, so she went into exile alone.

Only one person could give her refuge, her brother Sultan Vahideddin, who lived in San Remo. So she went to Villa Magnolia, the deposed sultan's home, and lived there until his death in 1926, after which she was homeless. Knowing that some of her relatives lived not far away in Nice, she moved there.

Like most of the older imperial princesses, Seniha Sultan had no idea of life outside the palaces, nor did she know anything about money, or how to make a living. When she left Istanbul she was given one thousand pounds—like all the other members of the family—but she spent it all in a matter of weeks, and when she arrived in Nice she was utterly penniless. For a while, she tried to live on the charity of relatives of the Abdülmecid branch of the family, but they also had difficulties in making ends meet. At the age of nearly eighty, she was forced to spend several nights in the public gardens of Cimiez—she, the daughter of Sultan Abdülmecid, she who had pulled faces in disappointment at a residence that was assigned to her, and failed to appreciate the palaces of Istanbul, was left in the streets.

She hoped that people would not find out about her appalling condition, but somehow it became known and someone called her younger son Lutfullah Bey, who was trying to make a living in Paris: "Your mother is living in the streets, come and take matter into your hands."

Lutfullah Bey arrived immediately and took his mother to the residence of the caliph. "My mother is your first cousin, Your Highness. My brother and I are in no state to take care of her. It would bring shame to our family if it were known that the daughter of Sultan Mecid is living in the streets. Please have mercy and take her in with you," he implored.

Sabiha Sultan was among those who insisted most strongly that the caliph give the elderly princess a room in his house, even a small one. After all, Seniha Sultan was Sabiha Sultan's aunt, the sister of her deceased father, as well as his last living sibling.

She was given a room in the attic, next to the caliph's painting studio, where one of his wives, Şehsuvar Kadın, kept her old clothes—a room full of cupboards. Sabiha Sultan was upset that her aunt had to sleep on a mattress amid old dresses, but she was told that no other room was available. Of course, it was better than sleeping on the street. Neslishah recalled:

> I always remember Seniha Sultan dressed in black. She was quite thin, in fact really skinny, she had dry skin, and was very old. Even her headscarf was black. My mother was very sad that her aunt had to live in that manner, but there was nothing to be done. She always kissed her hand when she visited her and showed her great respect. Seniha Sultan knew that my grandfather disliked her, so she was not around much, and she hardly ever left her room.
>
> One day she went out on her own and walked to the public gardens in Cimiez. She sat there on a bench, probably reminiscing about Istanbul. Her clothes were rather shabby, old and black. A Frenchman passing by assumed that the poor woman was a beggar and gave her some money.
>
> Later, relating the incident to my mother, she said, "I accepted the charity, I even accepted it with a smile!" My mother was crying as she told us about it.

Seniha Sultan, the longest-lived of Sultan Abdülmecid's children, died at the Villa Carabacel on 15 September 1931. Where was she to be buried? In Nice at the time there were no Muslim cemeteries, so she must be buried in a Muslim country, but that was an expensive undertaking and no one had the money. Her mortal remains were embalmed at

Neslishah's maternal grandfather,
the last Ottoman sultan Vahideddin

Neslishah's paternal grandfather, the
last caliph of the Islamic world
Abdülmecid Efendi

Neslishah's two grandfathers at a ceremony in Istanbul: Sultan Vahideddin (far right) and
Abdülmecid Efendi (second from right), with Khedive Abbas Hilmi (sixth from right), who would
later become her father-in-law

Şehzade Ömer Faruk Efendi during the First World War, with his
Ottoman and German medals

Enver Paşa (front left) with Ömer Faruk Efendi
(front right) returning from a visit to the Dardanelles
Çanakkale frontline

Sabiha Sultan's wedding, Yıldız Palace, Istanbul, 1920: (from left) Ulviye Sultan, Dürrüşehvar
Sultan, Nazikeda Kadınefendi, Sabiha Sultan, Ertuğrul Efendi, and Mehisti Kadın

Neslishah at two months old

Neslishah at one year old

Neslishah with her nanny Miss Brunner, at her grandfather the caliph's mansion in Çamlıca

Sabiha Sultan with her daughters Hanzade (left) and Neslishah

Abdülmecid Efendi during the ceremony that confirmed him as caliph on 24 November 1922

Sultan Vahideddin in Alexandria, with Muqbil Pasha, governor of Alexandria, 24 November 1923

Neslishah Sultan, Hanzade Sultan, and Necla Sultan in the garden of the Palais Carabacel in Nice, the home of Caliph Abdülmecid, 1931

Nice, early 1930s: Caliph Abdülmecid with his daughter Dürrüşehvar, in his arms his granddaughter Necla, and beside him his two other granddaughters Neslishah Sultan and Hanzade Sultan

Dürrüşehvar Sultan with Nilüfer Hanımsultan during their wedding ceremony in Nice on 12 November 1931: (from left) Azam Jah, Dürrüşehvar Sultan, Nilüfer Hanımsultan, Muazzam Jah; (front row) Necla Sultan, Rana Hanımsultan, Neslishah Sultan, Türkan Hanımsultan, Hanzade Sultan

Dürrüşehvar Sultan with her husband Azam Jah

Necla Sultan, Neslishah Sultan, Ulviye Sultan, Sabiha Sultan, Hanzade Sultan, with Nazikeda Kadınefendi in Nice

Neslishah (back left) with her relatives and friends during an outing in Nice in the 1930s

Caliph Abdülmecid, late 1930s, on a beach in Nice with French painters; he is holding Necla in his arms, Hanzade Sultan is on the far right at the back, Neslishah Sultan beside her

Nice, late 1930s: (from left) Ertuğrul Efendi, Ömer Faruk Efendi, Hanzade Sultan, Sabiha Sultan, Şerif Abdülmecid, Neslishah Sultan, Necla Sultan

Ömer Faruk Efendi with
Neslishah Sultan, Nice, 1936

Princess Fethiye's wedding in Nice: (from left) Emire Hanımsultan, Necla Sultan, Giselle Durout, Hanzade Sultan, Fethiye Sultan, Neslishah Sultan, Kamran Sami, Melike Hanımsultan

Neslishah Sultan (left) with her father Şehzade Ömer Faruk Efendi and her sister Hanzade Sultan arriving at the port of Alexandria, fall 1938

From left: Princess Khadija Hassan, Sabiha Sultan, Neslishah Sultan, Şehzade Ali Vasıb Efendi, Princess Emine Tugay, Hanzade Sultan, Miss McCray (Emine Tugay's lady-in-waiting) on a boat trip

King Fuad of Egypt

Khedive Abbas Hilmi II of Egypt

Three children of King Fuad: Princess Fawzia,
Crown Prince Farouk, and Princess Faiza

King Farouk of Egypt

King Farouk at the opening of the Egyptian parliament; far right, back row: Prince Mohamed Ali Tewfik and Prince Abdel Moneim

Prince Mohamed Ali Tewfik, lifelong heir to the Egyptian throne

Members of the Egyptian royal family at the wedding of King Farouk and Queen Farida, al-Qubba Palace, 20 January 1938

Three Egyptian princesses: Tewfika, Zeyneb, and Nimet

Neslishah Sultan on her wedding day, 26 September 1940

At the wedding of Neslishah Sultan and Prince Abdel Moneim, Manyal Palace, Cairo, 26 September 1940: (from left) Şehzade Vasib Efendi, Şehzade Ömer Faruk Efendi, Prince Mohamed Ali Ibrahim, Prince Abdel Moneim, Şehzade Osman Fuad Efendi, Prince Youssef Kamal

Sabiha Sultan with Princess Wijdan Hilmi, Alexandria, 1940

At the wedding of Neslishah Sultan and Prince Abdel Moneim, Manyal Palace, Cairo, 26 September 1940: (from left) Şehzade Osman Fuad Efendi, Prince Mohamed Ali Tewfik, Şehzade Ömer Faruk Efendi, Şehzade Vasib Efendi, Prince Youssef Kamal, Prince Abdel Moneim, Prince Mohamed Ali Ibrahim

Prince Abdel Moneim with King Farouk attending memorial prayers for Mohamed Ali Pasha, Ras al-Tin Palace, Alexandria

King Farouk with Şehzade Ömer Faruk Efendi

Prince Abbas Halim

Switzerland, 1940: (from right) Sabiha Sultan, Neslishah Sultan, Queen Geraldine (wife of King Zog of Albania), and Prince Leka (heir apparent to the throne of Albania)

Khedive Abbas in exile in Switzerland, with his sister Princess Nimetullah, early 1940s

Princess Fawzia (left), sister of King Farouk and former empress of Iran, with princesses Hanzade, Necla, and Neslishah, inspecting a hospital of the Mabarrat Mohamed Ali

A fundraising meeting for one of the hospitals under the patronage of the princesses in Cairo, late 1940s: Princess Neslishah, her lady-in-waiting Nahid Reshad, King Farouk's sisters Princess Fawzia and Princess Faiza, with Hanzade Sultan

Princess Neslishah distributing health certificates to Egyptian fellaheen

Princess Neslishah on the cover of *Akher Sa'a* magazine, 1950 or 1951

Neslishah, Salzburg, late 1940s

Princess Neslishah and Prince Abdel Moneim in Austria, 1940s

Gstaad, 1947: (from left) Prince
Abbas Hilmi, Sabiha Sultan,
Neslishah Sultan, Prince Abdel
Moneim, Hanzade Sultan

Princess Neslishah with her children
in Venice, 1950

Neslishah's children at a birthday party together with other children of the Ottoman family

Neslishah at Topkapı Palace, the residence of her forefathers, 1947

Princess Neslishah with her mother Sabiha
Sultan, Cairo, 1949

Neslishah in Abu Qir, near
Alexandria, 1948

Lebanon, 1949: (from left) Sharif Abdel Majid (son of the emir of Mecca Ali Haidar Pasha and
husband of Rukiye Sultan), an unnamed family friend, Sharif Muhy al-Din al-Haidar, Sharifa
Nimet, Sabiha Sultan

An official reception in Cairo, early 1950s: Princess Emine Tugay (third from left), Princess Neslishah (seventh from left), Carmen Franco, the daughter of Spanish dictator General Franco (fifth from right), Prince Mohamed Ali Ibrahim (third from right), and Fuad Hulusi Tugay (second from right), ambassador of Turkey in Cairo

Ömer Faruk Efendi at his residence in Abu Qir, 1950

Chateau Tansonville, the khedive's villa in Illiers, France inherited by Prince Abdel Moneim and once owned by the family of Marcel Proust

Princess Neslishah with Amadeo Guillet, Cairo, 1950s

Neslishah with Şehzade Ömer Faruk Efendi seeing off Prince Abdel Moneim on his way to
London to attend the funeral of King George VI on behalf of Egypt in January 1952; the child
wearing the fez next to Neslishah is her son Prince Abbas Hilmi

the cheapest rate and deposited in the morgue until the necessary funds became available. The cost of the mortuary was fifty francs per day, but the family could not even afford that amount.

The caliph could not bear the thought of burying his cousin in a common grave. So he instructed his son, Ömer Faruk Efendi, and Şehzade Osman Fuad Efendi, a descendant of Sultan Murad V, to request the money for the burial from Jefferson Cohn & Ranz, the company that had been officially appointed to reclaim the properties of the Ottoman family on their behalf. The negotiations between the şehzades and the company were lengthy and tiring, and ended with a threat: "Should you refuse to pay, His Highness the Caliph will terminate the agreement he has signed with your company." They obtained the payment.

The body of Seniha Sultan followed the same route as that of her brother Sultan Vahideddin: to Beirut by boat, then from there to Syria, where she was buried in the courtyard of the Sultan Selim Mosque, alongside other members of her family who had passed away after 1924.

On 12 November 1931 two wedding ceremonies took place at the Villa Carabacel: Dürrüşehvar Sultan, the seventeen-year-old daughter of Caliph Abdülmecid Efendi, was married to Azam Jah, the elder son of Osman Khan, the nizam of Hyderabad and the richest man in the world; and Nilüfer Hanımsultan, the fifteen-year-old granddaughter of Sultan Murad V, was married to the nizam's younger son Muazzam Jah.

The local newspapers were full of photographs of the Indian princes when they arrived for the weddings, with headlines like *A Thousand and One Nights* and *A Muslim Wedding*.

In 1930 Hyderabad, a state of 223,000 square kilometers with a population of sixteen million, was the largest and wealthiest independent princely state of India. For centuries it had been an important political and cultural center of the eastern Islamic world, where many books were printed in its printing houses. The nizams of Hyderabad had been in contact with the Ottoman Empire since 1744, when the princely state was founded, and this relationship continued until the end of the empire. In the eighteenth century, when Shia Iran was seen as a danger to the Sunni state of Hyderabad, the nizams wrote to the Ottoman sultan, addressing him as "Caliph of the Prophet of God" and requesting his support. And in the nineteenth century when the Ottoman Empire was losing ground, the nizams requested the assistance of the British in support of the Ottomans, pointing out that if this were not to be granted the Muslims of Hyderabad would be most upset. Nevertheless, during the First World War when the Ottomans declared a jihad, the last nizam of Hyderabad Osman Khan sided with the British rather than with Istanbul.

Hyderabad became particularly important to the Ottomans in 1924, when it voiced its opposition to the abolition of the caliphate, and when despite this the Turkish parliament went ahead and sent the last caliph into exile together with the rest of the Ottoman family, Hyderabad was the first state to give the caliph its financial support. With a firman dated 7 May 1925, signed by Osman Khan, Abdülmecid Efendi was awarded a monthly allowance of three hundred pounds sterling.

The two sons of the nizam of Hyderabad, Azam Jah and Muazzam Jah, arrived in Nice from London by express train on 11 November 1931. Accompanying the princes were the finance and foreign affairs minister Sir Akbar Haydari, Nawab Osman, Nawab Bahadur Yar Jung, Salih Haydari and his wife, Sir Richard Chenevix-Trench, the Burnetts, and the head of the Indian Muslims, Shawkat Ali, who was one of the signatories of the letter addressed to the Turkish prime minister, İsmet Paşa, in 1923 about the future of the caliphate. The Englishmen in the group were advisors to the nizam, sent to Nice to keep an eye on the princes.

The delegation was met at the station by Ömer Faruk Efendi and the grandson of Sultan Murad V, Ali Vasib Efendi, and the guests were taken to the Negresco, the most luxurious hotel in Nice. The following day brought a surprise: one of the intended brides was replaced by another. Neslishah recalled:

My aunt's marriage was apparently destined from shortly after our expulsion from Turkey, when the person who most helped my grandfather financially was the nizam. He not only sent money himself but I believe he also obtained donations from the other Muslim rajas and sent that too. So it was more or less clear that the marriage between my aunt and the son of the nizam was decided seven years before the wedding, that is, back in 1924—in other words, my aunt was considered to be engaged at the age of ten.

Several weeks before the wedding, Shawkat Ali visited my grandfather in Nice, officially requesting the hand of my aunt for the elder son of the nizam. Meanwhile, the younger son was also a bachelor, and it had been decided that he would marry Mahpeyker, the daughter of Enver Paşa. When the princes arrived in Nice, all the arrangements for the weddings had been made: Azam Jah was to marry my aunt Dürrüşehvar, and Muazzam Jah was to wed Mahpeyker.

However, my uncle Fuad[40] and his wife the Egyptian princess Karima wanted the nizam's younger son to marry their niece, Nilüfer (Fuad was the brother of Nilüfer's mother, Adile Sultan), whom they had prepared to marry someone rich.

They dressed her up, made her pretty, and introduced her to Muazzam Jah. Nilüfer was then fifteen years old and a ravishing beauty. She was so attractive that Mahpeyker could not compare. When Muazzam Jah saw her, he was breathless. He immediately forgot all about Mahpeyker and insisted: "This is the one I want."

My grandfather was furious, of course, but what could he do? Muazzam cabled his father: "There is a much prettier girl here, can I have her?" And the nizam replied, "Take her." At that point, all my grandfather could do was to accept.

The Indians had reserved a whole floor at the Negresco. "What is the point of so much expense?" My father had asked. "It is the honor of Hyderabad," they replied.

The marriage ceremony of my aunt and Nilüfer took place in my grandfather's villa. They were engaged one day and married the next. It was not a lavish wedding, just the family, my grandfather's entourage, and some close friends, but nearly all the inhabitants of Cimiez clustered around our villa, trying to see what was going on inside.

The Indian princes arrived in two yellow convertible Mercedes. The princely color of Hyderabad was yellow, hence this choice of color for the cars. The Mercedes were covered with flowers, and in the front of each car were large hooters like loudspeakers, and they hooted all the way to the villa!

The princes wore very narrow white trousers, with Indian kameezes that came down to their knees. On their heads were turbans with aigrettes and around their necks were necklaces of flowers.

The spectators gathered around the house were astonished by what they saw, but enjoyed every moment. We children also had a good time, except for poor Mahpeyker, who was quite miserable—the night of the wedding she did not leave her room, and cried all night long.

The marriage ceremony was performed by my grandfather's uncle Damad Şerif Paşa, who was married to Emine Sultan, the daughter of Sultan Abdülaziz. Many photographs were taken. When the congratulations to the newlyweds were over, the princes took their brides and their entourage back to the Negresco. A few days later they all flew back to India—my grandfather was quite upset by the departure of his beloved daughter.

My sister Necla, who was five years old at the time, just loved Shawkat Ali, who had come together with the princes. She kept on saying, "I shall marry him." [She didn't, instead marrying Prince Amr Ibrahim of Egypt.]

According to Indian rumor, it seemed that the nizam thought the dowry the caliph had requested for his daughter was excessive, and he is supposed to have said, "You will also give a girl to my younger son Muazzam Jah, and I shall pay the dowry you request for both brides. You can settle the amount to give each one of them among yourselves." Then he cabled Muazzam Jah, who was traveling to Nice with his older brother, instructing him to "choose a princess for yourself. I shall pay for her." When the caliph heard about the nizam's offer he was furious, and he did everything in his power to stop the second wedding, but to no avail, as eventually he had no choice but to accept the inevitable. The first choice and second choice of bride took place in one day.

After the religious ceremonies, the newlyweds went to the British consulate to complete their civil marriages and to validate their prenuptial agreements, according to which, in the event of divorce or the death of the husband, Dürrüşehvar Sultan would receive two hundred thousand dollars in compensation and Nilüfer Hanımsultan seventy-five thousand.

After the marriages, the nizam increased Abdülmecid Efendi's allowance by one-third and granted a monthly salary of twenty-five thousand pounds to Şehzade Fuad Efendi for having enabled the marriage of Muazzam Jah to Nilüfer Hanımsultan. The şehzade received this amount regularly until 1952, when the couple divorced, after which the payments were immediately stopped.

Fifty years later, in a conversation I had with Nilüfer Hanımsultan in the drawing room of her Paris apartment, she described her life in Hyderabad, her husband Muazzam Jah, whom she called "Şecaat" ('Hero'), and her father-in-law Osman Khan:

When we were thrown out of Turkey we went to Budapest with my mother; from there we moved to France and settled in Nice. We rented a small apartment, where we tried to live by selling the little we had. Eventually, we had nothing more to sell. My mother was ill, but we did not have the money for a doctor. It was in these conditions that Şecaat, the son of the nizam of Hyderabad, found me. He was extremely wealthy, and he could save my mother and me from the situation we were in.

When I first saw Şecaat, he looked at me as if he were inspecting a racehorse. He eyed me from head to toe and probably thought, "When this horse grows up it will run fast and win the race."

To escape poverty, I married him when I was fifteen-and-a-half years old. I went to Hyderabad with just a small copy of the Qur'an clutched to my chest, and for the next fifteen years I lived as if I were living in the Middle Ages. I experienced two very different ways of life, in two worlds that were four hundred years apart.

For us, Hyderabad was like a prison. The nizam was very conservative and very strict. He would call us—his daughters-in-law—"Big" and "Small." In his presence we would place our hands together under our chins and stand in the Indian manner. We were forbidden to speak: all we were allowed to reply was "Yes, Father" or "No, Father." I never heard the nizam speak softly: he always screamed at the top of his voice.

One day he decided we should have nose rings, which apparently was an old Indian custom. I wrote to my mother about it, who was so utterly shocked that she replied, "If you ever dare do such a thing, I shall disown you." A few days later the nizam took Dürrüşehvar and me to the place where they pierced noses. We watched a thin Indian woman with a needle in her hand as she stuck it into a young girl's nose and pulled a thread through. The poor girl was afraid of her father, who was standing beside her, and did not utter a word. Then my father-in-law turned toward us and said, "Big! Small! Look, it doesn't hurt. Now you will do it, right?" We both said, "No, Father." He started to shout louder than ever. He first threatened us, but then seeing that we were not afraid, he tried to persuade us by offering us jewels. He said he would cover us in diamonds, but still he did not manage to convince us. You can imagine the hell that broke loose.

My life in Hyderabad was a nightmare: I spent fifteen years behind a curtain. Wherever I went the nizam's spies would follow me. My own servants would listen to my conversations and report them to him. In spite of everything, I managed to leave a legacy behind by having an excellent hospital and a cancer research center built in my name, which I donated to the people of Hyderabad. I had created a health committee, which I presided over myself, and I collected two hundred and fifty thousand pounds to build the hospital, which they named after me. Years later when I divorced Şecaat and moved to Paris, they wanted to change the name, but the hospital management refused. Today, in the modern part of Hyderabad that institution still bears my name.

During the war, there was an outbreak of venereal disease among the women of Hyderabad. I went from village to village, trying to inform the women on the matter. When the epidemic became public, journalists, news reporters, and television broadcasters from Europe and the United States swarmed into Hyderabad. The nizam told me, "Beware, don't you dare speak to them." In spite of his interdiction, he could not prevent me from being interviewed by each one of them.

Having spent some time going through the villages, I fell ill with typhoid fever. In India, back in those days, they were still using rather primitive ways of curing diseases. They believed witchdoctors had healing powers. The nizam sent me his healers. Instead of medicine, they tried to make me swallow crushed pearls. Thank God I didn't take any of that, and I am still alive today.

I patiently endured fifteen years in Hyderabad, until I could not take it any longer, and I left Hyderabad and came to Paris. When I decided on divorce, Nehru had just been elected prime minister of India. So I wrote to Nehru asking him to speak to my father-in-law for his consent to our divorce. Nehru agreed and went to see the nizam, who said, "I shall not come between my son and my daughter-in-law."

Şecaat came to Paris. He tried to convince me to go back with him for ten days. He coaxed me and threatened me. I didn't know whether I was alive or whether I was in hell during those ten days. Eventually, he accepted to divorce. However, because I was the one who had left him, he negated our prenuptial agreement, did not give me a single penny of alimony, and took back all my titles.

The young Turkish republic was eight years old when Dürrüşehvar Sultan married the son of the richest man in the world, and the event was followed closely in Ankara. This marriage was of great concern for Turkey, because Hyderabad appeared to be one of the driving forces behind the revival of the caliphate, and the heir apparent to the throne of the rich state of Hyderabad was marrying the daughter of the deposed caliph. This could create a significant impact in the Muslim world, which might go as far as aspiring to reinstall the caliphate in another country. Furthermore, two of the nizam's sons were marrying Ottoman princesses at the same time, which could also mean that they wished to keep the institution of the caliphate within the family.

What worried Turkey was the possibility that being now related to the nizam, Abdülmecid Efendi could have access to greater wealth. Although he lived in a large mansion in Nice, he was barely making ends meet, and even that was thanks to the financial help of Muslim rulers, among which the nizam was the main provider.

The Turkish consulate in Nice, which opened just after Abdülmecid Efendi settled there, with the sole purpose of keeping an eye on the caliph, was frantically engaged in gathering information. Ankara, however, did not rely solely on its diplomatic envoys in France: they were also in close contact with London, which was considered to be in control of Hyderabad, and they went as far as informally requesting the British to prevent the weddings taking place. But Turkey's demands led to nothing, and in time the government in Ankara realized that its fears of a revived caliphate were unfounded.

Meanwhile, since the departure of his precious and cherished seventeen-year-old daughter to Hyderabad, Abdülmecid Efendi felt particularly lonely in his large mansion in Nice. He no longer took pleasure in music, or even in painting. When he held a paintbrush in his hand, or touched the keys of the piano, he was reminded of his daughter, and his eyes would fill with tears. He would then sit in a corner, secretly crying behind closed doors. He thought that if his granddaughters were to live with him, he would feel less lonely, and he said to his son Ömer Faruk Efendi, "If you could give me the children, . . . if they could stay with us . . . ."

To Ömer Faruk Efendi, his oldest daughter Neslishah was as precious as Dürrüşehvar was to his father. Of course, he loved his two other daughters Hanzade and Necla dearly, but Neslishah had a special place in his heart. So his answer to his father was, "I shall send you the little ones, sir. The little ones can stay with you, but I cannot give you Neslishah, she is mine!"

So it was that at the beginning of 1932, Hanzade Sultan, who was then eight years old, and Necla Sultan, who was six, were taken from the apartment at the Prince de Galles to the Villa Carabacel, where their grandfather the caliph resided. Hayrünisa Hanım, the caliph's second wife, who was childless, was to take care of Hanzade, while Behruze Kalfa, Abdülmecid Efendi's last sweetheart, would look after Necla. Neslishah recalled:

Hayrünisa Hanım was an angel. Because she never had a child, her position with my grandfather was a little behind the other wives, so she had her meals in the second sitting. On the other hand, Behruze, a Circassian woman, was much younger than the other ladies of the house, and there were rumors that there was still something going on between her and my grandfather, and that she hated my grandmother. She was also supposed to be a kleptomaniac. When she began to take care of Necla, she did her utmost to set Necla against my grandmother, but to no avail. Despite this negative side, she loved Necla and looked after her very well.

When Dürrüşehvar married and left for Hyderabad, my grandfather sent his private secretary Hüseyin Nakib Bey to accompany and keep an eye on her. The people at the court of the nizam, for some unknown reason, did not like him much. They kept asking him, "When are you going back?" Hüseyin Nakib Bey had no instructions from my grandfather about his return, so he gave vague answers such as, "Very soon, sir. I am preparing for my departure."

One day he injured his heel, and it grew worse as the days went by. The doctors could not find a cure. The poor man was in severe pain, when one of the nizam's men told him, "Take this as a warning. You have been poisoned—they will give you the antidote the moment you decide to go back, only then will you heal. On the other hand, if you decide to stay here you will die." So the poor man, running for his life, left India and went back to my grandfather in Nice.

Meanwhile, there was a housekeeper at the villa called Madame Grandjean. Hüseyin Nakib Bey and the housekeeper fell in love and hastily married. Both remained in the service of my grandfather, but they preferred to live elsewhere. So they rented a house where they slept, coming to work each morning, and there was now an empty room in the villa.

My great-uncle Seyfeddin Efendi had passed away a few years earlier and his family was scattered here and there. His twenty-year-old daughter Gevheri was living in Nice, striving to make ends meet. My grandfather was her uncle, and when he heard of her financial difficulties he brought her home with the intention of marrying her off, giving her the room that

Hüseyin Bey had left vacant. Gevheri lived with us for a few years, then became engaged to the son of a minor raja from India, but a short time before her wedding it was discovered that she was having an affair with someone else, so the engagement was canceled. My grandfather was so angry that he kicked her out, sending her to stay with her mother, who barely had anything to live on.[41]

When it was time for Neslishah to go to school there was no school for Muslim children in Nice, so she had to attend a French school. She recalled:

I started school late. One day my grandfather took me aside and said, "We all dream of returning to our country, my child, but we do not know what God has planned for us. We might go back, but we might have to live in exile forever. I don't know if in the future we shall be in a better position, or whether our lives will be even more challenging. Since our future is unknown, you should meet and befriend people from all walks of life. I shall send you to school, not to the one where only rich children go, but to a regular school where you will meet children from different backgrounds." So I was registered in a high school.

My nanny always spoke in French with me, so even when I lived in Istanbul, I could understand the language. In Nice everyone spoke French, and I became fluent in it, but I also learned how to read and write in old Turkish. Kamil Bey,[42] the brother of Enver Paşa, was married at the time to Enver Paşa's widow, Naciye Sultan, and they were living in Nice with their family. It was Kamil Bey who taught my sisters and me the old Turkish alphabet: every Sunday, when we had no school, he would come to our house with their children Türkan, Ali, Mahpeyker, and Rana[43] to teach us all how to read and write in old Turkish.

My mother and Madame Burdukoff taught me how to read and write in French, and in time I became quite good at it, with the result that in the high school in Nice I was older than most of the girls in my class: when they gave me an exam and realized I excelled in reading, writing, and even in grammar, they moved me up one class.

But I had been taught nothing at home about mathematics, and I have never been good at that subject. When they noticed at school that I was hopeless when it came to figures, they moved me down a class, though eventually when I did learn how to calculate, they moved me up again to the tenth grade.

The Popular Front came to power in France in April 1936, and Leon Blum became prime minister, leading a socialist government. At school there were several communist teachers, who talked to us about communism. One day one of the teachers told us something like, "Children belong to the state, not to their families. Never forget this, you are a property of the state." That evening, while having dinner with my family, my mother asked me what we had done at school that day. I innocently replied, quoting what the teacher had told us, "Actually, my sisters and I don't belong to you, but to the state!"

My father blew his top. He shot up from his chair and railed against the teacher, then said, "You are no longer to go to that school. We shall find you another school." The following morning he went to the school and raised hell, scolding the headmaster and the teachers alike. "I am not sending my daughter to such a terrible school. I am withdrawing her from here," he declared. And so I then joined a private school called Cours Moulin. It was a beautiful school in the middle of a lovely garden, where most of the students were foreigners.

My mother wanted me to become a solicitor, so she thought I should study Latin. She would dream of me wearing a barrister's robe, but I was a timid child, and becoming a lawyer was certainly not for me. Thankfully, my father intervened: "There is no way she will become a lawyer. She will not be part of that profession. I will not allow my daughter to be in law school alongside boys. Forget about Latin. Neslishah will first have to learn German and English!"

And of course we did what my father ordered. I gave up Latin and started to learn German and English. My school had the very best teachers. My English teacher was English and my German teacher was German. Both my French literature teacher and my history teacher were experts on their subjects, and my physics teacher had been an assistant to the famous physicist George Claude.[44] In other words, everything was perfect.

We were fifteen at most in class, but in some subjects we were even less. For example, in the German class there were only four or five of us. And being so small in number our teacher could spend more time with each one of us.

Aside from the monthly allowance that the caliph gave his son Ömer Faruk Efendi to support his family, he also paid for Neslishah's tuition fees. All her other expenses, such as food, clothes, and any additional expenditures for school, were paid by her father.

The house was always full of guests, and the table was always set for unexpected friends, but the money that the caliph gave his son was never sufficient, and his financial situation never improved: there were days when Neslishah did not have a skirt to go to school—the one she had was so worn out that she could not wear it any longer, and she had to stay home. Neslishah recalled:

> Every night the house was full of my father's flatterers. The table would be laid with all sorts of starters. My grandfather's allowance would be spent mainly on these dinner parties.
>
> My mother was no longer able to make ends meet with the house money she was receiving. My grandfather would ask my father, "Faruk, I give you enough money. Where on earth do you spend it all?" But he would not increase his allowance. He probably thought that if he gave my father more money he would spend it and invite even more strangers to the house.
>
> For a long time, our clothes were shabby, as we could not afford to buy new ones. We wore the sweaters that my mother would knit for us and she would darn our clothes that were threadbare. There were times when my skirt would be torn, and at school I would wear it back to front to conceal the hole.
>
> When I was about fifteen or sixteen years old, I only had one skirt to wear. It was a gray one. I wore it every day to school, but eventually it became so tattered that I could not go to school any longer! What do you

do when your clothes are so frayed and you have nothing else to wear?
You have no choice but to stay at home, so this is what I did. I could not
go to school. My mother was obliged to seek help from my grandmother,
her mother-in-law, when in tears she told her about our situation. My
grandmother, totally unaware of what we were going through, also cried,
then had some clothes made for me, thanks to which I was able to go back
to school again.

Neslishah was learning more at home than she was being taught at
school, where the lessons were harder, more challenging, and painful.
Her tutors at home were all members of the family: her grandfather, her
father, her mother, and other older relatives. She recalled:

I inevitably became aware of what kind of family I belonged to. At home
everyone kept on repeating, "You are a descendant of the sultans, you are
a princess, you are this, you are that. You are not like everybody else, you
have duties, your duties should come before anything else. Because you
are a princess, you must behave in this manner, you have to do this or
that," and so on. So you end up knowing who you are, you become conscious of your identity.

I was told that "to be a princess is a profession," and for years they
taught me this at home. "You are a princess, you must behave in this
manner, you must not act like that, you certainly must not think in this
manner, you have to hold yourself in this way . . ." The people around me
were to be my role models, and not just members of the family but the
*kalfa*s as well.

The most important among the things that were forbidden was to
show weakness. It was considered shameful to show your weakness. You
were not allowed to laugh out loud, and if you were to cry it had to be
done secretly—no one should see your sadness or your tears.

I was told that I had to be dignified and reserved at all times. I had to
be honest, think about others, and be as generous as possible. They had
raised my mother with these principles, so this is how she behaved. And
she was anyway a very kind-hearted woman. When we were about to go

out, at the threshold of the door with some small change in her hands, she would turn the coins round in circles above our heads, while saying a prayer, then she would give the money to the beggars in the street.

Later, we started to study history, but it was not proper history—we were just taught the lives of the sultans. My grandfather Abdülmecid Efendi wrote down for us a list of the sultans and told us, "Learn these off by heart."

I would sit in front of him and recite: Sultan Osman, Sultan Orhan, Sultan Murad, Sultan Bayezid, . . . "Well done my pretty girl," he would say, and give me a kiss.

At one point my mother also wanted to teach me history, but when we reached the period of Sultan Orhan, she came in with some large, thick books telling me, "Read these." So I learned history from books, though as they were forever talking about history at home, I have always felt as if I were living in it. Many books were read to my sisters as well. Kamil Bey, Enver Paşa's brother, would teach us the Ottoman alphabet on Sundays and Thursdays, but no one else taught us history. Thanks to my mother's insistence to "Read these books," I have learned to love reading and have been doing so all my life.

Of all the problems that noble families in exile had to face, the most important always related to financial difficulties. Next they had to worry about giving a good education to the younger generations, ensuring that the young ones would marry people worthy of their lineage.

Naturally, the only means of providing for all of this was money. Any noble family forced to leave their country of birth were doomed to live in misery if they did not possess a fortune of their own, if they did not know the world or how to work, or worse still if their family was a large one.

The Ottomans in exile endured all of this and more, since they were effectively penniless. Nearly all the palaces, mansions, and houses they lived in when in Istanbul belonged to the Hazine-i Hassa, which was established to manage the assets of the crown and the throne, and which distributed these estates to be used as lodgings for the members of the imperial family.

Property owners in the family were very few, and even then, shortly after their departure, they had to relinquish nearly all of their estates to their appointed proxies, some of whom cheated them, never sending on a penny of the money they obtained from the sale of these assets.

And they had no savings, as the subsidy they received from the state did not allow them to live in luxury. In fact, they lived quite modestly, while several members of the family were often up to their ears in debt. It was an old tradition of the Ottoman dynasty to provide as little as possible to the family, especially to the male descendants, to reduce their potential political power. This practice became particularly entrenched during the Tanzimat reforms of the nineteenth century. And after Sultan Abdülhamid was deposed in 1909, the outbreak of the Balkan Wars and the First World War that followed emptied the safes of the Ottoman Treasury. So the family was under financial strain—even if not to the same degree as the majority of the Turkish population.

The worst of it was that most members of the Ottoman family had no idea how to handle money, no experience of the outside world, and had never worked. And there were 155 of them in exile, making them more numerous than any other banished royal family of the time. This is why the life of the Ottoman family was so difficult. When they were expelled in March 1924, each of them received one thousand pounds sterling, which was rapidly spent. They then survived by selling their jewels or other personal objects, but eventually most of them faced extreme poverty. At night, on the deserted streets of Nice, it was not uncommon to come across some of the descendants of the sultans in search of food.

The Habsburgs, an older dynasty than the Ottomans, was faced with a similar misfortune. They had dominated Europe for centuries, and were the long-term adversaries of the Ottomans. The Austro-Hungarian Empire was the great loser of the First World War, alongside the Ottomans, and the Habsburgs, the ruling family of the empire, were blamed for the defeat: on 3 April 1919, the Austrian parliament exiled the family, confiscating all their properties.

Though not as considerable in number as the exiled Ottomans, they also endured hardship and poverty. After the death of the last emperor, Charles I, it was his wife Empress Zita who headed the family, and she followed common practice among other deposed European royal families in managing to provide her oldest son Otto, the heir to the throne, with an excellent education, bringing him up as a future emperor. Otto's brothers and sisters, meanwhile, received an ordinary education, growing up as the children of a middle-class—or even a poor—family. Nevertheless, in the event of a return of the Habsburgs to their country and throne, the princes and princesses of the family were taught not only several European languages, but also Hungarian and Croatian, which were the languages used in the old territories of their empire.[45]

Empress Zita's strategy in the education of the heir to the throne was not applicable in the Ottoman family, since in their case the throne was not passed from father to son, but was granted to the oldest şehzade, who also became the head of the family. And during those years of exile the youngest head of the family was well over fifty. It was thus rather difficult to provide the younger generation of the family with a good education and consequently with a good future.

The first to realize that something must be done was the caliph. In 1926, upon the death of Sultan Vahideddin, when he became the head of the Ottoman dynasty, he held a family council in Nice that included his son Ömer Faruk Efendi, his daughter-in-law Sabiha Sultan, Osman Fuad the grandson of Sultan Murad V, and Damad Şerif Paşa, who had been a minister in various governments during the reign of Sultan Vahideddin. The purpose of the council was to decide on family matters, such as how to help those family members in need, establishing what their needs might be, choosing which school the children should attend, and finding appropriate suitors for the girls.

Furthermore, the council would be responsible for undertaking legal procedures in various countries to obtain the return of the assets belonging to the Ottoman family after the collapse of the empire. This was an immense task, as these assets were spread out over a wide geographical area, and their location needed to be established before taking any legal measures. Abdülmecid Efendi initiated negotiations and made agreements with foreign companies, according to which they would be responsible for the expenses needed to open court cases, and they would also advance money to the caliph to be distributed among members of the family. Among the assets claimed were not just real estate—they also included some oil wells in Mosul, Iraq.

During the investigations to trace the properties there were setbacks. For example, after Sultan Yavuz Selim's conquest of Egypt in 1517, he established several foundations there that owned properties. With the aim of claiming a portion of the rent of these properties, contacts were made with the Egyptian government, but Cairo replied scornfully, "We have not come across anyone by the name of Sultan Selim in our records."

After signing agreements with the companies charged with restoring the assets, the family received some money in advance, helping them to overcome their immediate financial difficulties, at least for some time. Meanwhile, in 1930 the şehzades descended from Sultan Abdülhamid undertook another initiative independently from that of the caliph, and approached the British Petroleum Company (BP) to obtain a share of the oil recovered from the drilling of the Mosul wells registered in the name of Abdülhamid and opened lawsuits one after another to reclaim ownership of some land in Palestine that had belonged to the sultan.

The claim for the oil wells was led by the eldest son of Abdülhamid II, Şehzade Selim Efendi, who lived in Lebanon. But the caliph had made similar contacts, and eventually this dual approach led to a disagreement between the two cousins. Furthermore, some of the princes and princesses complained about the way the advance payment had been distributed, arguing over the amount they were each given, leading to an exchange of frank letters between them and the caliph, and several of them then quarreled among themselves and sued each other.

With the intervention of other members of the family the squabbling parties came to an agreement, and in 1936 the caliph signed a protocol with the disputants, thus ending the discussion. BP began to pay a regular monthly allowance to the Ottoman family after a court settlement over their shares in the oil fields. These payments were a blessing for the family, but at the outbreak of the Second World War in 1939 the payments stopped, and the old princesses, whose subsistence depended on these remittances, were left penniless again. After all these misfortunes, the family council was dissolved, some of the relatives quarreled once more, and the family was in even greater financial difficulties than before, with no prospect of further revenues from the oil wells of Mosul, or of other expected inheritances.[46]

Abdülmecid Efendi did his best to fill the position of head of the Ottoman family when in exile, and for a while he succeeded, but the circumstances were not easy, and after him the title of head of the family became merely symbolic.

Early one morning, Neslishah had just woken up as Ömer Faruk Efendi and Sabiha Sultan were about to leave the house, and they said, "You're up? Get dressed quickly and come with us." Soon the three of them left together, Faruk Efendi driving the Buick.

They headed for downtown Nice, then toward Saint Maurice and up into the mountains on an unpaved road, passing through villages and driving farther up among olive groves and terraced land, continuing on even steeper tracks until they reached a small, roughly built stone cottage.

On hearing the sound of the car, a feeble old man appeared in front of the cottage, with four women of various ages. The expression on their faces was one of bewilderment on seeing unexpected guests arrive, while what surprised the passengers of the car was the number of people who came out of such a tiny house.

Faruk Efendi, Sabiha Sultan, and Neslishah got out of the car, and Faruk Efendi took a few steps toward the hesitant but courteous-looking man, and after greeting him with a *temenna* said, "Good morning, Your Highness. We have come to take you with us. May your will be our command, and allow me to take you all back to Nice with us. Everything has been prepared for you!"

Then, without waiting for a reply, he addressed the women standing in front of the house, "Sabiha and Neslishah will help you gather your belongings, then we will drive back without wasting any more time."

There was not much to collect from the house: a few small suit-cases and the parrot that had never left the side of Tevfik Efendi since the days at Dolmabahçe Palace. They all squeezed into the Buick and drove back to Nice.

The man Faruk Efendi had come to collect was Şehzade İbrahim Tevfik Efendi, the grandson of Sultan Abdülmecid on his father's side—that is, the son of Şehzade Burhaneddin Efendi (1849–76). Tevfik Efendi had been born in 1874 at the Dolmabahçe Palace, and had five wives and seven children—five girls and two boys. Like the others, he had been exiled in March 1924, and had settled in the environs of Nice.

One of his wives had died when he was still in Istanbul, two had not followed him into exile, and another, the mother of his two sons, had left him, taking her children with her. Three of his daughters were married and led their own lives. Tevfik Efendi lived outside Nice in a village up in the hills with his last wife Hayriye, forty years his junior, his two daughters Fevziye and Fethiye, and an eighty-year-old *kalfa* by the name of Cenan, who had been with the family since the days of Sultan Abdülaziz. Neslishah recalled:

> Tevfik Efendi first moved to Paris with his family after leaving Turkey. They settled into an elegant hotel on the Champs Elysée, where they lived for some time. Then they moved to a large apartment. His wife had her clothes made by the most famous fashion designers in town. She dressed very ele-gantly and was often seen in dance halls, where she would merrily spend her husband's money with young men. She lived such an extravagant life that eventually there was no money left. Then she took her two sons and moved to the United States with an American man and settled there.
>
> Tevfik Efendi was left penniless. He could no longer live in Paris, so with his two daughters, his wife Hayriye, and Cenan Kalfa he went to Nice, where he found a small cottage in a village nearby. There was no electricity or running water in the cottage. When they needed water, they would go and collect it from one of the wells in the olive groves.
>
> They did not even have the money to buy gas for their lamps to light the house when it became dark. During their last few weeks in the hut,

they were fed through the generosity of the people of the village, who would bring them food now and then. These were the terrible conditions in which they were living.

My father was a quick-tempered person. He would flare up and raise hell, but five minutes later he would forget all about it, wanting everyone else to forget as well. Though he was a highly irascible person, strangely enough he was also very sensitive. If he ever saw someone in distress, his eyes would fill with tears. He would feel compassion and would want to help, but in helping others he would often find himself in an awkward situation. When we took Tevfik Efendi and his family home, we were not in a position to host guests and take care of them. We were also without money and had serious financial problems. But my father said, "We will bring Tevfik Efendi home. He will stay with us." For a while, we lived one on top of the other as if in a camp.

When they came to Nice Tevfik Efendi's wife Hayriye said, "I don't want to be a burden to you," and entrusting her daughter Fevziye to Faruk Efendi and Sabiha Sultan, she went to live with another relative.

The apartment was spacious, and there were two spare rooms. The large room used when Sabiha Sultan's mother, Nazikeda Kadınefendi, the widow of Sultan Vahideddin, came to stay was given to Tevfik Efendi and his parrot. Neslishah shared her room with Fethiye Sultan. Fevziye Sultan and Cenan Kalfa were put into Necla Sultan's room, as she was still very young. The person who suffered the most was Şehzade Ertuğrul Efendi, who would usually stay in the room assigned to Nazikeda Kadınefendi whenever he came back from Grasse: after the arrival of Tevfik Efendi, when he came to Nice the young şehzade had to sleep in one of the maid's rooms on the sixth floor.

Tevfik Efendi lived with his cousins Faruk Efendi and Sabiha Sultan for just one year. He was a quiet and peaceful person, whose presence was barely felt. On 31 December 1931 he died of a heart attack. Sabiha Sultan cried by his bedside as he passed away, while the parrot sang at the top of his voice an aria from *La Traviata*. The next day Tevfik Efendi was buried in a common grave next to a Christian. After the funeral, the first thing that Sabiha Sultan did was to open the cage of the parrot, which was still singing *La Traviata*, and set him free.

Following the death of Tevfik Efendi, his last wife Hayriye Hanım came back to Nice, took her daughter Fevziye, and went first to Paris and then to Egypt, where she married a Tatar by the name of Seyfulin Bey, who brought up Fevziye as if she were his own daughter. Fevziye lived for some time with Princess Wijdan, who in later years would become Sabiha Sultan's best friend. The princess's husband had just passed away and left her with a substantial fortune. Princess Wijdan wanted to raise the young Fevziye as her own and find her a suitable husband, but when she lost all her money gambling she was obliged to send her back to her mother. In 1951, when she was twenty-three years old, Fevziye Sultan married the Air Force officer Khayri Bey, the son of Qadriya Hussein, an Egyptian princess. Khayri Bey was later accused of taking part in the 1956 plot to overthrow President Nasser, arrested, and never seen again. Neslishah was among those accused of the same allegation, and she was arrested together with her husband at the same time; she was able to prove her innocence only after a long legal battle. Fevziye Sultan, who at the time of writing still lives in Paris, believes that her husband is still alive, and though sixty years have passed since his arrest, she is waiting for his return.

Fethiye Sultan and Cenan Kalfa had nowhere to go. They remained with Faruk Efendi and Sabiha Sultan, and around 1930 Fethiye married Rashid Shafiq Bey, from Egypt. The wedding (arranged by Faruk Efendi) was held in Nice, after which the couple left France for Egypt, and Cenan Kalfa stayed on with Faruk Efendi's family.

Cenan Kalfa had come from Sultan Abdülmecid's palace, where she was the favorite of the sultan's son Burhaneddin Efendi. She was an orphan and had no relatives, and she was in love with Burhaneddin Efendi, but when he passed away in 1876 Cenan Kalfa was told that she could marry a civil servant and leave the palace. Though she was still considered young at the time, the faithful *kalfa* did not agree to have another man in her life: she never married and preferred to stay at the Dolmabahçe Palace.

Cenan Kalfa would tell Neslishah about life at the palace during the reign of Sultan Mecid, and stories and the forgotten gossip of those days. When she reached and passed the age of a hundred, her mind was not all there and at times she would disclose to those around her details of the nights she spent with Burhaneddin Efendi, with whom she was still madly in love. In Egypt in 1942, when the *kalfa* heard that Field Marshal Rommel was approaching Cairo with the German army, she was terrified, and she would tell Faruk Efendi, who by this time had settled in Egypt with his family, "Oh my God, they will come to rape me! Your Highness, please you do it before Rommel's arrival, I don't want to be raped by an infidel!"

Neslishah lived in Nice for fifteen years. She had moments of joy and moments of sorrow in this pretty French town on the shores of the Mediterranean where she left behind her childhood—which was not an affluent one.

Her first suitor appeared in Nice, the Egyptian prince Amr Ibrahim, who was a descendant of Mohamed Ali Pasha through Ahmed Rifaat Pasha. He was rich, and one of the handsomest princes of that dynasty. Born in Cairo in 1905, he studied in France and in 1921 married Sarwat Hanem, the daughter of an Egyptian pasha. They separated, then remarried, and Sarwat passed away in 1935. The prince had three daughters from this marriage.

Members of the Egyptian royal family used to spend a few months each year in France, and like several of his relatives, Prince Amr was a friend of the Şehzade Ömer Faruk Efendi. Since the death of his wife he was spending more time in France than before, and he saw Neslishah for the first time in the fall of 1937. He wanted to remarry, and so thought of starting a new family with Neslishah, who was seventeen at the time.

There was a sixteen-year age difference between the prince and Neslishah, so Prince Amr was hesitant in his request to Faruk Efendi, but the latter found the proposal acceptable. "We favor such a marriage, which is a suitable one. However, I shall have to consult Neslishah and her mother," he replied. Sabiha Sultan also approved, while Neslishah was left to think about it for a few days, before accepting the proposal from the handsome prince.

Thus was the marriage between Neslishah and Prince Amr decided, but there was no engagement, only an agreement, while the details were to be discussed with the prince when he returned from a trip to Egypt. While in Cairo, however, the prince was struck down with partial paralysis and became bedridden. When the doctors told him he would never walk again, he made the elegant gesture of writing to Ömer Faruk Efendi saying: "I have no right to condemn Neslishah to spend her life with a bedbound person. Therefore, I withdraw my marriage request. Neslishah is thus free, and I wish her all the happiness she deserves."

Neslishah did not marry Prince Amr, but it was her destiny to be part of the Egyptian royal family, as eventually she was to marry another member of the family, Prince Mohamed Abdel Moneim.

Neslishah's life was soon to change, with a move to Egypt. In the 1930s in Europe, the Nazis were in power in Germany and the Fascists in Italy, and in some of the smaller countries, the Nazi and the Fascist movements were rapidly rising in popularity, while Britain was concerned with the consequences of these ideologies and their military ambitions. Eventually, war became inevitable. Adolf Hitler openly declared that Germany would no longer abide by the conditions imposed by the Allies at the end of the First World War with the Treaty of Versailles, and that he was preparing to reshape the borders of Europe.

Şehzade Ömer Faruk Efendi was a professional soldier and well knew that in the event of war, Germany would strike first and invade either France or Poland. Consequently, he decided to take his family to a country far from the imminent conflict—from now on, the exiled family would be living in Egypt. Neslishah recalled:

The situation in Europe was deteriorating; war was the only topic of conversation. My grandfather wanted to move to Paris, while my father was saying, "It smells of gunpowder here. If war begins, I do not want to be in Europe."

My father was aware that we were growing up and though he never openly mentioned it, I am sure he feared the possibility that we would marry foreigners. He probably thought, "What would I do if they fell in love with a Frenchman?"

Besides, suitors were already appearing at our door. In Nice there was a Persian prince by the name of Ishaq Khan, who was related to the Qajar family, though he was also on excellent terms with the Pahlavis, who had overthrown the Qajars. One day he came to see my grandfather, asking for the hand of Hanzade, who was then fourteen or fifteen, on behalf of the Pahlavi heir to the throne; that is, for the crown prince, Mohamed Reza, who later became the last shah. My grandfather kicked him out. The crown prince then married Princess Fawzia, the daughter of King Fuad of Egypt, then Soraya, and finally Farah Diba.

I then received another proposal: the Aga Khan sent an envoy to ask my grandfather for me to marry his son Ali Khan. My grandfather was even more irritated, "I find it insulting that an Ismaili requests the hand of the granddaughter of the caliph of the Sunnis," he said, and sent him away.

The Italians and the Germans became partners in the Axis alliance. My mother feared a sudden invasion of Nice. Until the nineteenth century, Nice had belonged to the Italians, and my mother was afraid that the Italians, backed by the Germans, would attempt to recapture the city when we least expected it. Every night she would go out into the garden and look up at the sky, saying, "Will the Italian planes come and bomb us?"

In September 1938 the British prime minister, Neville Chamberlain, went to Munich, met Hitler and Mussolini, and signed an agreement by which the Sudetenland was given to Germany. However, the situation deteriorated even further, and war was imminent.

Given what was happening, my father finally decided to leave France, but where to go? My maternal grandmother and my aunt Ulviye were living in Egypt. My parents thought about it at length and eventually said, "Let's go to Egypt, we have friends and relatives there."

They went to discuss the matter with my grandfather, who told them he would send us twelve thousand francs per month, from the allowance he was receiving from the nizam of Hyderabad, and that we should be able to live on it in Egypt. He then added, "If you go, I shall not stay here; I shall move to Paris."

Fortunately, we had acquired French passports so were able to travel to any country that would grant us a visa. When the family was expelled from Turkey in 1924, the passports that were given to us by the Turkish government were usable only for our departure, with no possibility of return, and valid for just one year. We had also been deprived of our citizenship, so a year later we had no passports.

Both my grandparents, Sultan Vahideddin and the Caliph Abdülmecid Efendi, contacted the French government to request passports for the family. When Vahideddin died in 1926, the caliph was in charge of following up on the matter. Edouard Herriot, a friend of my grandfather, became prime minister of France, and was re-elected several times, so thanks to his intervention we were granted our passports, though these were valid only for travel—we were not given citizenship. On our passports our status was registered as "Refugee" and our nationality as "Ottoman." In other words, we were all stateless, but under the protection of the French State. My name was registered as "Son Altesse Imperiale Princesse Neslishah Faruk."

When we decided to leave France we had already sold our flat at the Prince de Galles and rented a flat at the Ricardo. We then started to pack our belongings. I had to leave school, and never again had the opportunity to continue my studies. While my parents were organizing our move to Egypt, we girls were taken to my grandfather's house, and Cenan Kalfa was sent somewhere else for a few days. Necla slept in Behruze's room as in the past, Hanzade in Hayrünisa's room, while in another room they had prepared a large bed that I shared with Fethiye.

When the packing was over, we went back home and stayed for another few days. We had bought tickets on an Egyptian ship called *al-Nil*, which sailed from Marseilles to Alexandria, and we began our farewell visits.

My grandfather had a Saint Bernard dog, and he had given me one of the puppies. The warm weather in Nice was not suitable for the Saint Bernards, used to the mountains and the cold, so during the summer my grandfather would send his dogs up to the mountains, while my puppy would stay with me: we shaved his hair to make him feel the heat less, but he was still restless. A day before our farewell visit, I gave my dog back to my grandfather and a day before our departure, my sisters and I went to say goodbye to my grandfather. My parents did not come with us on that day. We spent the whole day with our grandparents, crying our eyes out together. We did not utter a word until dinner, we all just wept. After dinner my grandfather said, "Children let me take you back home," and he asked the driver to bring the car.

We left the house after saying goodbye to my grandmother. It was a difficult parting for both of us, since my grandmother had a very soft spot for me. Then my grandfather drove us home; on the way, he never stopped crying and embracing us.

The driver stopped in front of our house, my grandfather kissed us all for the last time, and shedding more tears said, "Come, children, get out of the car quickly." Then he drove off, still weeping.

That was the last time I saw my grandfather. I don't know about my sisters, but I was sure that I would never see him again, and I didn't. After our departure, he moved to Paris, where he lived for seven more years and then passed away.

I don't remember exactly when we left France, but it was about a month after Chamberlain returned to London from Munich, so it must have been in late 1938.

Fethiye, who had been living with us, had already married and moved to Egypt. Fevziye and her mother were in Paris. Ertuğrul Efendi, Madame Burdukoff, and Cenan Kalfa were still with us in Nice, so they came with us to Egypt.

The day after we bade my grandfather farewell we left for Marseilles to board the vessel that would take us to Alexandria. The voyage was not unpleasant. We all had separate cabins, and onboard we met quite a few people we knew.

Three days later we were in Alexandria.

Part Three

Egypt
A Bride in the Land of the Pharaohs

6

A Forced Engagement, a Marriage by Consent

Egypt, after the fall of the pharaohs, remained under foreign sovereignty for two thousand years—Egyptians were able to govern their own country only after 1952. After domination by Persians, Greeks, Romans, Byzantines, Arabs, and Mamluks, in 1517 the Ottoman sultan Selim I conquered the country, which then became part of the Ottoman Empire, to be ruled for centuries by governors appointed from Istanbul.

In the early nineteenth century Mohamed Ali Pasha came to Egypt as a young soldier, rising quickly to take control of the whole country, eventually in 1840 he and his successors being acknowledged as hereditary governors by the Sublime Porte: they would first use the title of 'governor,' then 'khedive,' 'sultan,' and finally 'king,' and would rule the country until the declaration of the republic on 18 June 1953.

However, from 1882 they had to share their rule with another power, the British, who had sent troops to the Suez Canal and would eventually occupy the whole country. In the ensuing years, most of the prominent ministers, undersecretaries, and chiefs of police of Egypt would all be British, and in Cairo there would even be a military garrison next to the royal palace.

Egypt was still nominally an Ottoman province, but totally under British jurisdiction. On 19 December 1914 the British deposed the last khedive, Abbas Hilmi II, whom they perceived as being pro-Turkish. He was replaced by his uncle, Hussein Kamil, with the title of 'sultan.'

When Sultan Hussein died in 1917, his brother Prince Fuad succeeded him, and when on 28 February 1922 Britain granted Egypt limited independence, Sultan Fuad became King Fuad.

On the death of Fuad in 1936, his only son Farouk, just sixteen, became king of a country in political turmoil: there were clashes between the king, the government, and the opposition, but it was still the British who ran the show—to the extent that in 1942, when the British threatened to depose the king if he did not do as they wished, as a token of earnest they sent their tanks to the royal palace in Abdin.

In the nineteenth century, despite insurgencies and foreign occupation, Cairo and Alexandria were known as the most modern cities in the Islamic world and the lifestyle of these cities was acknowledged to be well ahead of that of Istanbul. The palaces of Egypt were the epitome of luxury and splendor. Ottoman historians of the time wrote that "Istanbul society, which until then knew little about life outside its mansions, began to emulate the debauchery of the Egyptians," and that the Palace in Istanbul had learned from the Egyptian princes how to spend and live in luxury.

When Şehzade Ömer Faruk Efendi and his family left France for Alexandria, King Farouk reigned in Egypt. Neslishah was to become a bride to this royal family, that is, to the dynasty of Mohamed Ali Pasha.

When Ömer Faruk Efendi and his family (along with Ertuğrul Efendi and Mrs. Burdukoff) arrived at Alexandria in late 1938, they were met by their relatives living there: Sabiha Sultan's elder sister Ulviye Sultan and her husband Ali Haydar Bey, Şehzade Ali Vasib Efendi, Mukbile Sultan, and others. Sabiha Sultan wrote later in 1955:

> While sailing from the port of Marseilles toward Alexandria on the vessel *al-Nil*, the pain of parting from this beautiful country, where I left behind a large part of my life, was sinking deeply into my heart, bringing to my mind a sequence of memories. I was not wrong to love France,

which allowed me to live some of the dreams of my youth. When I left my homeland we first stayed in Switzerland, a country I later admired for its natural beauty, but at the time I was still very homesick. I recovered my inner peace only when we moved to Nice.

Ali Haydar Bey and Ali Vasib Efendi had rented a small villa that had a large garden with tangerines and orange groves for Faruk Efendi and his family, at twelve Egyptian pounds a month. The house was on Komanos Pasha Avenue, in the district of Ramleh. The Komanos Pasha who had given his name to the avenue was said to have been a kind of pirate, a seaman who long ago had sailed between the Italian ports and Alexandria.

Faruk Efendi and Sabiha Sultan had brought very few things with them from France, so they had to buy furniture for their new house, and Faruk Efendi had to spend a considerable amount of money. The twelve thousand francs a month that the caliph was sending his son, equivalent to sixty-four Egyptian pounds, was insufficient for his needs: in addition to the family, Ertuğrul Efendi, and Mrs. Burdukoff, Sabiha Sultan's mother Nazikeda Kadınefendi stayed with them now and then too, and at times there were ten people living in the household.

The children had started to go to school, and after paying twelve pounds a month for rent it became hard for Faruk Efendi to cover all other expenses with the remaining fifty-two pounds. He asked his father for an increase in his allowance, or at least to pay for the children's tuition separately, but the caliph did not reply, and worse was to come: with the war, communication was practically nonexistent and banks were unable to make transfers.

The family decided to find a cheaper place to live, and they rented an apartment in the district of Zizinya. They never liked the villa in Komanos Pasha Avenue anyway. Their relatives had rented the villa on their behalf when they were still in Nice, so they had not had an opportunity to see the house beforehand. Sabiha Sultan wanted an apartment, which would be less expensive and easier to manage, so they moved to a second-floor flat in a modern building with a lovely terrace, opposite the palace of Princess Fatma, which was surrounded by palm trees.

Financial problems were still a worry, and the only way to avoid even harder economic difficulties was to find rich sons-in-law!

In the midst of all this, Ömer Faruk Efendi had to give up his name. He was politely requested not to use the name Faruk again, but to go by just Ömer. The king of Egypt was Farouk, and the Palace did not want the şehzade, who was a guest in the country where he was now residing, sharing the same name as the king. Thus Ömer Faruk Efendi officially became Prince Ömer, the king calling him just plain Ömer.

Back in Nice, two years before their departure, Ömer Faruk Efendi had already made contacts with a view to settling in Alexandria. When Sabiha Sultan heard that her mother Emine Nazikeda Kadınefendi, who was living in Alexandria with her older sister Ulviye Sultan, was gravely ill, she immediately left Nice for Egypt, and stayed there for three months. In a letter to Ömer Faruk Efendi from Alexandria, at the beginning of 1937, Sabiha Sultan mentioned her wish to remain by her mother's side and to see whether she could also settle another matter: to provide her daughters with a bright future by finding them suitable husbands.

In 1898 Prince Fuad, future king of Egypt, was shot in the throat by his former brother-in-law and the wound never really healed, eventually turning to cancer that killed him in April 1936. His sixteen-year-old son Farouk, who was then studying in England, succeeded him. The young king was a bachelor, and the leading families of Egypt were competing for their daughters to become queen. Necla, the youngest daughter of Sabiha Sultan and Ömer Faruk Efendi, was twelve at the time, Hanzade was fourteen, while Neslishah was just seventeen. It was only natural that they first thought of the future of Neslishah, who for a short time had been more or less promised to poor Prince Amr. And it was not only the family who were in pursuit of a good match for Neslishah, but also their close friends in Egypt. At the top of the list was King Fuad's sister, Princess Nimet Muhtar, as well as Princess Wijdan Ibrahim, the wife of Prince Hilmi Ibrahim, a descendant of Khedive Ismail. Both princesses' first choice was the young king.

To begin with they had to ensure that the king saw Neslishah, and the first attempt had already been made by Princess Nimet in 1935, while the family was still living in Nice. During May of that year George V of England was commemorating the twenty-fifth anniversary of his reign. High-ranking dignitaries from all Britain's protectorates were to take part in the celebrations. Prince Farouk, heir to the Egyptian throne, was to represent his country, and the Prince and Princess of Berar—that is to say the elder son of Osman Khan, Azam Jah, and his wife Dürrüşehvar Sultan—were to represent Hyderabad.

Azam Jah and Dürrüşehvar Sultan had left India weeks before and gone to Nice. Princess Nimet told Sabiha Sultan, "Whatever you do, make sure that Neslishah goes to London. Our crown prince will be at the Jubilee, so they can meet. If Neslishah manages to go with Dürrüşehvar, our future king is bound to see her and one thing will lead to another. Convince Dürrüşehvar to take her niece with her when she goes to London."

The advice made sense, so Ömer Faruk Efendi took on the task of convincing Dürrüşehvar Sultan to take her niece along. He spent days trying to persuade his sister, even begging her, but never received a reply. A few days later it was Azam Jah who gave him the answer: "Please stop dreaming, my dear prince!" he said. "Don't you know your sister? Dürrüşehvar is a creature that would never accept a relative of hers to be in a higher position than her, not even if that person is her dearest niece. She could not even imagine Neslishah as queen of Egypt! So stop dreaming, Dürrüşehvar will not take Neslishah to London!" Azam Jah was right, and Dürrüşehvar and her husband left for London without Neslishah.

The festivities in London began on 6 May 1935. English protocol had divided the guests who were to congratulate King George V and Queen Mary at the reception room of Buckingham Palace into two groups. In the first group were the representatives of the sovereign states, while in the second were those representing the Commonwealth and countries under British protectorate. Hyderabad was an independent state in appearance but in fact under British protectorate, so Azam Jah and Dürrüşehvar Sultan had been placed in the second group.

Queen Mary had met Dürrüşehvar Sultan before and liked this young princess, who had imperial manners. When the guest list was brought to the queen for her approval, she reminded the protocol officer of the Palace that the princess was indeed married to the son of the maharajah of Hyderabad, but that she was also a member of the Turkish imperial family, and she wanted her to be part of the first group. Azam Jah, however, remained in the second group.

Dürrüşehvar Sultan was to enter the reception room of the palace with the representatives of the sovereign states and the kings and queens, but it was not appropriate for her to arrive unaccompanied. It was necessary to find her an escort, and so they did: Prince Mohamed Abdel Moneim, son of the former khedive of Egypt Abbas Hilmi II, who was in London together with Crown Prince Farouk, representing Egypt at the Jubilee. Dürrüşehvar Sultan was extremely elegant. She had Prince Abdel Moneim at her side, and around her neck the medal of the Order of the Ottoman Dynasty, a decoration granted only to members of her family. Azam Jah's place did not change: he entered the reception room with the second group.

At the entrance of the reception room, an embarrassing incident took place: Prime Minister İsmet İnönü was representing Turkey at the ceremony, and by pure coincidence he and Prince Abdel Moneim with Dürrüşehvar Sultan arrived at the same time. İnönü (then known as İsmet Paşa) had previously met the prince when the Ottomans were in power, so they greeted each other. İnönü shook hands with Prince Abdel Moneim and, wanting to behave like a gentleman, leaned forward to kiss Dürrüşehvar's hand. The response was quite unexpected: Dürrüşehvar Sultan, granddaughter of Sultan Abdülaziz, daughter of Caliph Abdülmecid Efendi, instead of extending her hand to the paşa, brought it to her chest, took hold of the medal she was wearing, and waved it toward him, glancing at him for a few seconds with her piercing blue eyes. She then turned her back and walked into the reception room.

Like a character in an old European legend holding up a cross in the face of a mythical monster to make it vanish, Dürrüşehvar had brandished her Ottoman medal at the prime minister of Turkey. Years later, Prince Abdel Moneim recalled, "I just wanted the ground to open and swallow me up!"

Princess Nimet still hoped to introduce Neslishah to Farouk, saying, "The king is still a bachelor, we have to settle this business." She, Sabiha Sultan, and Princess Wijdan racked their brains on how they could bring the meeting about.

In a letter to her husband from Egypt in 1937 Sabiha Sultan mentions the contacts she was making and describes how other families were also striving for their daughters to marry the king:

> In just a few days I have realized that the situation here is very positive. The members of our family living in this country are greatly respected by the Egyptian royal family. The attention shown to me by Toussoun Pasha is quite remarkable. There are a few families interested in the young king, who have brought their daughters here. Among them is the daughter of Princess Zeyneb and Yusri Pasha, as well as Selcuk, the daughter of Abdurrahim. Apparently, the queen would prefer to choose a local girl, while Mohamed Ali Pasha, the heir apparent to the throne, is more of the opinion that the king's bride should belong to a prominent family. However, the queen is supposed to have said, "I shall accept whoever my son likes and wishes to marry." I now believe that Princess Wijdan could be very useful in this matter. Nobody questions me, as it is quite obvious that I am here because of my mother's illness.
>
> You may all be certain that I am following this important mission that I have taken upon myself with the greatest care and attention. With the help of Almighty God, I hope to succeed. Since I have been here, my hopes of success have increased. We shall see, help comes from God.

Meanwhile Nazli, the queen mother, was looking for a bride who would obey her blindly, since she wished to remain effectively the only queen of Egypt even when her son married. So Nazli was the main obstacle preventing Neslishah from becoming queen of Egypt—it was not in her interest to have a daughter-in-law like Neslishah, a princess who belonged to the family that had ruled Egypt in the past, and who was of a nobler lineage than her son. If they were to marry, Nazli would not be able to dominate her, and her power would be diminished.

This is also why she did not accept any of the other candidates suggested to her, and did not even mention them to her son. Instead, she selected the bride herself: Safinaz Zulfiqar, the daughter of Youssef Zulfiqar Pasha, a high-ranking civil servant, and Zeinab Said, one of Nazli's ladies-in-waiting.

It had been a custom since the reign of King Fuad for all members of the royal family to have names beginning with the letter F, so Safinaz Zulfiqar became Farida, and she and King Farouk married in Cairo at Saray al-Qubba (the Dome Palace) on 20 January 1938.

Farida became the new queen of Egypt, and at the beginning of her marriage she bent to Nazli's will, but in time she managed to overshadow her mother-in-law, becoming the first lady of the Palace in Cairo. Her marriage, however, would last only ten years, as Farouk divorced her in 1948.

Much later, when King Farouk finally saw Neslishah and her sisters, he snapped at his mother and his entourage, "Why did you not tell me that these princesses were living in Egypt, and why were they not introduced to me?"

In late November 1938, when Faruk Efendi was still struggling to make ends meet after moving with the family to the apartment in Zizinya, Neslishah received a sorrowful letter from her grandfather in France that had her in tears. After his daughter left for Hyderabad and his son and grandchildren for Egypt, the caliph was alone in France with his wives. He missed his granddaughters terribly, but knew he would never see them again and had no choice but to accept the separation:

> We are here praying for the health and the happiness of all of you. We hope to God that your father will provide you with good and promising futures, which would be of great consolation to our wounded hearts. May Almighty God always bring you good omens and joy. From now on

you must forget about your old grandfather and grandmother. Your sick grandmother cries for you every day. On three occasions she recovered, but her illness has now recurred. She is in great pain. I kiss your sparkling eyes, which are as bright as your beautiful and compassionate heart, and I ask you again to forget us. We have greatly aged. Our weary hearts are not suited for emotions. I kiss the beautiful eyes of the three of you, and I ask God Almighty to bring you health and happiness.

Around this time Neslishah received another marriage proposal: Prince Hassan Toussoun wished to marry her. She recalled:

Hassan was the son of Prince Omar Toussoun, the "King of Alexandria," known as such because he was the richest man in town. His wealth and properties were countless. He was exceedingly generous, and he would help anyone in need. This is why they also called him "Abu al-Fellahin," the father of the peasants. He was very religious, and was one of the leading Egyptian intellectuals of his time. He had a huge library. He was treated like a king because of his generosity toward the poor.

I think it was King Fuad's sister Princess Nimet Muhtar who thought of Hassan, once it became evident that I would not be marrying King Farouk. They invited my parents to Cairo: Tahir Pasha, the son of Princess Emine, another sister of King Fuad, told them, "Princess Nimet wants to see you," and sent a private plane to Alexandria to take them to Cairo.

I had seen Hassan before. He was twenty years older than me. He drank a lot, in fact he drank so much that when he entered a room you would instantly smell the alcohol. His hands were covered with sores. As soon as I saw him, I was truly disgusted. I told my father, "I will not marry this man. I would rather die than marry him!"

While I was protesting in this manner, in Cairo my father told Princess Nimet, "Neslishah has accepted the proposal." All of a sudden, at the age of eighteen, I found myself engaged to Prince Hassan Toussoun.

I asked my mother, "My father made this decision, but how could you betray me? Knowing perfectly well what my feelings were, how could you possibly do this to me?" "Your father was very insistent, and you know how I can never say no to him. What could I do?" she replied, and burst into tears.

Meanwhile, the Toussouns sent a huge diamond ring and a rather ugly Sèvres porcelain filled with chocolates, as well as an incredible amount of sweets. After buying me some elegant clothes, we went to visit Queen Farida at the Montazah Palace in Alexandria, together with Princess Bahija, Hassan's mother.

The queen greeted us warmly. We spoke in French, and chatted away pleasantly. Then we went to the house of Princess Emine, Hassan's sister, where my engagement took place. Members of my family in Egypt, like my aunt Ulviye Sultan, her husband Ali Bey, Lutfiye Sultan, Namık Efendi, Mukbile Sultan, and her husband Vassib Efendi, were present. The Toussouns had also invited some of their relatives.

The engagement party was over, but I just could not stand Hassan. One day while I was sitting on the sofa he tried to kiss me—I pushed him so hard that he fell to the ground.

We stayed engaged for a few months, during which I was unbearable, as if I had lost my mind, and I was crying from morning to night. I must admit that both he and his parents were very kind to me, but I just could not do it!

It was my cousin Namık Efendi who saved me from this agony. One day he said to me, "Neslishah, you cannot go on like this. If you do, you will die. I cannot bear to see you in such a state!" I told him I was helpless and that I was afraid of my father's reaction if I tried to break the engagement. "Leave this matter to me," he said. "Write Hassan a letter, give me the ring and all the other presents he has given you, and under no circumstances leave your room. In fact, have your meals in your room. I shall calm your father down."

I did what Namık told me to do, I wrote the letter, and I gave it to him along with all the presents. He gave Hassan the letter and returned the gifts. Hassan was upset, of course, but once he understood that I was adamant in my decision he gave up on the engagement.

What worried me was what my father's reaction would be, but my fears were unfounded. I don't know what Namık told him, but as a result my father did not utter a word, acting as if nothing had happened. The people of Alexandria were very displeased with me for rejecting the son of their "king."

When the caliph heard that Neslishah had broken her engagement, he sent her a letter from Nice on 2 July 1939, in which he wrote that turning back from a decision did not conform with Islamic tradition. He was clearly angry with Neslishah for ending her engagement:

> I was very upset by the distressing news. Before taking such an important step one has to think thoroughly, but once the decision is made, to turn back is totally against the tradition of Islam.
>
> When the nizam of Hyderabad sent an envoy to ask me for my daughter's hand, I told him, "I am perfectly happy to give my daughter to the son of His Majesty the Nizam, who is a religious monarch and a distinguished son of Islam. However, the most important condition is that they should like each other, be in harmony with one another, and decide for themselves. So let them meet, and if they like each other and agree to get married, we shall perform the wedding ceremony the following day." This is how I dealt with the proposal.
>
> My advice to you, based on seventy-one years of life experience, which has had both good and bad moments, is not to choose a husband among people of your own age. That flame sparkles instantly and then burns out just as quickly.

The dust had settled in Alexandria, and the days passed, when a friend of the family from Cairo, Aziza Shafiq, told them, "Come and stay with us in Cairo for a while. You can go around, and the girls will see Cairo." Aziza Shafiq was a Circassian lady who had come to Egypt from Turkey and married Ahmed Shafiq Pasha, the minister for religious endowments and a member of the khedivial tribunals during the reign of the last khedive, Abbas Hilmi II. Emine Tawfiq, the mother of the khedive, and all the ladies close to her loved Aziza. Everyone liked her. She had five sons and a daughter; her youngest son, Rashid Shafiq, was married to Fethiye Sultan, one of the daughters of Tevfik Efendi, the grandson of Sultan Abdülmecid who Ömer Faruk Efendi had brought to Nice from the miserable village hut in the mountains.[47] So the families of Ömer Faruk Efendi and Aziza Shafiq were distantly related through marriage, and they were close friends.

Neslishah and Hanzade had been to Cairo once before, at the invitation of Princess Nimet Muhtar, but their younger sister Necla had not been allowed to accompany them. Now, in November 1939, the whole family was able to spend a few months in Cairo, at the large house of Aziza Shafiq in the district of al-Qubba. They went around the city nearly every day, visiting the historic places and ancient pharaonic sites or attending receptions given in their honor by the aristocracy and the high society of Cairo.

Though they had planned to spend only a couple of months in Cairo, they ended up staying four, for two reasons. The first was that, as they had feared, the war that had started in Europe before their departure for Cairo had taken a much more violent turn. But the second and more important reason was that because of the war, communications were unavailable, banks were inoperative, and the caliph, who had hitherto been regularly sending his son twelve thousand francs each month, was no longer able to do so—and the family had no money, either to take them back to Alexandria or to allow them to live there.

Ömer Faruk Efendi was broke, in a country where he could not even speak the language and where he knew very few people. As a last resort, he sent a cable to his sister Dürrüşehvar Sultan in Hyderabad asking for help, and followed it with a letter on 12 March 1940, explaining the situation in which he found himself:

> At the outbreak of the war, we were without money for two whole
> months, and we went through very hard times. The expected allowance
> never arrived. Then, in a more or less regular manner, I received the
> monthly payments on the twenty-second of each month; I received last
> month's payment on the twenty-seventh. We are still waiting for this
> month's transfer.
>
> Even when payments are made, we have difficulties in making ends
> meet, so what will happen to us if the money doesn't arrive? I beg you,

have a heart and think about it. My father wrote to me about his allowance not coming on time as well—so since the money to France does not arrive regularly, instead of being transferred to two different countries, mine could be sent to me directly from India.

I shall now explain the reason for my telegram: At the beginning of the winter, Fethiye's mother-in-law invited us to her house in Cairo. We have now been her guests for four months, for which we are extremely grateful of course. Thus, we have been able to save money and repay a significant amount of the debts we had in Alexandria. As we can no longer abuse her hospitality, and while I was pondering on how to return home, Fethiye's husband Rashid, who was working in a large Egyptian sugar factory, fell ill and they came here.

Now there is no more room in the house for all of us. We are therefore obliged to get back as quickly as possible, yet we have the money neither to pay for our return nor to live on when we arrive home. Hence I had no option but to contact you urgently for help.

So, Dear Sister, I think I have explained quite openly the situation we are faced with. The rest is left to your conscience and in your hands. In other words, it is up to you to save us or break us. God forbid we should be obliged to beg from the people here; it would be both terrible and shameful. Unfortunately, several members of our family live in this manner, but I just can't and I don't want to either, as it would tarnish our reputation—not only my reputation, but both our father's reputation and yours. Please believe me, Dürrüşehvar, when I say that I am totally disheartened. There is nothing that I would wish from this world, nothing that would still give me pleasure, if it were not for the responsibility and the duty of providing my children with a prosperous future. You may love me or not, but don't forget that my children's salvation depends on you. You know perfectly well what their feelings are for you. Don't turn away from them, don't hinder the future of these three innocent girls, who have committed no offence and whose lives, like mine, are at all times filled with so much uncertainty.

I leave all of this to your conscience, and while urgently awaiting your reply, I fondly kiss you and your children.

It is not known whether Dürrüşehvar replied to her brother, as there is no relevant document in the family archives.

In the course of these hard days, they decided one morning to visit the famous Step Pyramid of Saqqara. While wandering around the pyramid, they came across another group, led by a rather large, bespectacled man of average height, in his late thirties. On seeing Ömer Faruk Efendi, he burst into loud laughter, which was echoed by the şehzade, and the two men fell into each other's arms.

Ömer Faruk Efendi turned to Sabiha Sultan and introduced the man to her as "Prince Mohamed Abdel Moneim, the son of His Majesty Khedive Abbas Hilmi Pasha. He has been my friend since my student years in Europe." The prince, who at the time was second-in-line to the Egyptian throne, bowed politely and kissed Sabiha Sultan's hand.

This unexpected encounter would change Neslishah's life and destiny, as a few months later the prince she had met at Saqqara for the first time would become her husband. Naturally, she did not know then that she would take the name of Princess Abdel Moneim, or that she would remain married for forty years.

Unable to return to Alexandria, and waiting to receive a response from his sister, Ömer Faruk Efendi had no choice but to seek help from the Egyptian establishment, in particular from members of the royal family. So he approached Prince Mohamed Ali Tewfik, Egypt's heir apparent.

Born in 1875, Prince Mohamed Ali was the son of Khedive Tewfik and the younger brother (by one year) of Abbas Hilmi II, who became khedive in 1892, being his heir apparent for seven years until the birth of Abbas Hilmi's son Abdel Moneim in 1899. When Farouk became king at sixteen in 1936, Mohamed Ali became the prince regent of the young king for a year, and from 1937 he was once again heir apparent, a position he retained for fifteen years until the birth of Farouk's son Ahmed Fuad in 1952.

Eventually, Prince Mohamed Ali's dreams of becoming king ended forever with the Revolution of 1952 and the abolition of the monarchy in 1953. The prince, who had prepared his throne room at the Manyal Palace, "just in case," died in Lausanne in 1955.

Prince Mohamed Ali was not only a very wealthy man but also one of the leading intellectuals of his time, as well as a renowned collector: Manyal Palace was built with the intention of eventually turning it into a museum. During his lifetime he completed the legal formalities so that on his death the property would be transferred to the state, and not to his inheritors. After the 1952 Revolution, even though some of the objects in the mansion had been looted, the Manyal Palace still held important collections and today it is one of Egypt's foremost museums. The prince was also a notable botanist, and the palace is surrounded by an immense garden that includes many rare trees and plants.

The prince did not turn down Ömer Faruk Efendi's request for assistance, and with the funds he provided the family was able to return to Alexandria and somewhat improve their financial situation.

When the family met Prince Abdel Moneim at Saqqara that spring morning in 1940, he was second-in-line to the throne. He had been born in Alexandria on 20 February 1899, at Montazah Palace, the private residence of his father, Khedive Abbas Hilmi II, and from his birth until 1914, when the British deposed his father, he was the crown prince of Egypt and the Sudan and prince of Darfur. The khedives of Egypt, descendants of Mohamed Ali Pasha, ruled not only Egypt but also Sudan's provinces of Darfur and Kordofan. King Fuad and King Farouk, who followed the khedives, used the title King of Egypt and the Sudan, Ruler of Darfur and Kordofan; one of the three stars on the Egyptian flag of the time represented Darfur, another Kordofan. The khedive's heir to the throne had held the title Prince of Darfur, and the king's heir was titled Prince of Upper Egypt.

Abdel Moneim, once heir to the khedivial throne, had studied in Switzerland and after spending some time in Europe returned to Egypt. When his father Khedive Abbas was deposed and exiled to Switzerland he had financial problems (all his assets had been confiscated), and so did Abdel Moneim: he received a small pension from the Palace, but this was not enough to live on, so he was obliged to count on the handouts that his uncle, Prince Mohamed Ali Tewfik, gave him now and then.

Sometimes the Palace would entrust the prince with diplomatic missions, or would want him to represent Egypt at international meetings. In 1935 he attended the reception for the twenty-fifth anniversary of the reign of King George V in London on behalf of the Kingdom of Egypt, and in October 1946, at the end of the Second World War, he headed the Egyptian delegation to the talks with the Americans at the Conference on Palestine, again in London.

Prince Mohamed Ali Tewfik, who was helping both his nephew Abdel Moneim and Şehzade Ömer Faruk Efendi, decided to pay a visit to the şehzade's home in Alexandria, and told them, "Abdel Moneim, the son of my older brother, His Highness Khedive Abbas Hilmi, wishes to marry your eldest daughter." Neslishah recalled:

My grandfather could not send us money because of the war, so we were penniless. My father was asking for financial help here and there, and he also asked Prince Mohamed Ali, who agreed immediately, and we became indebted to him.

One day, he came to our home and told my father that Prince Abdel Moneim wanted to marry me. There was an age difference of twenty years between the prince and me, and when my father told me about the proposal, I immediately refused categorically, saying, "Daddy, I want to marry someone of my own age, someone who will like the same things that I do, someone with whom I can have fun, someone young. The prince is much older than me. I just can't marry him."

My father insisted, while I kept on repeating, "I will not accept, I shall not marry him." We had a terrible row, and we did not speak to each other for three months. I spent the whole day in my room, joining the others only at mealtimes. If I had to go out, Madame Burdukoff accompanied me.

I saw my father only during meals. My place at the dining table was next to him. I would sit at the table, but we would ignore each other. We both acted as if the seat next to us were empty. We ate, but whether it was food that we ate or poison, I am not sure.

This situation went on unchanged for three months; my father was insufferable, bickering and arguing with my mother. Then he stopped picking on my mother and he quarreled with everybody else, except with me.

Life at home became impossible as days went by, while my father was giving my mother and my sisters a very hard time; he even had an argument with my grandmother, for whom he had the greatest respect. Meanwhile, the one who was shattered was my uncle Ertuğrul Efendi, because he was not used to so much drama.

This went on, as I said, for three months. As life was becoming unbearable, I finally gave in and said, "Fine, I will do it," upon which my father sent word that I had accepted the marriage proposal.

However, making the decision was just the first step. Abdel Moneim had to obtain permission from his father the khedive and from King Farouk, since according to protocol, a prince could not marry without the consent of the king. Abdel Moneim sent a telegram to his father in Switzerland and waited weeks for the reply.

Meanwhile, quite unexpectedly, Hanzade married before I did.

At the time, Hanzade was sixteen years old and another Egyptian prince, Mohamed Ali Ibrahim, wished to marry her. He was the brother of Amr Ibrahim, who had been as good as engaged to Neslishah, and who would eventually marry Necla Sultan, the youngest of the three sisters. Neslishah recalled:

The prince knew Hanzade back in the days when we were still living in Nice; he was a friend of my father. Before making his official proposal, he had spoken to Hanzade, and she had agreed to marry him.

I told Hanzade, "Don't do it, don't marry him. The prince is much older than you. You can't understand what it means. I was engaged before, and I know what I am talking about, but you don't. Later on, you will suffer a great deal. I would not advise you to marry someone so much older than yourself." I pleaded with her, "They are forcing me into marriage, but no one is forcing you, so please don't accept."

"I am fed up with darning my socks, with darning things all the time. I want to have a comfortable life," she said, and she married him.

She meant what she said: she did not want to leave home just because of the upsetting situation we were in, she wanted to marry to escape from poverty.

We were having serious money problems. We could not afford new clothes; we were constantly mending what we had. We had to iron our own things. There was a Greek woman in our service, but she only knew how to cook—whenever she tried to iron she would ruin our dresses. Consequently, we ironed our own clothes, and if we were going somewhere important we asked Madame Burdukoff to help us.

Hanzade wanted to get away from all this and marry immediately. My father initially said, "The eldest marries first, then the younger ones. Let us wait for the khedive's response, let Neslishah marry, and then we can get on with Hanzade's wedding." But then he changed his mind, because communications were difficult and no one knew when the reply would arrive from Switzerland. We could be waiting for months.

Prince Mohamed Ali was an excellent husband to Hanzade. In the years that followed, he would be of great help to my husband and me when we were in serious trouble. My children lived with them for years.

The whole family went to Cairo for Hanzade Sultan's wedding, staying again at Aziza Hanem's house in al-Qubba. The prince rented a large house in Gezira from a Jewish landlord, with antique furniture and a library full of beautifully bound books of famous writers such as Balzac and Zola. The marriage was pronounced in that house, on 19 September 1940. Neslishah recalled:

In Egypt, Thursday is considered to be a lucky day for weddings. So Hanzade married on a Thursday. The ceremony took place in the morning. Mohamed Ali gave a big ball in the magnificent house he had rented in Gezira. When we went to the reception, we found that the telegram from my future father-in-law that we had been expecting for weeks had just arrived. Because of the war the mail was not functioning, as only military planes could fly—these were the only ones to provide the postal service, and this was the reason for the delay.

The khedive's reply said, "Congratulations, I am very happy."

The khedive's sister, Princess Khadija, sent me her gift at Hanzade's house: a magnificent necklace, covered with colored diamonds. It had belonged to Catherine I of Russia. According to rumors, when the commander of the Turkish army Baltacı Mehmed Paşa encircled the Russian army in Pruth in 1711, Catherine and her husband Peter the Great, to save their army, sent gifts to the paşa. This necklace was one of them. On his return to Istanbul Baltacı gave all the gifts to Sultan Ahmed III, and they became part of the treasury. When my great-grandfather Sultan Abdülaziz and Khedive Ismail of Egypt became friends they exchanged gifts, and Abdülaziz gave the necklace to Ismail. Later on, it was passed on to Khedive Tewfik, who gave it to his daughter Princess Khadija. Thus the necklace was returned to the Ottoman family—that is, to my family—two hundred years after it had first been acquired.

This superb piece of jewelry was truly exceptional, and on the night of my wedding it was exhibited in its box on one of the tables in the reception room. Years later I was obliged to sell it in London because I needed money, but sadly it went for nearly nothing.

That evening, Moneim gave me a beautiful ring, and the next day he requested permission from King Farouk to marry me on the following Thursday.

The Palace granted permission at once, and Neslishah married Prince Abdel Moneim on 26 September 1940. The wedding preparations were done in a hurry. Even her wedding dress was hastily prepared: Neslishah wore her mother's wedding gown, enhanced with some old lace.

The marriage ceremony took place in Cairo at Prince Mohamed Ali Tewfik's Manyal Palace on Roda Island, at five-thirty in the afternoon. Mohamed Imam Sherif, who performed all the weddings of the Egyptian aristocracy, prepared the necessary documents, according to the Islamic faith and its principles.

It was not a custom in Egypt for brides to attend the religious ceremony, so Neslishah was not present; instead, her father represented her. Prince Abdel Moneim and Şehzade Ömer Faruk Efendi, acting on behalf of Neslishah, signed the marriage certificate, while the witnesses were Prince Mohamed Ali Tewfik, the groom's uncle, and Youssef Kamal, another Egyptian prince. Two şehzades of the Ottoman family, Ali Vasib Efendi and Osman Fuad Efendi, the grandsons of Murad V, were also present at the ceremony, as well as Prince Mohamed Ali Ibrahim, Neslishah's brother-in-law as of one week.

The bride price that Neslishah received on signature of the marriage certificate was two thousand Egyptian pounds, and the sum to be paid in case of divorce was one thousand pounds. These amounts were considered a fortune at that time.

Neslishah's marriage was arranged thus, but in the prenuptial agreement there was no mention of the *ismet hakkı*, the right to divorce, which traditionally was given to the Ottoman imperial princesses. According to Islamic law, the right to divorce is a man's prerogative, though in certain cases a woman can demand a divorce by requesting permission from the *qadi*, a Muslim judge of religious law, who may agree to annul the marriage. But in the family of the Ottoman dynasty, *ismet hakkı* was an exclusive right accorded to the imperial princesses, because it was considered both unpleasant and unthinkable for a husband to divorce a direct descendant of the sultan, and this right was enshrined in Ottoman legislation. But since the empire no longer existed, and the family lived in exile, the custom was forgotten.

Neslishah's wedding reception also took place at the Manyal Palace, a few hours after the religious ceremony. She recalled:

> Prince Mohamed Ali Tewfik, my husband's uncle, took care of all the wedding expenses. He arranged everything.
>
> From the entrance of Manyal Palace there was a staircase on the left leading up to a large reception room. The prince had brought wooden panels from Damascus that decorated the ceiling. Our wedding party took place there. In the middle of the reception room there was a huge banquet table, where all sorts of cakes and a wide variety of appetizing dishes were on display.

They had allocated me a room to dress next to the reception room. I was to don my wedding gown there and then join the others. When I entered the room, I just could not stop crying. I cried so much that I was in no condition to go anywhere. It was then, in that very room, that I realized how much I did not want to be married, but it was too late. My mother came and tried to calm me down. "Come on darling," she kept saying, "The guests are arriving, everyone is waiting for you." It took my mother quite some time to soothe me, and for me to stop crying. Then I dressed and joined the guests.

All the members of our family living in Egypt were present, with the exception of my youngest sister Necla, as Prince Mohamed Ali, the host of the wedding, had said, "I don't want children in the house." Necla was fourteen years old then and when she was told that she could not come with us she was very upset. "How is it possible that I am not attending my sister's wedding?" she asked, and cried for days. The Egyptian side of the family was also not allowed to bring the king's younger sister Faiza, who was seventeen, but still considered a child!

Eventually, all the guests arrived, including King Farouk, Queen Farida, Queen Mother Nazli, and Sultana Melek, the wife of the former sultan of Egypt Hussein Kamil—everyone was there.

I was the bride, but the most beautiful woman of the evening was my grandmother Nazikeda Kadınefendi. She wore a purple dress with a *hotoz*, a kind of cap covered with a scarf, on her head, and her presence inspired great respect. My mother helped her to cover her headwear with embroidery and other adornments. She was so elegant that when King Farouk saw her he was stunned. Imagine—my grandmother was then eighty-odd years old, a very tired lady, just skin and bones, yet she still had such an imposing presence that all the guests, including the king, were terribly impressed. As I said, the king was there, the elder queen was there, the younger queen was there, but the only majesty present was my grandmother. Her outfit was simple, yet her appearance in that purple dress, her demeanor, her posture, and the way she looked around, made everyone realize that she was the empress. The guests forgot about the bride, having eyes only for my imperial grandmother.

King Farouk was taken aback. He usually had a very disdainful attitude, and looked down at people when he addressed them; when he sat on a chair it was as if he were lying down. Yet even he, when he saw my grandmother, pulled himself together, sat on the very edge of his seat, his feet together, and during the entire evening looked very proper.

Then the guests gave us their wedding presents: Princess Khadija, my father-in-law's sister, had given me the tsarina's diamond necklace a week before at Hanzade's wedding. Prince Mohamed Ali Tewfik gave me a sapphire ring and a blue Lincoln car. The two queens each gave me a brooch.

When the reception was over and the guests departed, we also left Manyal Palace. The odd thing was that I did not go with my husband, we left separately. I followed my parents to Aziza Hanem's mansion, while my husband went home to Heliopolis. The reason was that the house was not yet ready for me to live in—when my mother first saw it, she said, "How will you ever live here, Neslishah?" and cried.

The house in Heliopolis was a grand building in a huge garden, giving the impression of an imposing mansion. Years before, the wife of the khedive, that is, Neslishah's mother-in-law had bought it, and the khedive had brought a very ornate gate with an embossed crown from his mother's palace in Cairo and had it mounted here as the garden gate.

Prince Abdel Moneim had a passion for animals: inside the house was an aquarium with exotic fish from the Red Sea, and a parrot, and in the garden were various species of doves and pigeons, flamingos, a desert gazelle, and dogs of various breeds. He had even once kept a cheetah in the garden as a pet, but when he found that the cheetah was growling at passing herds of sheep and young children on their way to school, he sent it to the zoo.

The house looked magnificent from the outside, but the interior was old and in great need of restoration. Repairs began a few days before the wedding. There was a lot to be done, but only the fittings were to be renewed; the furniture would remain unchanged. Neslishah recalled:

Moneim's uncle gave him money as a wedding present. "This money is to restore your home," he said, and repairs were begun, but as we had married in a hurry the house was not ready in time. For instance, my husband's bed-room had been downstairs and a new bedroom was being built upstairs, but the staircase could not be used so I could not go up there. The construction was never-ending, so two weeks later we went to Lebanon.

Neslishah's title according to Ottoman protocol was *Devletlû İsmetlû Neslişah Sultan Âliyetü'ş-şân Hazretleri* (Her Imperial Highness Princess Neslishah), but in Egypt her title in Arabic was *Sahibat al-Sumuw al-Amira Neslishah* (Her Highness Princess Neslishah). In other words, her title would no longer include the words 'imperial' or 'royal.' Prince Abdel Moneim, the son of the last khedive, kept his title of prince, and though he was the second-in-line to the throne he was not considered to be part of the royal family.

But although Neslishah was now just a princess, not a royal princess, everyone knew to which family she belonged and everybody showed great respect, not only to her but also to Ömer Faruk Efendi and Sabiha Sultan. However, the fact that Neslishah and her sisters, who were also married to Egyptian princes, were imperial princesses had no relevance in the protocol: their status came from their husbands.

Abdülmecid Efendi was extremely pleased with Neslishah's mar-riage: the father of the groom, Khedive Abbas Hilmi, had been deposed because of his allegiance to the Ottoman Empire, so the caliph was very happy that his granddaughter had married the son of a sovereign loyal to his family.

One of the wedding gifts led to a confrontation with King Farouk. Everyone in Cairo knew that when Farouk saw something he liked in someone's home, he would overtly announce that he wanted it, and would say, "Send it to the palace tomorrow." Or if the object was small he would just take it—"I'm taking this." It was also known that at times he would send a truck to a house when the owners were not there, load-ing it with whatever took his fancy.

For example, a wealthy pasha, a member of the Yegen family, who had held important positions in the Egyptian administration, spent his retirement taking care of his antiques and collections. Rumors that he had a beautiful pair of silver-mounted ivory horns in his living room reached the king, who one day sent a message saying, "I am coming to see you tomorrow." The poor pasha immediately understood that the king was after his ivory horns, so he called in the builders and had a wall built in front of the horns to conceal them. The wall was then painted, pictures were hung, and furniture was placed in front of the new wall. When the king arrived the following day, he went all around the house in search of the ivory horns, and not finding them he left without a word.

Prince Kamal al-Din, a member of the Egyptian royal family, had given Neslishah as a wedding present a beautiful table made from an elephant's ear. During one of the king's rare visits to their house in Heliopolis, the king saw the table and said as he was leaving, "Send the table to the palace!" That evening, while Abdel Moneim was talking to Prince Youssef Kamal, he mentioned the incident with the table, and the prince, who was one of the wealthiest men in Egypt, said, "I have the same table. Keep yours and send him mine; I am not using it." The king did not like the table he received, and told Neslishah and Abdel Moneim, "I do not like this table, the other one is nicer. I don't want this one, send me yours." But in the end he did not get the table.

Then there was the matter of the sword of Sultan Suleiman the Magnificent. It was an old Ottoman tradition to give precious gifts to the sovereigns of the states subject to the empire. Following this custom, Sultan Abdülhamid gave Khedive Abbas Hilmi one of the swords that had belonged to Sultan Suleiman, and which was kept in the treasury of Topkapı Palace. This gift was not only the most precious gift that the sultan could have bestowed on one of his vassal rulers, it was also evidence of the importance that he gave to the khediviate of Abbas Hilmi and to the policies he was implementing.

Traditionally in the Islamic world, it was the male members of the family who inherited the weapons, and this custom was also followed in Egypt. The deposed khedive had taken the sword to Switzerland and kept it in his safe at the bank (the sword of Ibrahim Pasha, the son of Mohamed Ali Pasha the Great, was also kept in the same safe), and in his will he left it to his newborn grandson, Abbas Hilmi, fearing that something might happen to his son Prince Abdel Moneim. He had registered the safe in the name of his daughter Princess Shawkat, who was instructed to remit the sword to Abbas Hilmi on his twenty-fifth birthday.

Eventually, King Farouk came to hear of the existence of Suleiman's sword and said to Prince Abdel Moneim, "Give it to me!" At which point Neslishah intervened, saying, "The sword is not here, it is in a safe in Switzerland in the name of Princess Shawkat." The king then sent an envoy, asking again for the sword, and Neslishah said, "The sword belonged to my ancestor Sultan Suleiman. It is a family heirloom, and under no circumstance will I give it to the king."

Ilhami Pasha, King Farouk's first chamberlain, returned on several occasions to the house in Heliopolis, and unable to convince Neslishah to relinquish the sword he threatened her: "We are talking abut the king! If you continue to refuse, you will end up in tears."

Exasperated, Neslishah replied, "What is he going to do? Will he remove my husband's title? He is already sitting on his throne, he has taken his properties and has gone as far as taking his mother's jewels. He has taken everything, and now he wants the sword of my ancestors! Go and tell him I will not give it."

Prince Abbas Hilmi, the son of Prince Abdel Moneim and Neslishah, duly received the sword of Sultan Suleiman on his twenty-fifth birthday in 1966, and it is now kept safely in his residence in London.

The ongoing restoration of the house in Heliopolis never seemed to end. After her wedding Neslishah spent two weeks as a guest of Aziza Hanem, but not wanting to impose any longer, went with her husband to Lebanon on their honeymoon. She recalled:

> At the time there was only one hotel where one could stay in Beirut, and that was the Saint Georges. We settled in and immediately began calling our relatives: Dürrüşehvar, my mother-in-law İkbal Hanım, and my sister-in-law were all in Lebanon when we arrived.

We went to my mother-in-law's to kiss her hand and pay our respects. She was there with her daughter Princess Atiya. When I entered the living room, they both stood up and did the *temenna*. I was very embarrassed, and tried to say something like, "Please don't get up." But Princess Atiya replied, "You are an imperial princess, even if you are our bride, and this is the way we were taught to greet an imperial princess. We are accustomed to it."

Even much later, Princess Atiya never addressed me as Neslishah, always Sultan. I was very uncomfortable, and on several occasions I told her, "Please, call me by my name, call me Neslishah." "I can't help it," she replied, "I was not brought up like this, my upbringing will not allow me to call you otherwise."

Then we visited the older generation of our family, starting with my great-aunt Nazime Sultan, the daughter of Sultan Abdülaziz. Nazime Sultan and my grandfather Abdülmecid Efendi were full siblings, from the same mother and father. She was tiny, rather ugly, with large lips like her father's, but quite impressive. Nazime Sultan and her husband Halid Paşa lived in a mansion surrounded by a large garden, and I went there to kiss the hand of this grand lady.

When Dürrüşehvar married, Nazime Sultan gave her a diamond tiara, and to me she offered a beautiful bracelet embossed with three diamonds as my wedding present. The funny thing was that my husband sat in front of Nazime Sultan like a well-behaved child, just like the king in front of my grandmother at our wedding.

A few weeks later, word came from Cairo that the house was finished, and Neslishah and her husband returned to Egypt.

One might think that in a country like Egypt, where the royal family took an active part in the social life of the country, a princess married to the second-in-line to the throne would lead a fabulous life, attending parties and having fun. But this was not the case for Neslishah: they did not see many people, and lived more or less on their own.

The reason was that the Palace, and in particular King Farouk, did not want Prince Abdel Moneim to be seen too much: he was the son of the last khedive of Egypt, whom the British had deposed in 1914 in favor of Sultan Hussein, who was then succeeded by King Fuad, and the legitimacy of the throne had been the subject of discussion for years, because despite his early dismissal by the British the khedive did not actually renounce the throne until May 1931. So King Fuad was only then able to establish his dynasty, and even though the king's family was closely related to the deposed khedive, he did not wish the children of the khedive, such as Abdel Moneim, to be in the limelight. There were still people in Egypt who considered the khedive and his son Prince Abdel Moneim as the rightful owners of the throne, so the prince's regular appearance could be perceived as a danger to the Palace. Neslishah recalled:

The British deposed my father-in-law because of his allegiance to Turkey, replacing him with Sultan Hussein, another member of the family. Then they made Fuad king, and Fuad did not want the past to be remembered.

In Egypt, one hardly spoke about the khedive, but he was still loved. For instance, no one addressed my husband as Prince Moneim but as Efendina, meaning 'Your Highness.' He was Efendina to everybody.

Fuad was afraid of the past, as essentially he was not very sure of himself. He wanted Moneim to live in a restricted circle of people, without being seen in public too often. His son Farouk did the same. It was more or less forbidden for us to get close to high-ranking civil servants, to pashas and their families, and in particular to foreign diplomats.

The king's chamberlain, Hassanein Pasha, told my husband personally that the Palace did not want us to be in contact with others. Hassanein Pasha was married to one of the daughters of Princess Shiwikar, King Fuad's first wife. He had studied in England, he was interested in sports, and he had made some discoveries in the desert. When the young Farouk was sent to study in England, Hassanein accompanied him as his guardian, and after Farouk's ascent to the throne, Hassanein became one of the most influential figures in the royal court, where he was also the chamberlain of the Queen Mother Nazli—there were even rumors that he was having an affair with her.

Now and then we would attend the official receptions at the palace, as we were obliged to do, but these occasions were rare.

I think that the bar on appearing in public imposed on my husband also had something to do with me, as I was the granddaughter of the last caliph, and it had been King Fuad's aspiration to become caliph.

Farouk also fell under the same spell: in 1941 he grew a beard, and with his prayer beads in one hand he would go to the mosque on Fridays to pray together with his pashas. His father had fantasized about becoming caliph, and so did Farouk. It was a kind of megalomania.

My grandfather the caliph of course was still alive at the time. I told my husband that if it were true that the king dreamed of becoming caliph, I would never again step foot in the palace. My husband was surprised. "What do you mean?" he said. "You are my wife, you are obliged to come with me." "Not at all," I replied, "The caliph is alive, and what's more he is my grandfather. I will not tolerate such a thing."

Some years later I again clashed with King Farouk. In 1948 he divorced Queen Farida, and two years later he was engaged to Nariman Sadik, a young commoner. The king's birthday was 11 February, and on that day each year we all had to go to the palace to sign the register. When I went to the palace on 11 February 1950 I saw that there were two registers: one for the king's birthday, the other to congratulate his future bride. I signed only the birthday book, and one of the King's Chamberlains approached me, telling me that I had forgotten to sign the congratulations one.

"I have not forgotten," I said, "I have deliberately not signed it." "His Majesty's fiancée lives in Heliopolis, you can go to her house to pay your respects," the man suggested, at which point I could not stop myself and said, "I am not signing the register, and I shall not go to her house. Presently, this young lady is not yet the queen! I was born an imperial princess. Therefore, I will not go to pay my respects to Mademoiselle Sadik.

We led a quiet life, sometimes with a couple of friends, but most of the time by ourselves. We had very few friends coming to our house. Those of my age had husbands of their age, who liked to have fun—they were part of a different crowd and would probably get bored with us. The only people who came were Ebubekir Rateb and his wife Ceyda.

At one point I took drawing lessons to keep me busy. There was a middle-aged Turkish painter called Hidayet in Cairo. He came to Cairo from Istanbul during the war and never went back. He made his living by giving drawing lessons to the rich in their homes, and occasionally he would sell one of his paintings for a pittance. He became my teacher as well. Taking lessons helped me pass the time and earned him a few more pounds, which is what my husband wanted. He never actually taught me how to draw: when the lesson began he would say, "Look, this is how you do it," and he would sit and draw himself. I continued these sessions until I became pregnant.

Before the birth of my children, I would also go horse riding at the Equestrian Club early in the morning. I would then return home, where I spent most of the day, and sometimes I would go to the cinema. The Equestrian Club was in Zamalek, on the other side of town: the driver would take me there. In those days, there were several foreign clubs in Cairo, but we never went to those. The most famous one was the Gezira Sporting Club, where I went only once. My husband wanted to show me this club, so we went one day, but we came back without even sitting down, as we were not supposed to make public appearances!

Neslishah and her husband led a more or less solitary life, but under the control and the protection of Prince Mohamed Ali Tewfik. Neslishah recalled:

My husband called Prince Mohamed Ali Tewfik 'Uncle,' and eventually I did the same. He had no children of his own, so he treated my husband as his son and had taken him under his protection. He loved him, but he was constantly interfering in our lives, and my husband had no choice but to follow his uncle's advice, as at the end of the day he was the one who gave him money.

King Fuad gave all Egyptian princes a monthly salary, including my husband, but the money that came from the Palace was just to keep their loyalty, it was not an amount on which one could live. Nonetheless, my husband gave great importance to the allowance he received from King Fuad. "The king was very kind to me, he even paid me a salary," he would say. Several times when he spoke in this manner I would reply: "The king gave you that money to keep you on his side. He could have exiled you if he had wished, but I think he preferred to have your gratitude."

Moneim would send half the amount he received from the Palace to his mother and sister, who were living in Istanbul, and what was left was quickly spent. His uncle provided for all his expenses.

On Fridays, he would go to his uncle's residence at the Manyal Palace. They would pray in his uncle's private mosque and then have lunch together. This continued for years.

The Egyptian royal family enjoyed a much freer lifestyle than the Ottoman dynasty had done when they ruled in Istanbul. Since the nineteenth century, balls, concerts, and entertainment had been frequent events in Cairo. The Egyptian princes and princesses would attend such events almost nightly, and their attire was more European in style than that of the Ottomans.

This relative freedom at times—and often without cause—gave rise to rumors, even to scandals, and the high society of Cairo thrived on the gossip. Prince Mohamed Ali Tewfik knew this society well, and was concerned that they might gossip about Neslishah and make up stories, especially those who attended the Equestrian Club. And he was troubled that Neslishah continued to ride in spite of her pregnancy. She recalled:

One of the ladies at the Equestrian Club in Zamalek fell in love with a young officer there. She divorced her husband and married the officer, which gave rise to a terrible scandal. Uncle started to worry, so he summoned my husband and said, "Your wife will no longer go to the Equestrian Club. Anyway, riding is for men, women don't ride!"

I loved riding, so I took my horse from the club to Prince Youssef Kamal's mansion, where he had built a riding track on the grounds of his property, and I rode there every day.

The following year when my son Abbas was born, I saw a magnificent white horse entering the garden one morning, while I was still in bed. "Where has this horse come from?" I asked Moneim. He told me that Tahir Pasha had sent it to me as a gift. The best trainer in Egypt had trained him. The saddle, the reins, and I don't remember what else, all came from Paris. He was a magnificent Arab horse. Trained as a circus stallion, he was a fabulous animal. Tahir Pasha was the son of Princess Emine Ismail, one of the daughters of King Fuad, who later became one of our closest friends in Cairo.

But as soon as the horse arrived Moneim sent it back, without saying a word to me. "My uncle does not want you to ride, so I was obliged to send it back," he said. I was furious, and we had a terrible fight.

With the money that my husband received from his uncle for our wedding he repaired the house, but I needed to redecorate the interior. My mother-in-law had bought the building, but it had not been used much. At one point it became a hospital, and Doctor Moro, a Syrian doctor who took care of my grandmother's affairs, moved into the top floor with his family and used the ground floor as his clinic, leaving it in ruins. Not only was the furniture ugly, but nothing matched. In one corner there was a horrendous sofa inlaid with mother of pearl, next to it an old-fashioned sideboard, and the rest was also quite random.

I had no money, so I sent a pair of earrings to the goldsmith to be sold. I was going to use that money for the repairs of the house. When the man called to say that he had sold the earrings all hell broke loose! 'Uncle' was furious and said things like, "Those terrible people in the Equestrian Club have confused your mind." Then he would not allow us to see Ebubekir and Ceyda, and he also prohibited us from seeing Şerife Hanım, the daughter of Şerif Paşa the Kurd, who used to be Sultan Abdülhamid's ambassador in Stockholm, as well as his son-in-law Salih Bey, whom we had recently befriended.

I could not even move the furniture around. I would take a chair and place it somewhere else, then the housemaid would appear saying, "No! The master put it here, it must stay here!"

"I am the lady of the house," I would retort, "I am the master here." But she just would not understand and repeat, "This is how the master wants it, we cannot change it."

Naturally, after all these incidents, my relationship with Moneim became quite strained, and things continued in this manner for a year. It took me a full year to establish my authority, but from then on I was able to do everything I wanted.

In spite of the difficulties at the beginning of their marriage, Neslishah and Prince Abdel Moneim had a happy married life that lasted forty-one years until the prince's death in 1981. Neslishah said of her late husband:

I refused Moneim's proposal as soon as I was told of it, because of our age difference. But my fears were unfounded. Moneim was always very kind toward my family and toward me. For instance, he called my mother "Sultan" and my father "Your Highness," even though they had been friends since their youth, while my mother called him "Prince." He was a very understanding man; he accepted everything I said, and he was a good husband to me, but more importantly he was an excellent friend, with whom I could talk freely about anything.

7
Moonlight and Nights of Fear

During the first months of 1941, Neslishah realized she was pregnant. Prince Abdel Moneim immediately cabled his father in Switzerland to inform him that they were expecting a child. The postal services were very slow because of the war, and the khedive's telegram arrived a few months later, reading, "May God grant you a son and may his name be Abbas Hilmi." Neslishah and Prince Abdel Moneim's first child was born on 16 January 1941. It was indeed a boy, and he was named Abbas Hilmi after his grandfather, as the khedive had wished. Three years later, on 22 December 1944, their second child was born. This time it was a girl, and she was given the name of Prince Abdel Moneim's mother, İkbal.

One of the fronts of the Second World War was on Egyptian soil. King Farouk right from the beginning had declared his country's neutrality, but this would not stop the British and German troops running up against each other in Egypt's Western Desert, and in 1941 Field Marshal Erwin Rommel, commanding the German forces in North Africa, began their advance toward Egypt. The Egyptians, tired of being under British domination since the nineteenth century, were hopeful that this advance might change things.

In Cairo Neslishah's father, Şehzade Ömer Faruk Efendi, followed the movement of the German troops closely. He had graduated from the Military Academy of Potsdam as a professional officer, and had fought during the First World War in Galicia and Verdun. He had also been part of the regiment of the German First Guard Cavalry Division, where he received two war medals from Kaiser Wilhelm II.

At home, he had a large map spread out on a table, on which he would follow the movement of the German troops day by day. As a member of the dynasty that in the past had been allied with the Germans, he thought about the day when Egypt would be saved from the British. He was not alone in front of the map. With him were Abbas Halim, an Egyptian prince who had also trained as a soldier in Germany, and the grandson of King Fuad, Tahir Pasha, who was also pro-German.

Ömer Faruk Efendi and his family had left France for Egypt because of the threat of war, but the war caught up with them in Cairo. One morning, British soldiers came to the şehzade's house in Maadi. The officer in charge, after saluting him in a courteous manner, said, "The English command has taken the decision to intern you until the end of the war. You will be kept under surveillance in a villa. All your needs will be taken care of, while your family will be granted permission to visit you once a week."

According to rumor, the Turkish government feared that in the event of a German victory, Ömer Faruk Efendi could use this against Ankara. To avoid this possibility, and to prevent the şehzade from being in contact with foreigners, they requested the British to intern him. Sabiha Sultan bade farewell to her husband in tears. Neslishah recalled:

> My father, Prince Abbas Halim, and Tahir Pasha were first taken and locked up in a villa south of Cairo in a place called al-Ayyat, where they stayed for a year. Then they were moved to another villa in Saqqara, south of Giza, which belonged to the Ghali family.
>
> My father and Prince Halim were once German soldiers, but Tahir Pasha was a civilian, and his title was not a military one. The reason he was arrested together with my father was because he had lived in Germany and Austria for several years, where he knew a great number of Germans. The three of them spoke perfect German. During their stay in al-Ayyat, Tahir Pasha became ill and was taken to a military hospital, where he preferred to remain as it was in the city, making it easier for his family to visit him.

We would see my father once a week on Fridays: my mother, Prince Ismail Daoud, and myself. It was not possible for my husband to accompany us, since it was not suitable for the second-in-line to the Egyptian throne to visit a German sympathizer imprisoned by the British. But as he did not want my mother and me to go on our own, he had asked Prince Ismail Daoud to accompany us. The prince would sit in front, next to the driver, and my mother and I would sit in the back. After a journey of five or six hours, we would finally see my father. The wife of Prince Abbas Halim would come on the same day, but in a different car. We would leave early in the morning and arrive around noon. On the way, we drove through rice fields where the light of the sun shining on the growing rice was just magnificent. We would have lunch with my father and then drive back to Cairo in another five or six hours.

In those days I had an excellent cook at home, and I would ask him to prepare my father's favorite dishes, which I would carry along with me. He loved stuffed vegetables and Umm Ali ('Mother of Ali,' a traditional Egyptian dessert). To keep the Umm Ali warm, the cook would cover it with various cloths, and even several hours later it was still fresh as if it had just come out of the oven, and in spite of the water, milk, and cream in it, it stayed crispy.

The villa they lived in was quite spacious and comfortable. Soldiers surrounded the building, but they were Egyptian, not British. They had a radio, on which they could follow the news of the ongoing battles. The strange thing was that although my father was imprisoned, he still carried a gun. He felt naked without his gun, so when the British came to take him away, he said, "I cannot live without my gun," refusing to hand it over, and the British did not insist. Once, when we lived in Alexandria, a burglar broke into our house. My father went after the thief, who climbed the wall to jump off, when my father fired his gun. Thank God, he misfired. Who knows what would have happened, if he had shot the man!

A year later, my father and his friends were moved to a villa near Saqqara, closer to Cairo. The villa used to belong to the Ghali family, and I think it had been requisitioned by the British. It had a large garden, and compared to al-Ayyat it was easier for us to get there.

Abbas Halim at the time was married to an awful woman, who managed to turn my father against Hanzade and Necla's husbands. She would let loose her tongue, telling him, "Your daughters and sons-in-law don't care about you," and she convinced her husband, who was imprisoned with my father, of what she was saying. On Fridays when we visited, they would both make sarcastic remarks about it. Abbas Halim would start, and his wife would continue making comments against my sister, until the day Necla stopped visiting my father, who was furious with her.

While my father was imprisoned in the villa, Prince Mohamed Ali Tewfik did not want me to ride or to appear at the receptions that I was normally obliged to attend. He told Moneim, "She should not be seen around—people will talk. While her father is in prison, she should also live like a prisoner."

Life went on like this. My father remained locked up for two years, and when İkbal was born in December 1944 he was still in Saqqara, where during the last months of my pregnancy I could no longer go to see him. The British released him and Prince Halim in the spring of 1945, when the Germans withdrew entirely from all the European fronts.

There were also rumors that the British were about to arrest Prince Abdel Moneim. Everyone knew that he disliked the British, and of course he was the son of the deposed khedive, who during his reign had always been against British interests. In addition, the prince had been heir to the throne before becoming second-in-line, and his family might still harbor claims to rule Egypt. Thus there was a fear that he could be of interest to the Germans, and that Berlin could make contact with him regarding the future of Egypt.

The first to get wind of the British intention to arrest and intern the prince until the end of the war, as they had done with his father-in-law, was Prince Mohamed Ali. He then went to some lengths to vouch for him and convince the British that his nephew had nothing to do with politics. Thanks to his uncle's intervention, Prince Abdel Moneim avoided being imprisoned.

On the assumption that the prince might one day ascend to the throne, efforts had been made to give him a broad education and a far-sighted understanding of politics, so that when his time to rule came he would be able to reign wisely. As a result, and in spite of narrowly escaping internment by the British, he was able to perceptively follow world events. Before the beginning of the war, when Nazi Germany signed a treaty of non-aggression with the Soviet Union on 23 August 1939, the prince established an "Operations Room" on the ground floor of his house in Heliopolis, in which he spread out large maps of Germany and Russia on a table, with green and red flags showing the positions of German and Russian troops.

One evening, when the Şehzade Ömer Faruk Efendi came to have dinner at the house, the prince took the şehzade to his Operations Room. Faruk Efendi, who was a professional soldier, asked his son-in-law, "Mon cher, what are these?" To which the prince replied, "One day the Germans will invade Russia. The indications are there." Faruk Efendi laughed, "Come on, mon cher, how can that be?" But two years later, on 22 June 1941, when German troops attacked Russia, Prince Abdel Moneim coud say to Faruk Efendi and others who had not taken him seriously, "You see?"

Besides his Operations Room, the prince also set up a private radio station in Cairo, through which he broadcast the news on the ongoing war. One day British soldiers stormed into his house: "You must get rid of those maps and stop your radio transmissions," they said, forcing him to shut his activities down—though even then they did not arrest him.

Years later, after he moved to Turkey, when the Arab–Israeli war of 1967 broke out, Prince Abdel Moneim followed the conflict over the radio, hour by hour, and when Egypt was defeated and lost the Sinai Peninsula he locked himself up in a room, not wanting others to see his sorrow—but when he eventually emerged the redness of his eyes was noticeable.

Then in November 1971, when Iran annexed three small islands in the Arabian Gulf known as Greater and Lesser Tunb and Abu Musa in a fait accompli, the prince predicted, "This action will be disastrous for Iran." Eventually, this was one of the causes of the war between Iran and Iraq that started in 1980 and lasted seven years.

Wartime Cairo, which later became the subject of various novels and films, was a bustling capital, and while British and German spies were swarming around the city, Egyptian high society and resident foreigners were living it up. The officers of the Allied Forces were popular with the socialites of Cairo and in great demand at dinner parties. The finest parties were given by Princess Shiwikar, who had been the first wife of King Fuad. Even King Farouk often attended the receptions given by his father's former wife—he also visited her regularly to hear the latest gossip or find out where and when the top soirees in town were taking place and which ones were worth attending.

But while the rich of Cairo lived an endless round of receptions, balls, and wild desert parties, Neslishah and Abdel Moneim did not attend any of them, preferring to keep a lower profile. They chose instead to attend the concerts of European musicians who came to perform in the city. Neslishah recalled:

> We didn't feel as if we were living in wartime. The world was in turmoil because of the war, and one of the battlefronts was in Egypt, yet in the cities we were not aware of it.
>
> Cairo was like the Allies' headquarters; soldiers of all the Allied nations were in Cairo. There were Canadians, New Zealanders, Australians, South Africans, and even General Smart came and went.[48] Officers and soldiers of countries invaded by the Germans, who wanted to fight for their independence, also gathered in Cairo: Poles, Serbs, Greeks, French—they were all there. You saw men in colored uniforms everywhere.
>
> The city was chaotic but very lively. Every night there were big receptions or balls, where people would dance and have fun until the early hours of the morning. Parties were given in the desert. Cairo was the most exciting city in the world; people loved to come here, and they came from all over the world.

Of course, there were also those who were exiled and had nowhere else to go. The kings of Serbia, Greece, and Italy and Queen Giovanna of Bulgaria and her son Simeon—all sought shelter in Egypt.

We did not feel the war, and we were not terribly burdened by it. For instance, meat was sold three times a week. Only potatoes were difficult to find. When my son was born, a friend sent me a sack of potatoes as a present. Of all the gifts I had received, this was the most precious.

Now and then the Germans would make bombing raids with their Stukas,[49] but even then no one seemed to mind. They bombed the port of Alexandria extensively, but they did not touch the city. Sometimes they came to Cairo and bombed the British military airports. One of these airports was at Abbasiya, only about a kilometer from our house. The Stukas struck at a very low altitude, and they would start their dive over the roof of our building. They came so close that we could practically see the faces of the pilots. A couple of times my husband and I were foolish enough to go up on the roof to watch them bomb the airbase! They would first fire flares, and then they would begin bombing. As the planes approached, the British would light their projectors to scan the sky and fire their anti-aircraft artillery. The scene was beautiful; we would see all sorts of colors, white, yellow, green, ...

The most frightening nights were those when there was a moon, as the bombing raids would take place then. My dog would wake me up, showing me the way to the door well before the planes approached, even before the sound of the air-raid sirens. There was a cellar in the house with no windows where we would take shelter: if a bomb were to fall near the house shattering the windows, we could all be injured. So we used the cellar as a refuge, and I would take my son and run down there.

In the garden there were giant eucalyptus trees, at least seventy years old, which we would find lying on the ground, just like that. It was quite a frightening sight. We witnessed quite a number of bombings, but thank God the Germans only hit the airport. They were very careful not to bomb the city: their intention was to occupy Egypt and get rid of the British, so they did not want to antagonize the Egyptian population.

Meanwhile, the troops of Field Marshal Rommel were getting closer to Egypt. They planned to cross the desert and approach from two directions to reach Cairo from Asyut, and Alexandria from al-Alamein.

That is when we got scared. The British panicked when they heard that Rommel was on his way: the Egyptians supported the Germans, hoping that they would deliver the country from the British.

The British withdrew their money from the banks and, taking their families and even their furniture with them, began to escape. They were trying to reach Palestine via Port Said, the Suez Canal, and the Sinai Peninsula. The roads were full of trucks loaded with beds, fridges, tables, and all the rest. At one point, it was not possible to go from Heliopolis to downtown Cairo, as the congestion on the roads made it impossible for anyone who went to the city to get back. The inhabitants of Cairo were exultant. There were even people dancing in the streets, celebrating the imminent arrival of the Germans.

We had a small sheikh's shrine in our garden, known as Sheikh Abu Noor. It was a single-story construction with several rooms. My husband filled the shrine with containers of gasoline and diesel oil, saying, "If the Germans come we might not find any fuel, this will help us get around." On several occasions, I told him, "Moneim, please don't—if the Germans do come they'll take the fuel from us, they won't leave it to us." But he would not listen.

Later on, I used the other rooms in the shrine as an emergency pantry. I stacked all sorts of durable goods such as rice and biscuits there. I put salt in the rice, so it would not spoil. I also stocked up on soap and toothpaste.

Moneim had gold that he had inherited from his father, kept in the safe of a bank. One day he removed all the gold from the bank, piled it in his car, and brought it home. The roads were so crammed with the British running away from the city that it took him some time to get back, while the trunk of the Citroen was so full that it nearly collapsed. We had a huge safe at home where we placed the gold. Then we waited.

At the end of 1942, the British managed to halt Rommel's advance at al-Alamein, forcing the Germans to withdraw. Moving forward had been easy for Rommel, but he had to fight before retreating, even though his casualties were not immense. His real victory was in this magnificent retreat.

After the war, we visited the battlefields of al-Alamein. There were graveyards everywhere. Italian, English, German, ... When I saw the tombs of four German brothers, one next to the other, I thought of their mother, and I cried.

While Rommel was advancing everybody was pro-German, but upon his defeat and retreat to Libya, suddenly all the pro-Germans became pro-British!

Egypt had become a refuge for deposed royal families and royals of occupied countries. Since the khedives, the Egyptian royal family had had personal friends among members of the European ruling elites, and King Fuad and King Farouk allowed all sovereigns of countries invaded by the Germans or the Italians to seek asylum in Egypt.

When the Nazis invaded Yugoslavia and tore the country apart, King Peter II left Belgrade together with his government. He first went to Jerusalem, staying in Palestine, which was under British mandate, then moved to Cairo, where he lived for a while, and eventually he settled in London. When the Germans occupied Greece in 1941, King George II left for Egypt and stayed in Alexandria, where he had no financial problems since he was under the patronage of the Benakis, one of the richest Greek families in the country.

The deposed King Zog of Albania was another of the few monarchs who lived comfortably during his years in exile. When the Italians invaded his country in 1939, he took the State Treasury with him and fled first to England, then from there to Egypt, where he rented a beautiful villa in Alexandria. After the Egyptian Revolution of 1952 King Zog became involved in activities against the revolutionary government. This was brought to the attention of Gamal Abd al-Nasser, who expelled him from Egypt, so King Zog then settled in France.

In Alexandria, the king of Italy and his grandson the infant king of Bulgaria both took refuge, both of them quite broke. In 1946 King Victor

Emmanuel III of Italy was obliged to abdicate in favor of his son Umberto, and he sought asylum in Egypt. His daughter, Princess Giovanna soon followed him, with her young son King Simeon of Bulgaria.

Giovanna had married King Boris III of Bulgaria in 1930, and Simeon was born in 1937. In 1943, the king was poisoned, probably on the order of Adolf Hitler. Simeon, just six years old, succeeded him to the throne, but as he was still an infant a regency council was established, headed by the late king's brother, Prince Kirill. Following the Communist revolution in 1944, Kirill was executed by firing squad. Giovanna was imprisoned in her castle with her son and daughter for a year and in 1946 was ordered to leave Bulgaria within forty-eight hours. She left for Egypt via Istanbul, to join her father, who was living in Alexandria.

Giovanna had left her jewels and some documents behind in Sofia and wished to have them brought to Egypt. She asked an Italian who had previously been in the service of her husband to contact the Communist government. Surprisingly, the Communists gave her permission to retrieve her jewelry and documents, which were packed in a sealed trunk, which the Italian was charged to bring by plane from Sofia to Egypt. But the aircraft exploded in midair, killing all on board—and the jewels and the documents were scattered in the sea.

Giovanna raised her son Simeon in Alexandria, with great financial difficulty: the young king went around with holes in his shoes, and when at school he would cover the holes in his soles with newspaper. Only after the collapse of the Eastern Bloc, and fifty years in exile, was Simeon able to return to the country of his birth in 1996. He was elected prime minister of Bulgaria in 2001 and for four years governed the country where he was once king.

The English Patient—both the 1992 novel by Michael Ondaatje and the 1996 film by Anthony Minghella—was loosely based on the life of a Hungarian aristocrat, László Ede Almásy de Zsadány et Törökszentmiklós, who did not die of burns in the war in an Italian hospital but of dysentery in Austria in 1951, and whose life was even more colorful than that of the fictional character.

Almásy, born in 1895, was a well-educated man whose main hobbies were motorsports, trekking, flying, and desert exploration. Over the years, he became one of the leading explorers of the Egyptian desert, in his search for the mythical oasis of Zerzura. During the war the Germans appointed him as an intelligence officer in Africa, under the command of Field Marshal Rommel. Because of his knowledge of the desert, he was able to carry out his assignments satisfactorily, and he was decorated with the Iron Cross.

After the war, when the Communists took over the government in Hungary, Almásy was accused of treason and was imprisoned. He was then acquitted, but not released, and eventually escaped to Austria with the help of British Intelligence and a member of the Egyptian royal family. The Communist death squads were after him, though, so the British sent him secretly to Egypt, where King Farouk appointed him director of the newly established Institute for Desert Research in Cairo.

Back in Europe, when Neslishah went there on holiday, Almásy would often accompany her to concerts and the opera. He died of dysentery in Salzburg, Austria on 22 March 1951, and was buried there. Neslishah recalled:

> László was a close friend of mine, even though he was older than I was. During the war, he would come and go to Cairo secretly. But after the war I met him, and that is when we became friends.
>
> He was a friend of my husband, as well as of some of his relatives; through them, he got to know the desert, falling in love with it. He would often ride off to explore the desert with Prince Youssef and Prince Kamal al-Din. Both princes had worked on the topography of Africa: they had drawn maps of the desert and were members of the Royal Geographical Society in London. By going around with them László came to know the desert like the back of his hand. He knew where you could cross, where you could not, where to hunt—he knew everything about it; he even discovered the long-lost oasis of Zerzura, in the Gilf Kebir. He also discovered caves with paintings on the walls in Wadi Sura, including the famous Cave of the Swimmers.

When he was born, Hungary was not yet an independent country, but part of the Austro-Hungarian Empire. After the First World War when the empire collapsed and the country was divided, the region where his castle was located was given to Austria, so László became Austrian. Then when Hitler annexed Austria to Germany, he automatically became German.

As he was a pilot, he was drafted in the German Air Force, and since he knew the desert so well, he was sent immediately to assist Rommel in North Africa. The Germans planned to reach Alexandria via al-Alamein, and to Cairo via Asyut. Rommel put Almásy in charge of establishing the best route for the tanks to use when crossing the desert. He took a few friends and together they reached Cairo across the desert. They were wearing German uniforms, but in Cairo so many wore uniforms that no one noticed they were German. They moved around freely, going back the way they came, providing Rommel with the information he needed.

Later, I asked Almásy, "How did you dare to come all the way to Cairo in a German uniform?" "I was obliged to come in uniform," he replied. "Besides, so many people were in uniform in Cairo that they didn't recognize us. I knew exactly how to cross the desert, I knew where the cars could drive, which path the tanks had to follow, I knew it all. We reached Asyut, and from there we went down to Cairo. I never took my uniform off. Had I been caught while wearing civilian clothes I would have been executed immediately as a spy, while in uniform I would have been arrested as a prisoner of war. In Cairo there were soldiers from England, Canada, Greece, Czechoslovakia, France, Holland, New Zealand, Australia, India, and from all the occupied countries. There were so many uniforms, and they all wore different ones, so we got lost among them, that is why nobody realized we were German."

After the war, Almásy stayed in Cairo for a while. The chief of police in Cairo was an Englishman, who we used to call Russell Pasha. Almásy was flirting with his daughter; or rather, it was more than a flirtation, since they were living together. He had a brother called Yanos, and both Yanos and László were great friends with Tahir Pasha.

When in Cairo, he would often come to dinner at our house, so we would see him quite regularly. When we went to Europe, he would frequently escort me to the concerts in Salzburg. My husband did not like some of the operas, such as *Der Rosenkavalier*, so I would go to those operas with Almásy.

After the birth of her children, Neslishah went back to a sport she loved but had to give up for a long time: horse-riding. Her instructor was Amedeo Guillet, one of the most renowned equestrian trainers. He was born into an aristocratic family in the Italian region of Piedmont in 1909. He became a cavalry officer, and in the Berlin Olympics of 1936 he broke several new records. He took part in Italy's wars in North Africa and the Spanish Civil War, but it was in Abyssinia that he became famous, during the Second World War, fighting victoriously against the British with just a sword in his hand, alongside cavalry troops formed mainly by local recruits. After organizing guerrilla wars in Ethiopia and Eritrea he moved on to Yemen, where he trained the troops of the imam.

After the war, he left the army with the aim of teaching anthropology at university. Instead, he joined the Italian foreign ministry, becoming a diplomat in various countries. He retired in 1975, after serving as Italy's ambassador to India. He died in Rome in June 2010, at the age of 101, and was honored with a state funeral. Unusually, his coffin was draped with the royal flag of the House of Savoy, the deposed Italian royal family, to whom he had remained faithful until the end of his life, and the Royal Anthem was played instead of the Italian National Anthem. Neslishah recalled:

> Amedeo was one of the best cavalry officers in the world. He trained Piero d'Inzeo, the famous Italian rider who won one gold medal after another at the Olympic Games. At home, he had a photograph signed by d'Inzeo with the inscription: "To my teacher Amedeo."
>
> He devoted his life to Italy, but entirely to the monarchy. When Italy abolished the monarchy in 1946, Amedeo retired from the army and told King Umberto, "I have resigned from the army as I cannot serve this republic," requesting permission from the king to join him in exile.

Umberto replied as a real statesman would, "No, you were not serving me, you were serving Italy, and you shall continue to do so." Then the king told Amadeo that he was not at the service of the republic, but of Italy, and since he had resigned from the army he would join the diplomatic service. The king asked him to serve in the foreign ministry, since he knew so many different countries.

Unable to refuse the former king's order, Amedeo became a diplomat. He served as the fourth secretary at the Italian Embassy in Egypt, then very rapidly he became second, then first secretary, then ambassador, and he even managed the embassy on his own, now and then going back and forth to Ethiopia.

He taught me riding, jumping, and dressage when we met twice a week at the Equestrian Club. He didn't just teach me to jump, though: he taught me how to be a good rider.

I later befriended an English officer by the name of Billy McLean,[50] who during the war had been stationed in Cairo. Billy and Amedeo were both in Ethiopia during the war, on opposite sides, but they never met. Previously, Billy had told me how Amedeo had "attacked tanks with a cavalry." And I had seen a photograph of a battle taken by an English pilot from the air, where you could see Amadeo with his cavalry on one side and the British tanks on the other.

They were two old enemies who had fought on opposite sides, yet Billy admired the military mastery of Amedeo, especially the fact that he was a cavalry officer. In the 1970s, when I used to go to London to visit my son Abbas, I would also see Amedeo. Billy heard about it and said, "Please introduce me to my wonderful enemy." One evening we invited both of them to dinner at Abbas's house, and at the threshold of the house they had already fallen into each other's arms.

The one person who played a significant role in Neslishah's upbringing apart from her family was Madame Burdukoff. When at the end of 1938 the family had moved from France to Egypt, Madame Burdukoff had gone to England to live with her daughter and son-in-law, but she was unable to cope with them so during the war she returned to Ömer Faruk Efendi and Sabiha Sultan in Egypt. Neslishah recalled:

Madame Burdukoff came back and, as in the past, lived with my parents again. One day a German bomb fell on her balcony, but fortunately it did not explode, so no one was hurt. After the war she went back to London, where at the time, her daughter and son-in-law were involved in some kind of fraud and were about to run away to Australia.

Madame Burdukoff had inherited several diamond rings from her father-in-law. "All fake diamonds are white," he used to say, and only bought yellow or discolored ones. So Madame Burdukoff's diamonds were not worth a fortune, yet they still had some value. Her daughter and son-in-law stole her diamonds, her brooches, and all her other belongings that could be sold for money, leaving her with a few worthless trinkets. Worst of all, they dumped her in an old people's home outside of London and left.

A few years later, when I was in London, I wanted to see Auntie Katya—that is, Madame Burdukoff—so I looked for her and found her with great difficulty. She was in a place quite far from the city: I took a taxi and gave the driver the address. "It's too far out," the driver complained. "Far out or not, we are still going," I replied, and off we went.

I shall never forget, it was an awfully foggy day. We drove on and on. Eventually we reached the old people's home. It was a very dreary place, with five or six people sleeping in the same room, filled only with beds. They would wake the poor women up at six in the morning and turn the lights off at nine o'clock at night. God knows what they did in the dark until morning! They could not even go to the toilet.

On the way, I had bought her a basket of fruit and seeing the fruit, Madame Burdukoff—as well as the other women in her dorm—went wild. Apparently they had not eaten fruit for months!

Auntie Katya hugged me. "Dushka!" she said, "Please get me out of here, take me to Egypt. You are my only family. I have no one else. My daughter has stolen everything I had and left me here." She cried, and I felt dreadful.

So I took her back to Cairo. She could no longer walk. In Maadi, there was a nicely furnished hospital run by German nurses, and we put her there. The nuns gave her a large room and took good care of her. Both my parents and I often visited her. And not only us, but all those who knew her when we lived in Nice.

After the Revolution, however, Nasser closed the hospital down. The Germans had another, large hospital in Alexandria, and the nuns took their furniture, Madame Burdukoff, and the other patients, and moved to Alexandria. There again Burdukoff was given a very nice room, and she was well looked after until the end of her life.

In her last days an odd thing happened. Apart from Turkish, she spoke several languages fluently, but as she grew older she started to forget the languages she learned last. First she forgot English, then French—when I visited her instead of French, she spoke to me in German. Her memory was also slowly failing her, but she always recognized me and would hug and kiss me, crying, "Ah Dushka!"

After that, she also forgot German and spoke only Russian. That was not a problem, as there were Russian nurses at the hospital who had come during the time of the king. But when I visited her, we could no longer speak to each other. All she could say was "Ah Dushka," and she would hug me. Other members of the family visiting her could not understand what she was saying, but she recognized all of them.

One day the Mother Superior of the hospital called me: "Princess, Madame Burdukoff is in a terrible state, she does not understand us, and she speaks a language that none of us know. Please come quickly!" I rushed to Alexandria. "We have just found out what language she is speaking. It's Polish," the nurses told me. I approached her, she recognized me, she hugged me and kissed me, and said a few words in Polish, that was all.

Years earlier, when we were children, we wanted Madame Burdukoff to teach us bad words in Polish that nobody would understand. "I have forgotten Polish, I cannot remember a thing," she would reply. Not because she didn't want to teach us how to swear in Polish, she really had forgotten. But at the end of her life, when all the other languages had left her mind, she remembered only the one she had forgotten fifty years earlier.

When I saw Madame Burdukoff in such a state, I just could not bear it any longer, and I left. A few days later we were informed that she had passed away, and that they had buried her in Alexandria.

*

On the morning of 21 December 1944 there was a strange hustle and bustle in the house of Neslishah and Prince Abdel Moneim in Heliopolis. Cars were entering the garden one after the other, the doorbell was constantly sounding, the phone was ringing non-stop, and strangely Prince Abdel Moneim was not at home. In the early hours of the morning, after answering a phone call, he had left the house looking gloomy, taking his car and driving away without telling the servants where he was going.

Neslishah was in the late stages of her pregnancy and was resting in her room on the top floor when she heard voices coming from downstairs. She first thought someone had come to visit her husband, but the constant ringing of the doorbell and the telephone made her wonder what was happening. She dressed and went downstairs, where she was faced with people running in all directions, and her husband was nowhere to be seen, while the servants seemed to be trying to avoid her.

The phone was ringing again, and this time she picked it up. It was Aziza Shafiq. "We heard something, but we don't know if it's true," she said on the other end of the line. Neslishah was puzzled. "What did you hear, Aziza Hanem?" Aziza Shafiq interrupted her, "Oh my God, I think I messed it up, it means you don't know. It would not be appropriate for me to tell you," she said, and hung up.

Neslishah was baffled, but more than that she was worried, as all sorts of dark thoughts came to her mind. She first thought of her father, Ömer Faruk Efendi, imprisoned in a villa near Saqqara, who had not handed in his gun. "Oh dear, oh dear, he probably lost his temper and shot someone." Then she thought of her sister Hanzade, who had recently given birth, but the newborn had not lived, and they were barely able to save the mother. "My sister must be dead!" Addressing one of the servants, she asked, "What has happened? Why are you all running around like this?" But the servant did something quite unprecedented: she turned around and left the room without replying.

The doorbell was now ringing incessantly, but the callers were not entering the house. Instead, they were leaving their personal cards and driving away. Neslishah could not bear it any longer, and shouting at one of the servants she said, "For God's sake, what is going on?"

"Ah, Efendina, don't you know? His Majesty the Khedive has passed away," the servant replied. Thus did Neslishah learn about the death of her father-in-law, the last khedive, Abbas Hilmi II.

A little later her husband returned home. He had heard the news early in the morning and had done what he usually did when he was upset about something: he drove for hours on his own, and came home only once he had pulled himself together.

Neslishah received the callers who came to express their condolences in the living room downstairs, then she would go upstairs to her room and come down again when another group of visitors arrived. She spent the whole day going up and down the stairs. In the evening, her labor pains began, and she gave birth the following day: their daughter İkbal was born prematurely on 22 December 1944.

Even more people came that day—to offer their condolences or their congratulations, or both.

On the afternoon of the 22nd Queen Nazli sent her lady-in-waiting Madame Cattaoui to express her condolences to Prince Abdel Moneim. Madame Cattaoui was a wealthy and worldly lady from a leading Jewish family of Cairo. The fact that she had not come the day before when the news of the death of the former ruler was first heard meant that the Palace was sending a subtle message.

As Prince Abdel Moneim was receiving the condolences from Madame Cattaoui on behalf of the queen mother, a servant entered the room and leaning toward the prince whispered in his ear. The prince jumped up from his seat, embraced and kissed the man, who kissed him back in front of the bewildered Madame Cattaoui. "Am I in a lunatic asylum?" she thought, when the prince explained: "My wife was giving birth upstairs, and we now have a daughter!" Madame Cattaoui was even more perplexed, unable to both commemorate the deceased and congratulate the prince on the birth of the newborn. Neslishah recalled:

When Abbas was one year old he was ill with diarrhea at the beginning of the summer, and it lasted a long time and was difficult to stop. Later the same thing happened with İkbal, who was then only six months old. We decided that the heat of the Egyptian summer was unsuitable for the children, so for three years we spent the summers in Lebanon.

We rented a large house in Souk el Gharb, in the mountains. The children, the nanny, the servants, my boxer dog, we all went together. My mother also joined us. There was not enough room for the servants, so we set up two large tents in the garden: they worked in the house during the day and slept in these tents at night.

There were hyenas in that area. At night, they would come close to the house and howl. The servants were too frightened of these animals and their shining eyes in the dark to go outside to the toilet.

Souk el Gharb had a very pleasant climate, and it was near enough to Beirut for my mother and I to call on our relatives. Now and then, we would go to Damascus with my mother, to visit the tomb of my Şahbaba.

We were in Lebanon when the Americans bombed Hiroshima, and we returned to Egypt when all the peace treaties were signed.

When Caliph Abdülmecid's daughter, Dürrüşehvar, moved to India and his son Ömer Faruk Efendi moved with his family to Egypt, he was lonely in Nice so he moved to Paris during the first years of the Second World War, when the city was under German occupation. During the First World War the Turks had sided with the Germans, so when they occupied Paris they were very respectful to the head of the deposed dynasty whose country had once been their ally. Occasionally when Abdülmecid Efendi would make a request for something, they would try to satisfy his demands.

And the caliph would call upon the Germans to intercede in favor of members of his family: the exiled Ottoman family had no nationality, no passports, and most of them had no money to live on. With the outbreak of the war, life had become even more difficult, especially for those living in occupied territories.

Abdülmecid Efendi distributed a kind of certificate to members of the family who requested it, proving their identity, in which it was also mentioned that "this person is a member of the Ottoman family," and it was signed "The Sultan–Caliph Abdulmedjid II." The caliph used the titles of prince and princess for all family members, without distinction of status, such as şehzade, sultan, hanımsultan, or sultanzade—even for the sons-in-law.

But Abdülmecid Efendi did not see the end of the war, since he died in Paris on 23 August 1944, at nine o'clock in the evening. The death certificate issued by the police department of the 13th Arrondissement a week after his death, on 1 September 1944, recorded: "His Imperial Majesty Abdülmecid II, born in Istanbul in 1868, husband of Şehsuvar and Mehisti, passed away on 23 August 1944, at 9.00 p.m., at his residence on Marechal Maunory Avenue, no. 15."

Five years earlier, on 2 May 1939, the caliph had written a letter to his daughter's father-in-law, the nizam of Hyderabad, about his wishes regarding his burial. He specifically did not want to be buried in the Ottoman family tomb in Damascus, because Sultan Vahideddin was buried there: "Sultan Vahideddin was the cause of our downfall. Therefore, I do not wish to be buried in the same place as him." Instead, he asked to be buried in either India or Beirut. His wishes, however, were not executed. The nizam made no attempt to follow the caliph's request, and his body was embalmed and interred in a room in the Paris Mosque.

After the war, Dürrüşehvar Sultan and the caliph's private secretary Salih Keramet Bey contacted the Turkish government on several occasions, asking for permission to re-inter the caliph in Turkey. Dürrüşehvar, as a member of the exiled Ottoman family, was banned from entering Turkey, but in 1945, as an Indian princess she went to Istanbul and from there to Ankara, where she visited the president at the presidential palace in Çankaya. The president at the time was none other than İsmet İnönü, who had been the prime minister of Turkey to whom she had refused to extend her hand, brandishing instead her Ottoman medal and turning her back on him at the reception in London for the silver jubilee of King George V. When they met at the presidential palace, both the President and the Indian princess acted as if they had forgotten about that regretful event, behaving as if it had never happened. Dürrüşehvar Sultan's request to bury her father in Turkey, however, was refused.

Dürrüşehvar redoubled her efforts when the Democrat Party came to power in Turkey in 1950. With the assistance of Salih Keramet, she addressed one petition after another to the Turkish parliament. But even if the government of Adnan Menderes saw no harm in the burial of the caliph in his country of birth, some Democratic Party members of parliament were against it.

Ten years later, as a last resort, Dürrüşehvar was able to send her father's remains to Medina in Saudi Arabia, and he was buried in the Jannat al-Baqi graveyard after the afternoon prayer of 30 March 1954. Neslishah recalled:

We only heard that my grandfather had passed away several months after it happened. Following our departure to Egypt the caliph did not stay in Nice but moved to Paris. He rented a villa around the Bois de Boulogne, close to the forest, where he lived with my grandmother Şehsuvar Kadın, Behruze Hanım, his secretaries, and a few *kalfa*s. Mehisti Kadın, Dürrüşehvar's mother, went to India with her daughter.

Toward the end of August 1944, American troops entered Paris and they were battling the Germans very close to my grandfather's house. Later we were told that during one of these confrontations the bullets were flying into his house, and he had a heart attack while the shooting was going on.

My father's secretary Hüseyin Nakib Bey lived on the other side of town, somewhere near the Eiffel Tower. He was told to find a doctor and come as soon as possible, but by the time he and the doctor made their way to my grandfather's house, with the bullets still whistling over their heads, my grandfather was already dead.

We knew nothing about it. Months went by, and İkbal was about to be born, which means it must have been around November 1944, when one day while I was getting into the car to go somewhere, a man on a motorbike arrived and gave me a telegram. I opened it and learned that my grandfather had passed away in August. We were all devastated.

Caliph Abdülmecid Efendi had only one surviving sister, Nazime Sultan, who was living in Beirut. In the summer of 1945 when Neslishah

went to Lebanon with her husband and her children she visited her
great-aunt and had the shock of her life when she saw her. She recalled:

> One day we went to visit my great-aunt Nazime in Beirut with Moneim
> and the children. I always used to visit her whenever we were in Lebanon,
> and she and her husband Halid Paşa came to see us a couple of times.
>
> As soon as Halid Paşa saw me this time he embraced me and said, "So
> good of you to come, my child! You saved my life! While you keep Sultan
> Efendi company I will go to town with your husband and get some fresh
> air." And off they went.
>
> When the paşa said, "You saved my life," I did not understand what
> he meant, but when I saw my great-aunt I nearly fainted! That clear-
> headed, domineering, clever woman had lost her mind, and we had known
> nothing about it!
>
> A year earlier, when informed of the death of her brother, she had
> fainted; when she regained consciousness she was not herself any more.
> There was such a close bond between the two of them, as if they were
> twins, that losing her brother made her lose her mind with grief, and she
> became quite a different woman.
>
> It was impossible to talk to her—she did not understand me, nor
> could I understand her. She made sounds like "ha ha ha, ho ho ho." She
> was totally demented, and her eyes were the eyes of a madwoman.
>
> She held my hand while walking me around the house, then we went
> around the sofa, and then we sat. She understood more or less who we
> were, but she could not express herself. Then, again holding me by the
> hand, she led me from one room to another. The house tour became lon-
> ger and longer as we went in and out of various rooms, until we came to
> a smaller one in which there was just a piano, with a framed picture of my
> grandfather and a chair.
>
> She opened the lid of the piano, sat on the chair, and banged on the
> keyboard like a child. She was pressing on the keys while looking at me,
> making sounds like "he, he, ehe, be, be, be." Then, turning around, she
> noticed the photograph of her brother, and all of a sudden the expres-
> sion on her face changed. Her eyes, her mouth, her whole aspect became

normal again. She smiled at the photograph, her previously expressionless eyes lit up, her fingers slowly relaxed, and she played Chopin magnificently.

But then the spark in her eyes vanished once more, the smile on her face had gone, her fingers stiffened up, and she began to bang on the keys again. She turned toward me shouting, "He he he, ha ha," and leading me by the hand we wandered around the house one more time.

I didn't know what to do! I felt like crying, but I didn't. I was just trembling all over.

The next great shock came in 1948, taking by surprise not only Neslishah but the whole Ottoman family, and the king of Egypt too: Şehzade Ömer Faruk Efendi divorced his wife Sabiha Sultan on 5 March 1948 after twenty-nine years of marriage. He sent her a *boş kâğıdı*, an Islamic form of divorce, accompanied by a few written words.

Members of the family and friends including the deposed King Zog of Albania, who was living in Alexandria at the time, tried to dissuade him, but to no avail, as Faruk Efendi did not change his mind. Worse still, four months later he married his cousin Mihrişah Sultan, the daughter of his uncle the crown prince Yusuf İzzeddin Efendi. Neslishah recalled:

> My father had been a womanizer all his life, and my mother always pretended to ignore his infidelities. When Mihrişah appeared on the scene, things changed. While the trouble was brewing I was in Europe with my husband. And Madame Burdukoff, who had been living with my parents, was in London at the time. Had we been in Cairo, my father could never have divorced my mother, or had Madame Burdukoff been there, she would definitely have prevented it.

It was public knowledge that things had not been going well between Sabiha Sultan and Ömer Faruk Efendi during those last few years. Even if people were saying that their discord was due to disagreements over the establishment of a family council, everyone was well aware of the şehzade's increased interest in his cousin Mihrişah Sultan.

The first family council had been founded after the death of Sultan Vahideddin in 1926 by the caliph, Abdülmecid Efendi. He presided over the council and took in as members his son Ömer Faruk Efendi, his daughter-in-law Sabiha Sultan, Şehzade Ömer Fuad Efendi (a descendant of Sultan Murad V), and Sultan Abdülaziz's son-in-law Şerif Paşa. He had initiated legal procedures to reclaim properties outside Turkey belonging to the Ottoman family, but increasing disputes among the family members obliged him to dissolve the council without obtaining any positive result.

The need for a family council became clear in 1945, when Sabiha Sultan wished to have a shrine built for her father Sultan Vahideddin, who was buried in the courtyard of the Selimiye mosque in Damascus. The cost of construction was to be covered by Sabiha Sultan's three sons-in-law, Prince Abdel Moneim, Prince Amr, and Prince Mohamed Ali, and the plans were drawn by Mohamed Salah al-Din Albani, a Syrian architect who spoke Turkish, chosen by Prince Abdel Moneim. But the area where the shrine was to be built was constricted, so it was not going to look like the conventional shrines of the sultans—it would be a more modest one, three meters in height. Sabiha Sultan was not happy: "I want a dome," she said. The architect prepared a new plan, but there was turmoil in Syria and it was difficult for Sabiha Sultan to go to Lebanon. Administrative problems emerged, followed by wars in the Middle East, and the 1952 Revolution in Egypt. So the project never materialized.

The idea of a new family council had come from Necla Sultan's husband, Prince Amr Ibrahim. The members of the family living in Cairo met on 24 January 1948 at Prince Amr's home in Zamalek. There, the decision to establish a family council was taken and the oldest living şehzade of the Ottoman family, that is Sultan Murad V's grandson Ahmed Nihad Efendi, who was living in Lebanon at the time, was elected to chair it.

The council would work on five issues: to provide for the education of the children and the younger generation; to find suitable spouses for those who had reached the age of marriage; to warn and correct those who behaved in a manner inappropriate to the honor of the family; to provide treatment for the sick members of the family who had financial difficulties; and to provide proper funerals and build shrines.

Şehzade Ahmed Nihad Efendi was informed in writing of the decisions taken by the council during the meeting held in Prince Amr's home. But Ömer Faruk Efendi did not accept Ahmed Nihad Efendi as head of the family, while Sabiha Sultan—whose relationship with him was already tense—backed the council's decision and approved the choice of leader. Only the grandchildren of Sultan Abdülaziz—Şükriye Sultan, Mihrişah Sultan, and Şehzade Abdülaziz Efendi—sided with Ömer Faruk Efendi. Neslishah recalled:

After marrying Necla, Prince Amr felt very close to our family. He wanted to do something for the members of the family who were in need. This was the reason for the council.

I had broken my leg, and I was in a hospital in St. Moritz. The caliph had passed away some years previously, and the family was left without a leader. Amr thought, "The wealthy sons-in-law should donate money that will then be spent on ailing members of the family or on those who are getting married. We can organize the family to choose a leader, to whom we will deliver the funds, and he will provide for those in need." He liked Nihad Efendi, and once the council was established, he wanted him to be the leader.

Prince Amr and Hanzade's husband Prince Mohamed Ali could give money, and Moneim could also join in to some extent, but he was not as rich as the other two and would be giving less. Prince Youssef Kamal had also agreed to help, once the council was established.

Nihad Efendi was a very honest, gentle, and a polite person, but he spent the whole day sitting on a chair doing nothing. Besides, he did not have the capacity to fulfill such a role. My father on the other hand, who had always taken care of everybody's problems in the family, saw himself as the head of the family. Sultan Abdülaziz's branch of the family was on his side, but all the others supported Nihad Efendi.

Had I been present I would have said, "Nihad Efendi sits around all day, there is no way he will be able to head the family." I would have sided with my father and I would have made them change their minds, but I was in hospital. My mother was saying, "Nihad Efendi must be the leader, it is in the tradition of our family." She did not support my father, and my sisters were on her side, giving rise to a great commotion. The project fell through—and what's more, my parents divorced! My father accused my mother, "You have incited my daughters against me," he said. But he was already in love with Mihrişah, and the issue with the council was just an excuse.

Ömer Faruk Efendi believed that his sister, Dürrüşehvar Sultan, was behind the dispute of the council. He thought she was seeking revenge on him because their father's body, still in the vaults of the Paris Mosque, had not been taken to Hyderabad. And in promoting the issue of the council, he felt she had isolated him from the other members of the family and had broken up his marriage. He maintained this position even years later in Cairo, when he wrote to his historian friend İsmail Hakkı Danişmend on 21 August 1962:

> I was accused of ending my thirty years of marriage for Mihrişah. They destroyed me deep within my soul. They brought down my house, they destroyed everything. The world around me collapsed. To save the house, which she said belonged to her father, from being seized because of my debts, she took all the furniture and the objects saying, "These are mine," and left me with an empty house. Not a chair, not a table to dine on, remained. I would have been stranded in the street if it were not for the house I was building in Abu Qir. I immediately moved there, and my marriage with Mihrişah saved me from this distressing situation. Do you think anyone thought about it, or knows what I went through? On the contrary, I was accused of all sorts of felony, and this went on for years. If I hadn't been seriously ill, no one would have got in touch with Mihrişah. What good has all this damage done? The only purpose it served was to make a laughing stock out of us. Thank God it didn't end up in the newspapers. That would have been the last straw.
>
> To cut a long story short, I am deeply saddened by all that has happened. I am sorry to trouble you with the family gossips, but I wanted

you to know how unjustly I have been treated. Even if these events are now part of history, because of your close interest in history, I refer all the above to your judgment and your conscience.

Mihrişah Sultan married her cousin Ömer Faruk Efendi in a religious ceremony, and in the prenuptial agreement she asked that the *ismet hakkı*, the right to divorce her husband, be included in the contract. Their marriage did not last, and a few years later Mihrişah Sultan indeed divorced him, using her *ismet hakkı*. Later the şehzade would tell his friends, "I divorced the most beautiful woman in the world, to marry the ugliest one. Fate!"

On the other hand, Sabiha Sultan, in spite of the divorce, continued to love Ömer Faruk Efendi until the end of her life. Whenever someone came from Egypt to Istanbul or Europe when she was there, she would always ask, "How is Faruk?" And when Faruk Efendi died in Egypt in March 1969, she stopped greeting anyone who had not come to pay her their condolences. To Neslishah, who said, "Mummy, you were divorced, he was not your husband any longer, why do you expect them to come?" she replied, "Yes we were divorced, but he was still my cousin. They should have come to express their condolences."

The 1940s went by, with births, deaths, frictions, struggles, and divorces in the family. Neslishah's children were growing up, and toward the end of the 1940s she began working for charity, as the other prominent Egyptian princesses did. She recalled:

> The largest charitable foundation, known as Mabarrat Mohamed Ali, belonged to the royal family; it ran hospitals and schools to train people to work in the hospitals. The first president of the foundation was Princess Shiwikar, the first wife of King Fuad.[51] When she passed away, King Farouk's sister Fawzia[52] succeeded her. The deputy president was Princess Emine Tugay, the wife of the Turkish ambassador in Cairo. The committee also included some wives of pashas. They all knew well what they were doing, and worked hard.

I was also a member of the committee, and so were my two sisters. We had hospitals in various cities of Egypt: in Cairo, Alexandria, Benha, Zagazig, and Kafr al-Dawwar. After our committee meetings we would inspect the hospitals. We would go into the kitchen to see what they were cooking. We would go around the hospital wards, making sure that the linen was in good condition. The hospitals were running well, as experienced Italian nuns were taking care of the patients, while the girls we trained in our schools were helping the nuns. An English lady was teaching the girls.

Al-Mar'a al-Gadida ('The New Woman') was another charity we had, in which I was the deputy chairperson. We took care of orphans and sick children, giving priority to education, teaching children how to read and write, and trying to ensure that eventually each child would have a profession. Girls were taught sewing, embroidery, and carpet-weaving; boys were given classes according to their skills. Those who could continue their studies were sent to school, others were taught shoemaking, carpentry, even basket-weaving, or were given other similar courses.

The large hospital in Ataba was under my responsibility. Here, poor people were looked after free of charge, and we would also feed them. The workers of the Tramway Company, the Electricity Company, and workers in other companies were treated in this hospital, and these companies would pay for their care. We created luxury hospital rooms, as well as second-class ones. The luxury rooms were for single usage, while the second-class ones were for double occupancy. Patients in these rooms paid a fee. We treated the poor with the money that was generated from these rooms and from the companies.

We then established another outpatient unit called the extreme clinic, for those with no financial means. Here there were eye specialists, gynecologists, dermatologists, and a large pharmacy, which had a large laboratory where a considerable number of people worked. Eye drops and creams were distributed to the poor free of charge, and medicines frequently used were prepared here.

I was there every Sunday. Now and then, with one or two other ladies of the committee, we would visit the other hospitals unannounced, to determine their needs. When Queen Farida was pregnant she asked me, as deputy chairperson, to attend the opening ceremony of various departments on her behalf, which I did.

After 1950, when the young Egyptians began fighting the British, many were wounded, and our hospitals then really served their purpose. We were the ones treating the injured.

Neslishah and Prince Abdel Moneim now usually spent their summers in Europe. But in 1947 the prince decided to go to Istanbul, where he had lived for some time as a young man, and he wished to show Neslishah the country that had exiled her when she was three years old.

Law 431, which was ratified by parliament in 1924 and authorized the expulsion of all members of the Ottoman family from Turkey, was still strictly enforced in the 1940s. Not only were the Ottomans not allowed to enter Turkey but even transit travel was forbidden, and they were not permitted to bury their deceased in the country.

Until this time only one swaddled baby was secretly brought into the country, and in 1939 five people were allowed to return thanks to a special law that was applied only to them. The baby was Emel, the daughter of Rukiye Sultan (who was the daughter of the eldest son of Sultan Reşad, Mehmed Ziyaeddin Efendi) and İhsan Bey, a descendant of Sokullu Mehmed Paşa. İhsan Bey had taken part in the Turkish War of Independence, and while in Beirut he had met and married Rukiye Sultan, meaning that he too was stripped of his nationality, and forbidden from returning to Turkey. Their only daughter Emel was born in Beirut in 1925, and when a few months later her mother passed away İhsan Bey took the baby to Turkey, saying, "Whatever will happen, will happen."

He spent a few days at the police station in Istanbul, and just when it seemed certain that he would be sent back he appealed to Ankara, where the government granted him permission to stay in Turkey because he had fought in the War of Independence. There was however, one condition: he was not to reveal who his wife or his child were. In other words, he was not to mention his family ties with the Ottomans; even his daughter was not to know. And he and his family indeed kept this secret for many years: Emel Hanımsultan learned about her family only on the day she finished high school.

The first members of the Ottoman family who were legally allowed to return to Turkey were the children of Enver Paşa and Naciye Sultan: Mahpeyker Hanımsultan, Türkan Hanımsultan, and Sultanzade Ali, as well as Rana Hanımsultan, who was the daughter of Naciye Sultan and her second husband Kamil Bey, Enver Paşa's brother. The granddaughter of Sultan Vahideddin, Hümeyra Hanımsultan, was also granted permission to come back, as her father, İsmail Hakkı Bey, was a soldier who had fought in the War of Independence and who had later held important positions in the Turkish Foreign Ministry. On 5 July 1939 the parliament passed a special decree allowing these five young people to return, based on the status of their fathers as national figures. (At one point, Hümeyra Hanımsultan had earlier come to Turkey, registered on her father's diplomatic passport, but as soon as it was known who she was, she was hastily deported.)

Dürrüşehvar Sultan had entered Turkey in 1945 as a princess of India. And Neslishah became the second member of the dynasty to visit Turkey for the same reason, that is, as a princess of another country. Her visa application to the Turkish Embassy in Cairo was sent with the passport of "Princess Neslishah, wife of Egypt's second-in-line to the throne, Prince Mohamed Abdel Moneim." The embassy referred the request to Ankara, and on 3 April 1947 the Foreign Ministry instructed Cairo to grant a visa valid for fifteen days, extendable for three months.[53]

Neslishah was finally, after twenty-three years, able to return to her country of birth, from which she had been expelled at the age of three. She embarked on the *Aksu* in Alexandria with her husband, her children, and a servant, and docked at the port of Izmir on 30 May 1947. The officials who came on board greeted the prince of Egypt and his wife on behalf of the governor.

Neslishah's cousin Hümeyra Hanımsultan was waiting for them on the dock. The two spent the day together, while Prince Abdel Moneim paid a visit to the city governor, with the car that was put at his disposal.

They spent the night on board, and early the following morning sailed on to Istanbul. The daily Izmir paper of 31 May described Neslishah as "Egypt's most beautiful woman," and at the foot of the article a short sentence stated, "Neslishah is a member of the Ottoman dynasty."

The *Aksu* arrived at the port of Karaköy in Istanbul on 1 June. The journalist Metin Toker was on the same ship, and the following day he reported in the daily newspaper *Cumhuriyet*:

> As the *Aksu* approached Istanbul, Princess Neslishah, with her husband and children, was on the bridge, looking at the beautiful city she had to abandon twenty-three years ago, when she was just three-and-a-half years old. She wore a pale navy-blue dress, with a light pistachio-green coat, two strings of pearls around her neck, and on her head a navy-blue hat with a large white flower on the side and some tulle. Her high-heeled sandals were black. There was a larger crowd than usual at the passenger lounge of the pier. Waiting to see the princess were people connected to the old palace, and the eunuchs especially drew the most attention.
>
> A small room on the left was assigned to the relatives of our guests. Princess Atiya [Neslishah Sultan's sister-in-law] and others were there. The chief of the police Ahmed Demir and the governor's chief of protocol were also present to greet them.

A week later, a rumor in Istanbul that the owner of a magazine had asked Neslishah for a large sum of money in exchange for publicity and that Neslishah had refused the offer was published in the newspaper *Memleket*. There was no mention of the name of the magazine or of its owner. The Turkish Press Association immediately published a statement: "Our association has nothing to do with the journalists of *Meş'ale* ['The Torch'] or *Büyük Doğu* ['The Great East']." (The publisher of *Büyük Doğu* was the famous poet Necip Fazil Kisakürek.)

Then Neslishah herself was obliged to make a statement: "I have closely witnessed the Republic of Turkey, which has become a very modern and advanced country, and as a sister of yours born on this land I can only feel pleasure. Regarding the rumors concerning the magazine, you cannot imagine how upset I have been. I have not been personally contacted with such an offer, nor has a third party been approached to convey such a message to me."

The family stayed fifteen days in Istanbul, and on the evening of 16 June they sailed to Marseilles on board the *Ege*. At their departure, the quay in Karaköy was as crowded with reporters as it had been when they arrived, and before she embarked Neslishah declared, "I would like to thank all the government officials with whom we have been in contact and in particular the customs officers, who have shown great courtesy while doing their duty, which I can only reciprocate with my heartfelt gratitude." Neslishah recalled:

> Moneim wanted to show me the country of my birth, and we did what Dürrüşehvar had done: in 1945 she went to Turkey as an Indian princess, and two years later I came as an Egyptian princess.
>
> They had given me a fifteen-day visa. My children and Atifet Hanım, who was in my service, accompanied us. We boarded the vessel in Alexandria and first sailed to Izmir. My cousin Hümeyra met us at the harbor, and we had an excellent lunch in Kadifekale. Then we went back to the ship and sailed to Istanbul.
>
> The pier in Karaköy was very crowded with the people who had come to meet us and many ordinary people too. "We have seen princesses from all over the world, now we have come to see our own princess," they said, and there was considerable confusion around the quay. At first I did not realize that all those people had come for me, until I saw the reporters and the photographers.
>
> I really did not know what to do! Should I wave, should I not? After all, we had come to Istanbul with special permission from the government and I did not want to make a misstep. Then some of the ladies started to cry, and of course I cried too. I could not remember this city that I had left at the age of three, but I was aware of being in a beautiful country. I was crying on the one hand, and on the other my heart was pounding with excitement, so finally I was not conscious of how beautiful the city was.

Next, Hasan Shafiq, the consul of Egypt, met us. He took İkbal in his arms and we disembarked, bombarded by the flashes of photographers and the never-ending questions of the reporters. The consul was the brother-in-law of Fethiye Sultan. His wife had come with him.

As my husband was the second-in-line to the throne, the Egyptian ambassador and his wife were also waiting for us on the pier, and among all this commotion we managed to leave the quay and go to Tarabya on the Bosphorus, where there was an old wooden hotel belonging to the owner of the Pera Palace. We chose this hotel because it was away from the city, and we thought we would stay there undisturbed, but the reporters were waiting for us.

One evening Atifet said, "Sultan Efendi, some young people have come to see you." A group of students on a boat had come close to the hotel, chanting at the top of their voices, "Hip hip hurray for Neslishah, long live Neslishah!" Again I did not know what to do—should I greet them, should I not? Finally, I can't remember what I did.

We called on everyone we knew in Istanbul. We visited my husband's relatives, most of whom I knew from Egypt, but I had no relatives of my own here, as all of them were exiled and banned from entering the country. We visited the Topkapı Palace and the mosques, followed by journalists wherever we went.

One day a reporter asked me, "How did you learn to speak Turkish so well?" Dürrüşehvar had been asked the same question. I was truly irritated: "I am Turkish, sir," I replied. "Do not forget that I am a Turkish woman!"

Fifteen days went by quickly, and my visa was about to expire. The Egyptian consulate requested an extension on our behalf, and Ankara accepted. "We see no harm in prolonging the visa of a princess belonging to a friendly country for a few more months, and we could extend it even further, if she so wished." But we did not stay any longer, as the day our two-week visa expired we sailed for Europe, and then returned again to Cairo.

Neslishah had actually wanted to stay longer in Istanbul, and her visa had been extended so there was nothing to stop her. But her husband said, "Let's stay just two weeks, and then leave." Being close to the Egyptian throne, he felt their presence was sensitive. He was aware that Neslishah's arrival had disturbed Ankara, and he did not wish to inconvenience them further, or abuse their courtesy. This was also the reason for selecting a hotel in Tarabya, away from the center of the city. So they left as soon as their first visa expired.

Prince Abdel Moneim's assumptions were right. The earlier arrival of Dürrüşehvar in the country, followed now by Neslishah, had become a "matter of governance" in certain circles and provoked uproar in the more radical wing of the ruling Republican People's Party. Ahmed Remzi Yüregir, an MP of the party for the city of Seyhan, in a written question to his parliamentary group, requested an explanation from the minister of foreign affairs of why the government allowed the coming and going of individuals who in accordance with Law 431 had been expelled from Turkey and whose return had been prohibited indefinitely. He also complained about "republican Turkey allowing and tolerating press reports in favor of the sultanate. Serious precautions and forceful measures must be taken." On 26 November 1947 the minister, Necmeddin Sadak, replied that the said members of the Ottoman family had come to Turkey as "citizens of friendly countries" and "as a matter of political courtesy, they were given a fifteen-day transit visa."

Following the visit to Turkey, the family went to Montreux in Switzerland, and Neslishah's mother Sabiha Sultan came from Paris to stay with them. She wanted to visit the son of her aunt Seniha Sultan, Sabahaddin Bey,[54] who lived on his own in a village not far from Montreux, and she asked Prince Abdel Moneim to drive her to see her cousin. "With pleasure," he replied, and they informed Sabahaddin Bey of the day they would be visiting him.

On the morning of their departure Sabiha Sultan said, "Neslishah can join us if she wants to." To which Prince Abdel Moneim replied, "Absolutely not, Sultan Efendi. I cannot bear that man! I am his nephew, but he plotted against Sultan Hamid, against his country. This is why

I despise him. I am taking you because you requested it, but I will not allow Neslishah to come and see that man!"

Neslishah wanted very much to see her mother's cousin Prince Sabahaddin, since he was often mentioned in the last days of Ottoman rule, and he was known to be a Turkish intellectual. However, as her husband would not allow it, she never met him.

Neslishah, Cairo, 1952

Neslishah, Paris 1952

Neslishah, Paris, 1952

Princess Neslishah, First Lady of Egypt, 1953

Egypt's Regency Council (from left): Mohamed Bahey al-Din Barakat Pasha, Prince Abdel Moneim, and Colonel Rashad Mehanna, Cairo, Abdin Palace, 1952

Prince Regent Abdel Moneim, Princess Neslishah, and their children Abbas and İkbal at their residence in Heliopolis in 1953

Princess Neslishah with Egypt's first President, General Mohamed Naguib, Cairo, 1953

King Faisal II of Iraq and his fiancée Princess Fazile Ibrahim

Hanzade Sultan, Paris, 1950s

Prince Mohamed Ali Ibrahim, 1957

Necla Sultan, early 1950s

Necla Sultan with her husband Prince Amr and their son Prince Osman in Switzerland

Princess Neslishah and Prince Abdel Moneim at the military court in Cairo

Şehzade Namık Efendi in the Tora Prison, Cairo

Neslishah taking the oath at the military court in Cairo

The military judges at the trial of Princess Neslishah and her husband

Neslishah Sultan, Paris, late 1950s
(photograph by Laure Albin Guillot)

Neslishah, Paris, late 1950s

Neslishah, Paris, late 1950s

Sabiha Sultan, Neslishah Sultan, Prince Abbas,
and Princess İkbal, Mallorca, early 1960s

Montreux, early 1960s: (from left) Prince Amr, Prince Youssef Kemal, Neslishah Sultan, Necla Sultan

At Necla Sultan's home in Montreux, early 1960s: (from left) Hanzade Sultan, Sabiha Sultan, Princess İkbal, Princess Fazile, Prince Ahmed

Neslishah, Istanbul, 1966

Neslishah Sultan and Prince Abdel Moneim in their Messerschmitt car, 1960s

Neslishah in her mansion on the shores of the Bosphorus, Istanbul 1966

Neslishah, Istanbul, 1966

Neslishah Sultan, Hanzade Sultan, and Necla Sultan with their mother Sabiha Sultan, Istanbul, 1960s

Prince Abbas Hilmi's wedding, Istanbul, 1969: (from left) Prince Abdel Moneim, Princess Mediha Hilmi, Prince Abbas Hilmi, Neslishah Sultan

Neslishah, Istanbul, 1969

Prince Abdel Moneim in his later years,
Istanbul, 1970s

Neslishah with her son Prince Abbas
Hilmi, London, 1988

Neslishah Sultan, Hanzade Sultan, and
Necla Sultan in Kuşadası on the Aegean
coast, 1995

Neslishah Sultan, Nizam of Hyderabad Barakat Jah, Hanzade Sultan, 1996

Neslishah at her grandfather Sultan Vahideddin's tomb, Damascus, 1999

Istanbul, 1996: (from left) Azize Taylan, Prince Osman Vasıb Osmanoğlu, Neslisah Sultan, Prince Abbas Hilmi, Rahmi Koç

Istanbul, 1997: (from left) Neslishah Sultan, former Queen Dina of Jordan, Hanzade Sultan

Neslishah in Sharm al-Sheikh, Sinai, 1998

Neslishah with her son, daughter, son-in-law, daughter-in-law, and grandchildren at home in Istanbul, 2000

Neslishah Sultan with the speaker of the Turkish parliament at the opening of her grandfather Caliph Abdülmecid Efendi's restored library at Dolmabahçe Palace, 24 March 2004

Neslishah Sultan on her eighty-fifth birthday, 2006

Istanbul, August 2004: (from left) Princess İkbal, Neslishah Sultan, and Necla Sultan with a painting by Caliph Abdülmecid Efendi

Neslishah at a Byzantine archaeological site, Istanbul, 2006

Neslishah on her ninetieth birthday, 2011

Princess İkbal Moneim Saviç with her husband Dr. Mürsel Saviç

Neslishah with her son Prince Abbas Hilmi and daughter Princess İkbal, Istanbul, 2010

Neslishah's funeral, 3 April 2012

Neslishah's funeral, 3 April 2012

8

A First Lady Arrested

The stifling summer months in Cairo were unbearably hot, and the summer of 1952 was worse than ever.

Neslishah went to France with her family for the summer, to the country house that Prince Abdel Moneim had inherited from his father the khedive in a village named Illiers in north-central France. They decided to spend the summer exploring the region, and in the middle of July they drove to visit the chateaux of the Loire Valley. The prince loved the radio, and he always listened to the news on the radio every hour of the day, but this time, and for the first time in his life, he decided not to take his radio with him. "I am not going to listen to the news for a few days, and I am not going to buy any newspapers either," he said. They visited the chateaux, and enjoyed excellent meals in restaurants.

Back in Illiers a few days later, their Turkish maid was anxiously waiting for them, and quite confused asked, "Your Highness, have you not been told? Have you not been informed?"

And that is how they learned that there had been a revolution in Egypt, that King Farouk had abdicated in favor of his six-month-old son Ahmed Fuad, and that the Egyptian Embassy in Paris was calling nearly every day, wanting to speak to Prince Abdel Moneim.

The prince called the embassy immediately, and he was informed that General Mohamed Naguib had taken command of the Revolutionary

Council, and that a three-member regency body had been established for the infant king, to be presided by Prince Abdel Moneim. The other members of this council were Bahey al-Din Barakat Pasha, the former minister for education, and Colonel Rashad Mahanna, one of the revolutionary army officers. The ambassador told the prince, "They want you to return immediately and take office at once."

This meant that Neslishah had become Egypt's 'first lady,' but both she and her husband were worried, as the military were now in power and no one knew what might happen. Their apprehension was justified, as in time things did not turn out well for Neslishah and her husband. She recalled:

> Moneim was able to find a flight to take him back to Egypt only two days later. I stayed on for a few more days to close the house, then together with the children and the servants we flew to Cairo. From then on my life was completely changed.
>
> We did not move to the palace, preferring to stay in our house while my husband used Abdin Palace as his office. In the morning, a car escorted by police would pick Moneim up to drive him to the palace. There he would meet the prime minister, the other ministers, and the ambassadors, all of whom he had meetings with, and he would also take care of other matters related to the state. He would come home for lunch, again escorted by the police, returning to the palace after lunch. In other words, his working hours were like those of a civil servant.
>
> I was in charge of receiving the ambassadors' spouses, which I did at home, not at the palace, and I didn't even have a secretary. According to protocol, it was not appropriate to welcome the wives of the ambassadors on my own, so I asked my friends to help me, and they would join me in welcoming these ladies.
>
> The military had not yet touched our charities, but the sisters of the former king were not around, so I was in charge of all the work. I took care of the charities for some time before they were abolished.
>
> Moneim took on his role as chairman of the regency council in August 1952. Decrees were prepared in the name of the young king, and

my husband and the other two regents would sign them on his behalf. Barakat Pasha was loved and respected, but we did not know much about the third regent, Rashad Mahanna, as he was appointed by the military.

The council worked together for two months, but then Rashad Mahanna was arrested as allegedly "working for the Muslim Brothers." Barakat Pasha was frightened, and he resigned and retired somewhere around Alexandria, where he had some land. Before leaving Cairo he came to bid us farewell, apologizing to my husband for leaving him alone. Thus the council was dissolved in October, and my husband was appointed as the sole regent.

The military organized another ceremony, where Moneim was sworn in. He had to sign all the decrees that came in from the military; he tried to avoid signing the death penalties, but was forced to under the threats of the revolutionary officers.

Moneim's uncle, Prince Mohamed Ali Tewfik, who had been heir to the throne most of his life, was still expecting the military to put him on the throne, even after the revolution. He was not aware that things had changed drastically, or perhaps he was but did not wish to be. He was waiting for their call at Manyal Palace, with his suitcases packed.

On the few occasions when he visited Moneim at Abdin Palace he would always scold my husband, saying, "When I come here they are supposed to play the anthem of the crown prince—why don't they?" "There has been a revolution, nothing is as it used to be any more," Moneim would reply in vain, as his uncle would just not listen.

We had the position but not the power; it was just a show. For instance, my husband would drink coffee, and offer coffee to his guests, and at the end of each month, he was asked to pay for the coffee consumed.

The revolutionary officers had assigned an aide-de-camp to my husband, as in the time of the king. His name was Nugumi Pasha, and he was a distinguished, well-mannered, and pleasant Sudanese gentleman. But he was not only Moneim's aide-de-camp, he was also the director of the Cairo Zoo! To scorn the king's regent, the revolutionaries had purposely chosen the director of the zoo as his ADC.

The room at the palace used by my husband as his office had a broken toilet, which they would not repair. When he needed to use the bathroom, he had to go all the way to the other side of the palace and use Nugumi Pasha's toilet. All of this was meant to say: "The monarchy has ended, you are of no importance, we are now the masters of this country."

One day Moneim said to me, "Things are changing. I don't know what it is, but the general situation is not good, I don't like it, something is going to happen. I think they intend to abolish the monarchy, and they are getting ready to declare a republic." The wording of the decrees that Moneim was signing was changed; the young king's name was replaced by "Kingdom of Egypt."

My husband had great experience in understanding a political situation, and he sensed beforehand what would happen. After a short time, everything he had predicted occurred, and the revolutionary officers, less than a year after the revolution, proclaimed the republic on 18 June 1953. The reign of the dynasty of Mohamed Ali Pasha had come to an end after a century and a half and became part of history, while General Mohamed Naguib was appointed president of the new republic.

The first thing Naguib did on that day was to come to our house, where he said to my husband, "I told our boys over and over again not to abolish the monarchy, not to declare the republic, they just would not listen." He probably wanted to appease Moneim, and said things like, "We love you." He embraced Moneim several times before leaving. Years later at Moneim's funeral, he apologized in front of his coffin.

Our task had come to an end, after less than one year in office. We retired to our home, trying to stay away from everything.

Worse was to follow.

As happens throughout history, the leaders of the revolution of 1952 turned against each other, quarrelling bitterly. There were rumors that the driving force of the revolution was a thirty-four-year-old colonel called Gamal Abd al-Nasser, who was later to become one of the iconic names of Arab nationalism. At first, Nasser took care not to be in the limelight. While General Naguib appeared to be the leader of the takeover, Nasser was second in command of the Revolutionary Command Council (RCC). He then became deputy prime minister and minister of the interior, then prime minister. Next he overthrew President Naguib on 14 November 1954 to become head of the RCC, and finally, from 23 June 1956 until his death in September 1970, he was president of Egypt.

The problems for Neslishah and her family began in November 1953, when Gamal Abd al-Nasser effectively came to power, even if he was still then behind the scenes. First of all, the government confiscated all the properties of the royal family, of all the princes and princesses, of Mohamed Abdel Moneim, and consequently of his wife, Neslishah. They seized not only Neslishah's properties but also her money, her household goods, her personal belongings, and even her clothes! She recalled:

It was in November. I had woken up early and dressed to go riding. We had a black servant by the name of Abdu, who had been working for us for years. In the morning, he would bring my breakfast with the daily papers to my room and we always had a little chat. That morning he was acting strangely. He left the breakfast tray without uttering a word and, looking away from me, dumped the papers on the table before he left.

I was very surprised of course, and I sensed there was something odd going on, when without meaning to I glanced at one of the newspapers and learned that all our belongings were to be confiscated! They were taking everything from us . . . our homes, our money, our furniture, everything had to be handed over to the government. Abdu, trying not to catch my eye, was afraid he would burst into tears, so he had thrown the papers down and left the room!

I woke my husband to tell him what was happening. I knew I had to hide some of the valuables we had; I had to save them from being seized, even smuggle them away. After all, we had two children, and I had to keep my jewelry for their future. I filled my pockets with a few things and left them in a safe place. Then we called Prince Ismail Daoud, a relative of my husband. As soon as he heard the news, he did the same as I had done. He said that in order not to arouse suspicion, we had to show that we had not changed our habits. He came to pick me up and together we went riding for a short while. We first rode in the desert, then closer to town so that we would be seen, and then I went back home.

I could not bring the usual carrots to the horses that day, since my pockets were filled with small pieces of jewelry and other valuable objects. None of them had anything to do with Egypt; they were either family heirlooms or items that I had bought because I liked them. After leaving these valuables with a trustworthy friend, I came back home. Moneim was badly shaken.

The expropriation officers had not arrived yet, but our closest friends and the three ladies I worked with at the Mabarra, Emine, Hediye, and Batta, came to our house to help. They were running around the house asking, "What can we do, how can we help you?" We had some old enameled boxes in gold on a table in the living room. "Don't leave those!" they said, filling their pockets with a few objects. Although it was only November and the weather was still mild, each of the ladies left the house wearing a fur coat.

I had asked them to deliver what they had taken to Fahriye Hanım's house.[55] The confiscation law contained an article stating that concealing seizable goods would be punishable by two years in prison. At first, Fahriye refused to keep the objects I had sent, as she was afraid of getting herself into trouble, but then she was persuaded to accept and hid everything. I had a very beautiful set of gold-plated cutlery for thirty-six people, which I also found a way to send to Fahriye Hanım.

Even Abdu, who in the morning had almost thrown the papers at me, came back saying, "Efendina, whatever is in this house belongs to you, not to the state. Don't leave it to those thieves. I will help you." "Don't Abdu," I said, "They will send you to prison." "Halal, ya Efendina," he said, meaning it was not a sin, and he also took things to hide.

By lunchtime, we had completed these activities and we were waiting for the requisition to take place. Eventually, the officers in charge of the confiscation arrived, holding large ledgers in their arms and four sets of weighing scales, and the expropriation began. The first thing they

registered was the Patek Philippe watch on my wrist; then they opened
the safe and took what I had left there. They took away my silver dinner-
ware, weighing each piece one by one and listing it in the ledger. Hanging
on the walls, I had large illuminated firmans [imperial decrees] made for
my forefathers, which I had bought here and there over the years. They
wanted to take those too. "These belong to the history of my family, they
have nothing to do with Egypt, they all belong to my grandfathers," I
told them, but they would not listen and took them all the same. Then
they were about to register the children's toys. "What are you doing?" I
said. "These are toys, they are here one day and gone another." So they
did not include them in the ledger. They knew nothing about antiques or
furniture. For instance, when they measured my beautiful antique Persian
carpet, they listed it as 'blue carpet' and wrote down the measurements.

In the garden there was a one-story building between the garage and
the storage room; they moved the requisitioned items from the house,
dumping them all in that building, then they sealed the door and left a
soldier to guard it. The confiscated items and the guard remained there
for fifty years, while everything rotted away!

The worst came when all was over: "You must leave this house by
tomorrow. We are expropriating the house as well."

The house did not belong to the state; it was my husband's private
property. My mother-in-law, Iqbal Hanem the wife of the khedive, had
sold some of her jewelry and some land she owned in Kütahya to buy the
property, and my husband inherited the house from his mother. They
refused to take notice. "Tomorrow you must leave this place," they said,
and left.

We did not know where to go, we did not have the money to go to a
hotel. They had taken all the cash from our bank accounts. We were left
with nothing. A friend told us, "We have a large house, come and stay with
us." Then other friends called inviting us to their homes. But as we were
getting ready to leave, the same friends called one by one, saying, "Don't
come, our house has been taken, we are also in the street."

We knew a lawyer who was well informed on these matters. "What
can we do?" I asked him, "What can we take with us? What did they

confiscate, what did they leave to us?" "I really don't know," he replied, and burst into tears. "Leave the crying to me, just tell us what to do!" I said. But the man was both scared and confused. All he could mumble was, "You can take your clothes." "Can I take some blankets? I don't want the children to be cold," I asked. "They won't allow it; the blankets also belong to the state," he answered, and left. We packed until the early hours of the morning. When we closed the suitcases, the sun was about to rise, while we could hear the call to prayer. We had been up all night. We were ready to leave the house, without a clue where we were going to go. But a few hours later they told us, "You can stay home today." Then they told us, "You can stay another week." That week became a month, and eventually we stayed in our house for years as tenants.

Prince Abdel Moneim and Princess Neslishah were not the only victims of the RCC sequestration, all the other princes and princesses had their houses and properties confiscated, some of them having to leave their homes on the day the confiscation took place. Prince Daoud, the cousin of King Fuad, for instance, was ordered to leave his residence right away, with an allowance of eighteen Egyptian pounds a month. He was permitted to take only a few shirts with him, and he moved to a third-rate hotel. The money they had granted him was not enough to pay the bills of even this cheap hotel, but fortunately friends who in the past had been helped by the prince came to his aid, and paid for his lodging for some time.

European ambassadors began to intervene: as soon as they had wind of the situation they went to the RCC and said, "This decree is against human rights. If you throw people out from their homes, we will not recognize your republic, and we will not give you our support." The RCC took a step back from expropriation: instead of confiscating the houses they nationalized them, telling the owners, "You may go on living here, but don't forget that the houses and all the furniture are now the property of the state." In other words, they allowed the owners to live in their homes as guests of the state.

The government gave a monthly allowance of two hundred Egyptian pounds to Prince Abdel Moneim, because he had two children, which at least was more than his cousin Prince Daoud was receiving. Neslishah recalled:

> We had no money, as our bank accounts had been blocked. The state
> was giving a small monthly allowance to all the princes and princesses,
> including my husband. But it was such a small amount that it was just not
> possible to live on it. We had to economize on everything, even on food.
> Until then I had known nothing about grocery expenses, and I learned
> how expensive it was to eat in restaurants. Thank goodness friends helped
> us again. If it were not for their aid, we might have starved.
>
> We could no longer pay our servants, so we explained our situation
> quite openly to all the staff. They had gained experience by working in the
> service of a prince, so most of them found employment in princely homes
> of Saudi Arabia, as they were well trained. Our old and faithful Abdu, on
> the other hand, said, "I have spent my life with your family, and I will not
> leave you. I don't want a penny from you! Even if you kick me out, I will
> come back. If you are starving I will also starve, and if you are well fed I
> will also eat," and he stayed on.
>
> Before the revolution I had invited Mademoiselle Monet, who used
> to be my teacher when I was in Nice, to Cairo to teach my children
> French, and she was living with us. She was a difficult woman, always
> bickering with the servants, but she was an excellent teacher. When I told
> her about our difficulties, she replied, "I am staying. I have been your
> teacher, and I shall go on teaching your children."
>
> And there was a young man doing menial housework whom we did
> not want to get rid of. We knew that the military would be placing some-
> one in the house to spy on us, so we preferred to have someone we knew
> to do the job, and we did not fire him. But whenever he was around we
> spoke in Turkish so that he would not understand.
>
> The Egyptians were fond of my husband's family. They knew it was
> the family of Mohamed Ali Pasha that had enabled Egypt to develop and
> become a modern country. Besides, they still felt a certain loyalty toward

the khedive. Thus it was not just our friends who helped us out, but also people unknown to us and of moderate means, who would come saying, "We deplore the injustice you are made to suffer. Please accept our life savings." My husband would naturally refuse, thanking them with tears streaming down his cheeks.

The expropriation went on. They confiscated the house and belongings of Neslishah's sister Hanzade Sultan, who was in France at the time. She was married to Prince Mohamed Ali Ibrahim, a member of the Egyptian royal family, and the requisition included not only the prince's possessions but also his wife's.

It was not only the members of the Egyptian royal family and their spouses who suffered; even the in-laws of some of the princes were targeted, including Sabiha Sultan, who after the separation from her husband had closed up her house and gone to live for a while with her daughter Hanzade. Sabiha Sultan had a small Citroën, driven for her by one of her son-in-law's men. When the car was bought, for convenience it was registered not in her name but in the name of Prince Mohamed Ali Ibrahim. As the confiscations proceeded at Neslishah's house, the impounding officers arrived there deliberately driving her mother's requisitioned Citroën, just to show who now held the power in Egypt.

Even the children's toys were confiscated. "From now on these toys belong to the state," the officials declared as they left the house. Atifet Hanım gathered all of İkbal's toys and placed them in a room that she then locked, telling İkbal, "Forget the toys—if anything were to be broken, God knows what could happen to us."

Years later Neslishah was able to retrieve very nearly all the things she had managed to smuggle out of the house on the morning of the confiscation. She had asked Fahriye Brav and her other friends to whom she had entrusted her belongings to hand them to the Iraqi Embassy in Cairo. The Iraqi ambassador then sent them through a diplomatic courier to Baghdad, to Prince Regent Abd al-Ilah, who was a good friend of Prince Mohamed Ali Ibrahim. From Baghdad the prince regent forwarded them to Hanzade Sultan in Paris. When Neslishah's possessions finally arrived in Paris her jewelry, her furs, and her objects of sentimental value were all there. The only thing that had gone missing was part of the gold-plated silver cutlery set of thirty-six, and a reduced set of just twelve arrived.

9

Looking for a Gentleman to Shake Hands With

On 16 July 1952 in Turkey a new decree was issued: Law 431, which the parliament had ratified in 1924, imposing permanent exile on all members of the Ottoman family, was amended, and henceforth the return of female members of the family was permitted. The male members, meanwhile, would have to wait a further twenty-two years for decree 1803 of 18 May 1974 to be promulgated, finally authorizing them to return to Turkey after fifty years in exile. By then it was too late for most of the exiled şehzades, who were no longer alive; Ömer Faruk Efendi had passed away five years before the new law came into effect.

In the summer of 1952 Sabiha Sultan was staying with her daughter Hanzade in France. When the new regulation allowing her to return to Turkey came into effect, she went to the Turkish Embassy in Paris and applied for citizenship. Since the formalities at the embassy would take some time she was given an entry visa, and on the evening of 26 August 1952, the daughter of Sultan Vahideddin arrived in Istanbul after an absence of twenty-eight years. With no home in the city conquered by her ancestor Sultan Mehmed II in 1453, she stayed with friends.[56] She spent her first night in the Taksim apartment of Mahpeyker, the eldest daughter of her cousin Naciye Sultan and Enver Paşa. She made a note of her feelings that same night:

Such a blessing to be here in Istanbul, my one and only city.

Not everyone can understand what I mean. You need to have left the city as I did, you need to have yearned for your hometown as I did, and the feeling of coming back has to be savored little by little. As when lovers have lost each other, the venom of separation has also to be savored, drop by drop.

I am taking part now in the fate and the destiny of this city. I am quietly mourning the past with her. I don't want to share this. I am alone with Istanbul.

I understand her, and she understands me!

Sabiha Sultan was the first female member of the Ottoman family to return to Turkey under the new regulations, and the other princesses would soon follow her example.

Life in Egypt had now become rather difficult, and the days passed dismally for Neslishah and her family. President Naguib, the apparent leader of the revolution, had little power left. It was Gamal Abd al-Nasser who called the shots and who was imposing severe political measures both abroad and at home. He introduced land reform, which involved the confiscation of the vast estates of Egypt's big landowners, and he launched the movement of Arab nationalism, gaining the support of some of the Arab countries, though alienating the Arab monarchies.

The land reforms dealt a blow to what was until then Egypt's legendary cotton production, and a primary source of income. This was mainly because Nasser had the long-fiber cotton varieties replaced by seeds producing short fibers so that the British would no longer buy Egyptian cotton. Neslishah recalled:

Before the agrarian reform was introduced the Revolutionary Command Council invited Dr. Hjalmar Schacht to Cairo: he had been director of the Central Bank in Hitler's Germany. Moneim was still the king's regent at the time. Schacht said, "If you touch the arable land, Egypt's source of wealth will go. Huge funds are required to manage the farms and the mansions. If the state and the peasants embark on such a venture, the quality of the cotton will suffer, and you will be bankrupt." But they would not listen. They distributed land and seeds saying, "We are making reforms." Then Dr. Schacht's prediction came true. They misused the land, they did not irrigate it correctly, and the long-fiber cotton sold in Manchester was substandard, while the budget became insolvent.

In January 1954 a major diplomatic row blew up between Egypt and Turkey that simmered for years, when Fuad Hulûsi Tugay, the Turkish ambassador in Cairo, insulted Gamal Abd al-Nasser at a reception and was deported from the country.

It followed an earlier spat between the two countries in 1932, following an incident in Ankara involving the tarboosh, or fez, of the Egyptian ambassador. At an official reception held at the Ankara Palace to celebrate the anniversary of the Turkish republic on 29 October the ambassador of Egypt, Abd al-Malik Hamza, arrived wearing his national headgear, a fez. On President Mustafa Kemal's insistence, he was obliged to remove it, after which he hastily left the reception. Egypt filed an official complaint, arguing that the national headgear of their ambassador could not be removed on the orders of the president of another country, even if that country, Turkey, had itself abolished the fez. An exchange of letters of protest followed, over a period of two months, until eventually Turkey was able to mollify the Egyptians.

In 1954 the Turkish ambassador to Egypt was Fuad Hulûsi Tugay, the son of a well-known officer and diplomat of the Ottoman Empire known as 'Mad' Fuad Paşa. He was married to Princess Emine, daughter of King Fuad's sister Princess Nimet and so a cousin of the deposed King Farouk. Fuad Hulûsi Tugay was a hot-tempered man, a characteristic he probably inherited from his father. After the revolution, the Egyptian newspapers were publishing articles against the royal family, and what was written about Emine Tugay went beyond insults. Usually under such circumstances, the Turkish Foreign Ministry would replace their ambassador, but they did nothing. Fuad Tugay wrote personally to Ankara requesting his transfer, which was denied, and he was kept in Cairo for quite some time, practically forgotten.

Eventually Ankara appointed a new ambassador, and Fuad Tugay made his goodbye calls. On 21 December 1953 he gave a farewell reception at the ambassadorial residence. Nearly the whole corps diplomatique was present, but not a single representative from the Egyptian Foreign Ministry: Fuad Tugay had not invited them. Such an omission had no precedent in diplomatic circles, but worse was to come: the departing ambassador was heard telling his European friends, "You will never see me again in this filthy place."

And it got worse still: after a performance at the Opera House in Cairo on 2 January 1954, Gamal Abd al-Nasser, who was deputy prime minister at the time but the real leader of the country, gave a small cocktail party in one of the reception rooms of the Opera House for the diplomats in attendance. Fuad Tugay was among them, but that day the press had again published articles attacking his wife, using quite offensive language. When Nasser entered the room he shook hands with each of the diplomats in turn, but when he extended his hand to the ambassador of Turkey, Fuad Tugay said, "I only shake hands with gentlemen," and continued to address Nasser in an insulting manner, ending with, "You are leading Egypt to the brink of disaster." And without waiting for a reply, he turned and left the room.

The following day Nasser, who could not ignore the public affront, declared the Fuad Tugay persona non grata and ordered him to leave the country within forty-eight hours. At the airport the ambassador was not allowed to use the area reserved for diplomats, and was made to queue with all the other passengers, and before boarding the plane his luggage was thoroughly searched. And to make matters even worse for the man, reporters were taking one photograph after another, which were published the next day in all the national newspapers.

The incident provoked a strong reaction in Turkey. While the government and the minister of foreign affairs released statements one after the other, President Celâl Bayar received Ambassador Fuad Tugay in Ankara, asking to know what had happened at the Cairo Opera House. Ankara and Cairo went on blaming each other for weeks, and relations between Turkey and Egypt took years to improve.[57]

For Neslishah and her husband, in the midst of these difficult times, their main concern was the future of their children. She recalled:

> My daughter was ill, and everyone was telling me, "How can you keep your children in a country that has been through a revolution? Are you out of your mind? Take your children somewhere else."
>
> The women of the Ottoman family were now allowed to return to Turkey, and I could go there freely. I told the Egyptian authorities that I wished to travel to my country and because I was Turkish by birth, they could not refuse me an exit visa. When I received permission to leave, I flew to Istanbul with my children. My husband had to stay in Cairo.
>
> In Istanbul, we settled down in a friend's house. I spoke with everyone who was advising me to leave Egypt, one by one, but no one offered me help.
>
> One day, Prince Mohamed Ali, my sister Hanzade's husband, came to Istanbul from Paris. "Neslishah, you have offended me deeply," he said, "You have contacted everybody about the children, except for me. Don't forget that I am your sister's husband. So far I have two children: I will take yours as well, and from now on I will have four."
>
> So I sent my children to Paris with him, and he and Hanzade looked after them as if they were their own.
>
> I went back to Egypt, and every two years I was granted permission to go to Turkey, from where I would go to France to see my children, and then return to Egypt via Istanbul.

Neslishah was happy in Istanbul during her visits there, even if at times they were not easy. She was in her own country, and her beauty, her elegance, and the family she belonged to inspired respect.

In Turkey up until then the title of 'princess' brought to mind European royalty and Hollywood stars who portrayed princesses on film. This was particularly true for the younger generation, who now found that they had their own princess with Neslishah's arrival. Sparked partly by Neslishah's beauty, popular interest in Turkish princesses grew. An item that appeared in the gossip column of a Turkish magazine on 6 December 1956 illustrates the high esteem in which Neslishah was held:

On Sunday night, we were walking in Nişantaşı with a group of foreigners. We came across Neslishah Sultan, wrapped up in a mink shawl: her beauty was apparent even in the darkness of the night. She was walking slowly on her own toward her mother's house. Someone in our group said, "What a shame, is there no gallantry left among Turkish men, to leave this beauty to walk unaccompanied?" At which point a Turkish man in our group replied, "It is not because of lack of gallantry, but because we do not know our place."

In the autumn of 1956, the world was thrown into a panic by events in Egypt. In July, Gamal Abd al-Nasser, now president of the country, had nationalized the Suez Canal, which since the nineteenth century had been administered by the multinational Suez Canal Company, whose major shareholders were Britain and France. In October, British and French troops invaded and occupied the Canal Zone, helped by Israel, which invaded the Sinai Peninsula. The Soviet Union threatened to bomb Paris and London if the occupying troops were not removed. The United States intervened, and the fighting ceased, thanks to the diplomatic mediation of the two superpowers.

British domination of Egypt, which dated back to the nineteenth century, was now at an end. Nasser emerged from this crisis stronger than ever, becoming the most powerful leader of the Arab world, and his growth in stature allowed him to implement even harsher political measures than before.

Prince Abdel Moneim had been waiting with apprehension for the outcome of the Suez crisis. Everybody was aware that after the Sinai Peninsula, if Suez were also lost, Gamal Abd al-Nasser would not be able to remain in power, and the whole revolutionary regime would come tumbling down. If that happened, it seemed the only solution would be to revive the monarchy, since there was a growing dislike over the last few years for the current government. As the return of the deposed King Farouk was not possible, it would be imperative to find someone else, someone who was a descendant of the Mohamed Ali family, experienced in the affairs of the state, loved by the people, and whom no one would object to—in other words, Prince Abdel Moneim.

In Cairo, people were already talking about such a possibility, and this was why the prince was worried. For him to be forcibly enthroned by foreign powers that had occupied his country would be the equivalent of treason. His fears were dispelled when the British and the French troops withdrew from the Canal, and he was able to breathe freely when Sinai was completely evacuated.

In the spring of 1957 Neslishah, with a new exit visa from Egypt, had come to Istanbul and was staying at a friend's *yalı*. She had planned to spend a few days in Istanbul before going to Europe to see her children. While she was there two guests arrived: Nuri Said Pasha, at the time the prime minister of Iraq, and Şehzade Namık Efendi, Neslishah's cousin and the grandson of Sultan Reşad.

Nuri Said Pasha was a former Ottoman citizen. He had been born in Baghdad in 1888, and studied in Istanbul, graduating as an officer from the Military Academy. When Italy invaded Libya in 1911, he was among the officers who went to Libya with Mustafa Kemal and Enver Paşa, but when the First World War broke out he joined the Arab nationalists. After the war he went into politics, supported the British policies in the Middle East, and became prime minister of the Kingdom of Iraq, seven times.

Şehzade Namık Efendi was the son of Şehzade Ömer Hilmi Efendi, who was the son of Sultan Reşad. He was born in 1911 at the Dolmabahçe Palace. When he was eleven years old, he was exiled with the rest of the Ottoman family, and lived in France and Egypt and later he went into business, representing a British company in India. He also dealt in arms. He had a special place in Neslishah's heart, as he was the one who had saved her from marrying Prince Hassan Toussoun.

Nuri Said Pasha spoke fluent Turkish, since he had studied in Istanbul, and in the living room of the *yalı* he spoke in Turkish with Neslishah and Şehzade Namık Efendi. They began the conversation in a very Turkish manner: "We have come here for a very auspicious matter. As you know, Iraq has a major Shia population. King Faisal is barely twenty-two years old and to enhance the respect and the admiration among the Sunnis, he is compelled to marry the daughter of one of the most important Sunni families in the world. We thought that it would be very beneficial, both for your family as well as for the future of our kingdom, if Princess Fazile, the daughter of your sister Hanzade Sultan, were to marry the king and become the queen of Iraq."

Şehzade Namık Efendi also explained why this marriage would be suitable for other reasons, and he asked Neslishah to inform Hanzade Sultan and Prince Mohamed Ali of this request, convincing them to accept the proposal. Neslishah said she would convey the message to her sister, and leave it at that—which is what she did.

Hanzade Sultan and Prince Mohamed Ali were surprised when they heard the proposal, as Fazile was only sixteen and was still attending school. It must have been their astonishment that made them wait for a couple of weeks without giving a reply.

Dürrüşehvar, the daughter of Caliph Abdülmecid Efendi, was also in Istanbul at the time. Since the female members of the Ottoman family had been allowed to return to Turkey, she came and went freely. One day she paid a visit to her niece Neslishah, and said to her, "Tell Hanzade to make up her mind quickly. Some families in Istanbul have heard that the king wants to marry, and they are doing their utmost to push their daughters on him." She even gave the names of the families who were desperately looking for a matchmaker to introduce their daughters to the king.

Neslishah called her sister Hanzade again, telling her, "This is how things are: decide quickly, and inform the Iraqis of your decision." Then she went to Switzerland with her children, as she was unable to change her holiday plans.

A few days later Prince Mohamed Ali called the Iraqi ambassador in Paris, saying, "His Majesty has honored us with his request," and accepted the marriage proposal. In August he went to Istanbul with Hanzade Sultan and their daughter Fazile. Soon afterward, Faisal, the young king of Iraq, was welcomed at the airport in Yeşilköy with a military band and full state honors. He had come to Istanbul to meet his future wife. Some elderly members of the family accompanied him to discuss the details of the marriage, including Prince Abd al-Ilah, Faisal's uncle, who had acted as his regent until he was eighteen years old, and Iraq's most powerful man.

The yacht *Queen Alia* was sent to Istanbul before their arrival and was anchored in the bay of Bebek. Faisal spent his days with the family of his fiancée in the *yalı* that was hosting them, while at night he stayed on his boat. He remained in Istanbul for a month and a half. The families agreed on how the engagement and the wedding were to proceed, and on 14 September King Faisal returned to Baghdad. His future parents-in-law were at the airport to bid him farewell.

The engagement was announced the following day, that is, on 15 September 1957, at the royal palace in Baghdad. In June Nuri Said Pasha had been replaced as prime minister by Ali Jawdat, who now flew to Istanbul with the king's gifts and officially informed Princess Fazile of her engagement. Sadly, the flowers that Neslishah sent from Switzerland to congratulate Princess Fazile never arrived.

Turkey at this time was keen to strengthen relations with the countries of the Middle East, in particular wanting to bolster the Baghdad Pact they had made with Iran, Iraq, Pakistan, and Britain. Thus the engagement between King Faisal and Princess Fazile was in line with Turkey's foreign policy, and Ankara was very pleased with the engagement.

Meanwhile Gamal Abd al-Nasser was a source of apprehension for Ankara. He was targeting the regime in Iraq, and the Egyptian radio was constantly broadcasting messages urging the Iraqi army to rise up against King Faisal. And of course relations between Cairo and Ankara were already at their worst, following the diplomatic incident at the Cairo Opera House in 1954.

Sabiha Sultan was worried about the damage Egypt could provoke by inciting the Iraqi army against their government. Being the daughter of Sultan Vahideddin she had been very much aware of the intricate politics that went on around her from a very early age; she had witnessed all kinds of provocations, betrayals, and intrigues. She was therefore amazed by the lack of reaction that King Faisal and the Prince Abd al-Ilah showed to the provocative attitude of Egypt against Iraq.

After her granddaughter Fazile's engagement to Faisal she often spent time with the Iraqis, and she recorded her impressions of some of the exchanges she witnessed that demonstrated how unconcerned Iraq was about the effrontery of the Egyptians:

> One evening while we were sitting in the hallway, Abd al-Ilah tuned in to Radio Cairo. An Egyptian speaker was virulently criticizing the government in Baghdad. The prince smiled, saying that these attacks were a daily routine, and that Baghdad never neglected to respond.
>
> I did not understand something that the radio mentioned that evening, and asked the prince about it. They had said something about some Iraqi officers being arrested for siding with Egypt. "Yes," he said, "They are now making these kinds of allegations. I have asked for the newspapers that have published such accusations to be brought to me, and I shall show them to our aides-de-camp who are here with us. Nasser's doings again. It is pure fantasy. There is not one bit of truth in all this, how could this possibly happen?"
>
> The next day at lunchtime the whole family was there, with the king and his aides-de-camp. Prince Abd al-Ilah took a newspaper out of his pocket, handed it to Nuri Bey, the king's aide-de-camp, and said laughing, "Are you one of the officers that have been arrested?" I could feel that under what was meant as a joke lay a deep sense of trust, and I looked to the side of the table where the officers were sitting. They were all laughing, with expressions of astonishment on their faces. Abd al-Ilah then turned to Mohamed Ali and myself saying, "You see how much Radio Cairo is lying?" As if to say, "Did I not tell you?"

It was not many months later that Sabiha Sultan's fears became a reality.

The engaged couple saw a lot of each other during the months that followed. In December 1957, Fazile flew to Baghdad with her parents and her grandmother Sabiha Sultan, where the families went over the wedding preparations, after which the young princess was sent to a school in England for lessons in how to be a queen.

It had been decided that the wedding would take place in the autumn of 1958. The Iraqi side wanted the future queen to come to Baghdad a few months before the wedding to get to know her new country. But Hanzade Sultan did not wish to send her daughter to Iraq before the wedding. She herself did not know why she was against such a request, but a voice inside her was telling her, "Don't send her," so following her instinct she gave excuses, refusing the invitation.

On 14 July 1958 she discovered how right her instinct had been.

The member countries of the Baghdad Pact were to take part in a summit meeting at the Şale Pavilion in Istanbul on 15 July, hosted by President Celâl Bayar. Shah Reza Pahlavi of Iran, King Faisal of Iraq, and President Iskander Mirza of Pakistan were to attend the meeting. Great preparations were made for the conference. The heads of state were to be hosted in the palaces, the delegates in luxury hotels. Fifteen rooms were reserved at the Hilton Hotel, sixty-one at the Cinar Hotel, twenty at the Park Hotel, and thirteen at the Divan. During the meetings, military bands were to give concerts in the city's main squares, and the Janissary band would perform in the squares of Taksim and Beşiktaş.

The heads of state were expected to arrive on 14 July; the first to come was to be King Faisal. The red carpet had been rolled out early that morning at Yeşilköy Airport. President Celâl Bayar, Prime Minister Adnan Menderes, and various officials went to the airport to meet the guests. But as they waited for King Faisal's plane to land, news came that shocked and stunned everyone there: a bloody military coup had taken place in Iraq that morning. Nothing was said of the fate of the young king.

The news had come through a radio communication to an Iraqi commercial plane flown by an English pilot, John Everest, that had left Baghdad that morning at 6:15 for London. Everest received an urgent radio message at 7:15 from "The Commanding Council of the Revolution," which read: "A coup d'état has taken place against the government of Baghdad, and the traitors have been punished. King Faisal will not be sent to Turkey. Inform the Turkish government of the situation." Before landing at Yeşilköy at 9:20 to refuel, the pilot asked several times for a confirmation of the message he had received. Co-pilot Dowdy relayed the message to the officials waiting at the airport and to Najib al-Rawi, the Iraqi ambassador, after which the plane took off again for London.

The red carpet was folded back from the runway; the flags were lowered on the flagpoles. Radio messages were sent to the planes carrying the shah of Iran and the president of Pakistan, informing them of the revolution that had taken place in Iraq. Both leaders were notified that the meeting was now to be held in Ankara, and their planes were diverted there.

Details of the coup were revealed around noon: in the early hours of the morning, military troops led by General Abd al-Karim Qasim seized Baghdad, and raided the palace and the houses of the members of the government. Crown Prince Abd al-Ilah was killed together with his family. Nuri Said Pasha, who had been reappointed as prime minister on 3 March of that year, managed to escape hiding under a black burqa when his mansion was stormed. But he was later recognized and lynched, and his body was cut to pieces and fed to the dogs.

Radio Baghdad confirmed the rumors that circulated, repeating the same announcement: "There are now two corpses on the street. One of them belongs to the traitor Nuri Said Pasha, whose will was contrary to the will of the people, and the other to his master Crown Prince Abd al-Ilah."

This was one of the bloodiest armed coups in Arab history, and involved unprecedented barbarity: when some foreign news agency claimed that Abd al-Ilah had escaped and was leading an armed counter-revolution in the provinces, to disprove the reports the military displayed the prince's blood-soaked body on the door of a government building, announcing on the radio, "Go and see the body of Abd al-Ilah with your own eyes." The Middle East News Agency, which supported Abd al-Nasser, reported that "the body of Abd al-Ilah was dragged in the streets like the corpse of a dog by the people, who then tore it to pieces."

The fate of the twenty-three-year-old king was worse, and the details of his death were heard only days later. The revolutionary soldiers who broke into the palace fired at everyone they came across, shooting Faisal with a machine gun. But the king was not dead, and he was carried, covered in blood, to a hospital, where the doctors said, "If we treat him these guys will kill us without blinking an eye." So they did not touch King Faisal, or even put him on a bed, but left him in agony on the floor, where he bled to death.

That same day Iraq abolished the monarchy and proclaimed the republic. The first act of the new regime was to send a cable to Cairo, addressed to Gamal Abd al-Nasser, stating that they were "honored" to recognize the United Arab Republic, Nasser's new union of Egypt and Syria which Iraq had previously refused to acknowledge. Nasser was in Yugoslavia at the time of the coup. Back in Cairo he immediately replied to the telegram, informing them that he recognized the revolutionaries as the lawful government of Iraq.

The fate of General Abd al-Karim Qasim, who led the coup and who allowed the agony of the young king to go on for hours, was not to be so different. On 8 February 1963, when the Baath Party took power in another military coup, the general was put on trial the same day and condemned to death. He was executed the following day by machine gun while sitting at a table, and photographs of his body covered in blood were distributed to the world press.

Meanwhile in Istanbul, the day after the Iraqi revolution, a fight broke out among the crew of the royal yacht *Queen Alia*, which was moored in the bay of Bebek. Most of the crew and the staff considered that the yacht was now the property of the Iraqi state, and thought they should return to Iraq with the boat. A smaller group argued that the yacht was the property of the king, who was their employer, and they did not wish to go back. The argument turned into a fight. The Iraqi ambassador in Ankara and the consul in Istanbul had decided not to show which side they were on until the situation in Baghdad became clearer, so they did not interfere in the fight on the yacht. But as it turned out, there was no need to, since the majority of the crew eventually convinced the minority to return with the boat to Iraq: the royal yacht left Istanbul, and on the way the name was changed from *Queen Alia* to *Thawra*, meaning 'Revolution.'

As the revolution was taking place in Baghdad, Fazile was in London attending her school, Hanzade Sultan and Prince Mohamed Ali were in the south of France on their yacht *Rakkase*, and Neslishah was in Cairo, where she had only recently been prosecuted in a military court and acquitted, while her husband Prince Abdel Moneim was still under surveillance.

Hanzade Sultan and Prince Mohamed Ali heard about the tragic events in Baghdad as they were sailing from Cannes to Capri, and they immediately flew to London to be with their daughter. Fazile was now the unhappiest princess in the world, and an army of reporters followed her as soon as she set foot outside her home. This went on for days and weeks.

As soon as Sabiha Sultan, who was then in Istanbul, heard about the coup, she began trying to gather information. She noted in her diary:

14 July 1958: Princess Wijdan came this morning at ten o'clock and in a rather agitated manner told me she had heard that the arrival of the king had been postponed because of unrest in Baghdad. I immediately called the ambassador of Iraq, who informed me about the tragic events. The newspapers published contradicting news. It was not possible to understand exactly what was going on. I cabled my friends to find out Hanzade's whereabouts, and at the same time I called Cannes, where I was told that they had left. I sent another telegram to Dürrüşehvar, asking her to let me know how Fazile was. No additional information had been broadcast on the radio or reported in the papers.

15 July: Today I received a cable from Fazile, telling me that she was well and that her parents were on the island of Elba. My heart bleeds for the pain that my little one must be suffering. I went to see the wife of the ambassador, but she did not know much more than I did.

16 July: I received a cable from Hanzade, letting me know that they were now in London and asking me to contact the ambassador to obtain additional information. I phoned Ankara and the ambassador promised me he would call my daughter personally.

17 July: The ambassador was unable to get in touch with London. He told me he would be back in Istanbul in the evening and would call again from there.

18 July: The ambassador has spoken to Hanzade. Yesterday I sent her a letter in which I implied that there was not much to hope for. So far, there has been no encouraging news regarding the life of the king. I have accepted this painful tragedy. I am heartbroken at the outcome of the life of this pure and innocent young man, while I am in total disbelief when I think of the last conversation I had with Abd al-Ilah. I just cannot understand how they could have been so careless. The press conference given this evening by King Hussein [of Jordan] confirmed the painful disaster. Poor little innocent Faisal, you have been sacrificed like a lamb in this tragedy! So much negligence is shameful! I now believe that except for you, they are all to blame.

19 July: This morning I went to see the ambassador. We cried together. I wanted to speak to Hanzade. I was told that it would be possible at four o'clock. I went home with the intention of returning in the afternoon. As I was leaving the ambassador called me back, as a phone call had come from London. The line was bad, so Prince Mohamed Ali asked me to send them a cable telling them what I wanted to say. Since it was not possible for me to write on the various subjects I wanted to talk about, I decided to go back to the ambassador this evening and try to call again."[58]

10
Password: "Unnnnn!"

N eslishah and her husband were going through bad times of
their own: in the fall of 1957 they were placed under house
arrest, accused of "plotting against the government," and
faced a military court in two separate trials that lasted months.

Gamal Abd al-Nasser was now increasingly powerful, but the Suez
Crisis had given hope to the opposition, which had now been forced
underground, who believed that if things went on as they were, Egypt
would be further politically isolated and Nasser would become more
vulnerable—and they were searching for ways of getting rid of him at
the earliest opportunity. Already in some circles people were saying,
"Nasser's days are numbered."

Meanwhile, the *mukhabarat*, the secret services, announced that
they had unveiled a dangerous plot against the regime. The alleged
conspirators belonged to different walks of life, and were of various
nationalities—even the British secret services, as well as Zog the King
of Albania, who at one point was exiled in Alexandria, were supposed
to be involved. Also implicated were the son of a prominent religious
scholar and one-time Sheikh of al-Azhar, Mustafa al-Meragi, who had
fled Egypt after the 1952 revolution, accused of fraud; Air Force officer
Mohamed Khayri, the son of Princess Qadriya, who was the daughter
of Egypt's Sultan Hussein; and Mahmud Namık Efendi, Neslishah's
cousin and friend. According to the attorney general, Namık Efendi

had not taken part in the plot, but being a friend of the conspirators he knew the details of their plan.

The Egyptian intelligence service revealed the unprecedented precautions taken by the conspirators: they had apparently had a particular design of ring made that they wore to identify each other. One of the rings was said to have been given to Namık Efendi, who showed it off to everyone he came across in Europe, saying, "The wearers of this ring will overthrow Nasser."

The intelligence officers were even more impressed by the plotters' choice of secret password, which was allegedly not a word at all but a strange sound, something like "Unnnnn, unununnnn, unununununnnn!"—though in time they are said to have forgotten what intonation to use while uttering this sound.

The allegations were serious, and all the accused who were in Egypt at the time were immediately arrested. A warrant was issued for Namık Efendi's arrest in absentia. Mohamed Khayri was arrested, and nothing was ever heard of him again—there were plausible rumors that he had been quietly murdered, as it was feared he might disclose everything he knew about Nasser in court. The Egyptian authorities gave no adequate explanation of his whereabouts, beyond "He went missing." His wife Fevziye Sultan, who at the time of writing still lives in Paris, believes that her husband is alive and is waiting for his return.

As bewildered and intrigued Egyptians followed the revelations, two more names came to light: Prince Abdel Moneim and his wife, Neslishah. They were accused of having knowledge of the conspiracy from the start. While in Europe, Neslishah had met the conspirators through Namık Efendi, and had even been offered a role in the plot.

Also implicated was the deposed Albanian king Zog, who was a close friend of Neslishah's father Şehzade Ömer Faruk Efendi. They would often meet when they both lived in Alexandria, and the king had great respect for the şehzade: when at the threshold of a door Faruk Efendi would say, "After you, Your Majesty," King Zog would make way and reply, "Your Highness, please, after you. I am just the governor of your smallest province!"

While Neslishah was in Europe, Namık Efendi took her to see King Zog, who asked her to carry some secret documents. Neslishah refused, saying, "We are followed everywhere we go. It is not possible for me to help you." In Zog's house Neslishah also met the head of British Intelligence. He had just returned from Hungary, and he introduced himself to Neslishah under an assumed name. Neslishah understood immediately who he was, and realized that when the Russian tanks were trampling down Hungary he had been involved in British undercover work. He asked Neslishah, "Is your husband the heir to the throne, or should it be Prince Amr Ibrahim, your sister's husband?" To which she replied, "Go to Egypt and ask the Egyptians!"

In light of the accumulated evidence, one morning in the fall of 1957, the military stormed the house of Prince Abdel Moneim and Neslishah in Cairo, turned the house upside-down in the search for incriminating secret documents, and placed the couple under house arrest. Neslishah recalled:

My children were finally in France with Hanzade. My husband and I were living in Egypt. Every two years I was granted permission to leave the country, and I would first go to Turkey, from where after a short stay I would fly to France to be with my children. Then I would return to Egypt via Turkey.

My husband was not allowed to accompany me. It was as if he were being held hostage, so I traveled alone. I could not return to Egypt directly from France, as my exit visa was valid only to go to my country of origin, that is, to Turkey. So I had to go back via Istanbul, and I made this trip several times.

After the Suez Crisis of 1956 I went again to Paris via Istanbul. I wanted to spend a couple of months with my children, but I received a cable from my husband: "Your father is very ill, come back at once." I immediately returned to Cairo, and stayed by my father's side. He really was in a terrible state. He had had a heart attack, and to make matters worse he had pneumonia. His kidneys were also not functioning properly, and the doctor had lost all hope: "This man is medically dead, so be prepared for the worst." But then a miracle happened. My father suddenly recovered, and he lived another ten years!

After my father had divorced my mother to marry his cousin Mihrişah, we were not on very good terms. We still saw each other, but I would refuse to be anywhere near Mihrişah. She, however, took very good care of my father. For instance, while my father had pneumonia he would say, "It's very hot!" and would ask for the fan to be near his bed to cool him down. Was it possible not to do what he wished? He would raise hell, and they would bring the fan closer, but Mihrişah would take a chair and sit between the fan and my father, with the cold air against her back and risking pneumonia herself, just to stop my father from getting any worse.

Realizing how she was sacrificing herself for his sake, I decided to see her again. It was my father's habit to come to our house for lunch on Mondays, so now he began to bring Mihrişah with him. It was a Monday toward the end of December 1957, and my father and Mihrişah were due for lunch. I had just woken up, had breakfast in my room, and dressed, and I was about to go down to make the necessary preparations, when the maid came to my room, trembling all over: "Soldiers have surrounded the house, they are everywhere, and the phone has been cut off, it's not working," she mumbled.

Just then we heard a noise, and before we had time to realize what was going on, the bedroom door was thrust violently open, and in came an officer and a bunch of armed soldiers! In Egypt, it was unimaginable for men—even if they were soldiers or policemen—to barge unannounced into a lady's bedroom. So I understood that this was serious, and for the first time I was frightened!

"You are under arrest! We shall search the house," said the officer, and they turned my room topsy-turvy.

We did not know why we had been arrested, and no reason came to my mind. I asked the soldiers, who said they could not answer; they were just here to search the house and arrest me and my husband, that was all.

On the table in my bedroom I had an exquisite eighteenth-century box inlaid with porcelain. I had bought it in Salzburg that year, and it was where I kept the letters from my children. When I missed my children I would read their letters over and over again. First, they took the letters. "These are letters and postcards sent by my children," I said, "They are of no use to you, why are you taking them?" But they would not listen. They were taking anything that was written, not just my children's letters.

I became really angry! I went to the cupboard where I kept my underwear, opened the drawers to show them the contents, and shouted, "Take these as well!" They were very embarrassed and suddenly remembered they had invaded the room of a lady. They immediately closed the cupboard. "We apologize," they said. "We will continue after you have left the room." And they went out, but then when they came back they turned everything upside-down again.

Then they went to my husband's study. There they also turned everything inside-out, and removed the radios. "You are both under arrest. It has been decided that instead of going to prison you will be under house arrest. You are not to leave the house, not even to go into the garden," they declared, but again they did not tell us why we had been arrested!

They posted a squad of soldiers in front of the door and in the garden. Every few hours they would patrol the area. At night when there was a change of guard they would make as much noise as possible, just to annoy us.

There was a small house in the garden where my husband's secretary lived. They threw him out and replaced him with a police officer, who was in charge of us. Thank God, he was a polite and kind person, who treated us well.

No one was allowed to come to the house. Even when the maids arrived or left the house, they were thoroughly searched. They had to come empty-handed and they could not even bring us newspapers.

We were arrested on a Monday, a day when my father and Mihrişah were meant to come for lunch. They arrived around noon, Mihrişah driving the car. When they saw the soldiers and the policemen in front of the door they were alarmed. One of the soldiers told them, "You cannot enter, they are both under arrest." My father, who was just recovering from his heart attack, felt faint, and on the way back in the car he felt even worse. Later, when Mihrişah described the events of that day, she said, "On the one hand I was thinking of you, while on the other I thought your father was going to die in the car. I was very frightened, and we returned home with great difficulty."

When the soldiers left and took the radios with them, they had overlooked a small radio we had. It was from this radio that we learned that Moneim and I were accused of being part of a conspiracy to overthrow the government.

Soon Neslishah and Prince Abdel Moneim were taken to the military court. The charge was defined on 31 December 1957 by Sayyid Muafi, Cairo's chief prosecutor: "It is clearly understood that Neslishah has not taken part in the preparation of the conspiracy against the government, however being aware of such a plan she is accused of not informing the authorities." He added that Neslishah and Abdel Moneim were to stand trial, but that her Turkish nationality had been taken into account and instead of being imprisoned they would both remain under house arrest until the end of the hearings. During their house arrest they were taken regularly to the military court, where for six months they endured exhaustive interrogations. Neslishah recalled:

> A couple of days after our house arrest, the attorney general came to the house with a group of officers and soldiers, and my husband and I were questioned.
>
> The interrogation lasted a long time. As I wanted to speed things up, I answered the questions in Arabic, but in very short sentences, and my statements were naturally recorded in writing, in Arabic.
>
> When it was all over, I was given the written deposition and told, "Sign it!" "No, I won't," I replied. "Why not?" "Because I don't trust you, that is why! Let my husband read it and translate what I said, then I will. I can speak Arabic, but I don't understand written Arabic. I don't know what is written on that piece of paper, so I will not sign it before my husband reads and translates it!"
>
> We went on arguing for quite some time. The officers told me, "You are obliged to sign." And I replied, "You can't force me, I will only sign after

my husband has read it to me." "That is not possible," they retorted. "In that case, I will not sign it," I insisted, and I did not sign my deposition.

They had no proof, no clues, nothing at all. Some people had apparently conspired against Abd al-Nasser, and my husband and I were supposed to have known about this conspiracy and had not informed the authorities. They wanted my signed deposition admitting the crime of not reporting to the government what we knew. I did not sign!

Then they sent us to the Military Court. We were under house arrest for six months—that is, for the whole period of the trial.

Before each hearing, I would rehearse at home in front of the mirror what I would say in court. The words I would be using, my gestures, my expression, my posture—all had to be credible. This is why, like an actress working on a play, I would spend hours in front of the mirror, practicing my most persuasive attitude.

On the days of the hearing, a car would come to pick us up and take us to the courthouse. A policeman in plain clothes sat next to the driver, while my husband and I were in the back of the car. On our way we would chat with him, and eventually he began to like us.

On one occasion I was rather annoyed, and I was talking about someone behind their back. The policeman turned toward me and bringing his finger to his lips signaled to me not to talk. I kept silent, but I did not understand whether he was afraid of the driver or if it was something else, and I was intrigued.

I found out later and in a rather amusing way, the reason for his concern. Ever since my childhood, when I laugh I kick my feet forward; in other words, I laugh with my face and with my legs! On another occasion, again while we were driving to the courthouse and talking among ourselves, I started to laugh rather loudly, when my legs kicked the seat in front of me. The back of the front seat dropped toward us and out came a tape recorder, ejecting the tape. Apparently they were recording and listening to our conversations. This was the reason the policeman had made a sign to silence me!

You could not smoke in the courthouse, and there was nothing to drink besides tea or coffee. If I wanted to go to the bathroom, I had to tell the policeman escorting us, who would go and find someone else, who would fetch yet another policeman, who would also call on another person and eventually there would be four or five men accompanying me to the bathroom. They would all wait in front of the door, which would make me so nervous that I would come out of the bathroom without using it!

We spent most of the month of Ramadan in court, and during those days, whether by coincidence or not, the hearings were even tougher.

The court consisted of five men, led by a military judge. During the first hearing, the judge told me, "You don't speak Arabic well enough to defend yourself, so speak in English or in Turkish. Turkish would be better, as we have found a good translator for you," but I refused to speak in Turkish. "I shall speak in English," I said. "If I speak in English everybody will be able to understand what I say, while in Turkish your interpreter might translate in the manner that is most suitable for you. That is why I prefer to express myself in English."

"What do you mean, don't you trust us?" asked the judge. I could not resist: "No, of course I don't trust you! You are accusing us of incredible things, so I don't trust you," I replied, and spoke only in English. All the judges spoke English and whenever I said something that displeased them or inconvenienced them, they made me stop talking.

In one hearing they openly asked me, "Since you were aware of this conspiracy, why did you not report it?" I said, "So many rumors of conspiracies go around. In Cairo people are continually talking about such things. Moreover, the people who mentioned these plots are people that I like. Do you expect me to denounce them?" At which point the judge asked, "Do you mean to say that you do not like us?" Again I just could not resist and said, "No, I don't like you. How could I like you? You have treated us as thieves, as traitors, you have accused us of all sorts of things! And after all these accusations, how could you expect me to like you?"

They realized that they were getting nowhere with the allegation of conspiracy, so they tried to accuse us of smuggling money abroad. Just after the revolution, the military had issued a law obliging Egyptians who had previously sent money abroad to bring it all back immediately. In Egypt, the king, the princes, and the rich often spent a few months a year in Europe and so were always taking money with them. Even King Farouk once said jokingly, "I put my money in shoeboxes when I go abroad. How do you take yours?"

We had also transferred money abroad, though not in huge amounts, which we used during our stays in Europe and for my children's education. But our account in Switzerland was nothing compared to the other wealthy princes.

So the court brought up this issue, and the judge asked me, "We have verified that you have an account in Switzerland. Why have you kept your money there, in spite of the law issued by the government for the repatriation of funds abroad?" "For our children," I admitted. "We are responsible for our two children. That money is for their education. If you had money abroad for the education of your children, would you bring it back, just because the government had said so? You wouldn't, and nor have we."

Just then a Greek lady in the audience shouted, "Well done, Princess!" The judge screamed back at the woman, and there was total confusion in the courtroom.

Neslishah and Abdel Moneim remained under house arrest for six months, and they were taken back and forth to court several days each week. Then the military tribunal acquitted them both. Cairo's attorney general Sayyid Muafi declared their innocence with regard to the conspiracy, while completely ignoring the issue of the bank account in Switzerland.

The trial was over, but Neslishah's ordeal was not. Because of her sister Hanzade Sultan and her niece Fazile, she had yet to face another trial in Cairo.

A few days after the Iraqi revolution, a military plane flew from Baghdad and landed at Cairo airport, carrying a single handcuffed and chained passenger accompanied by a few heavily armed soldiers. The plane belonged to the Iraqi air force, and the passenger who disembarked was put into a waiting military vehicle that drove off rapidly to the Cairo Citadel, on the edge of the Muqattam Hills, which had long been used as a prison.

The passenger was Şehzade Mahmud Namık Efendi, grandson of Sultan Reşad. A year earlier he had visited Neslishah with the former prime minister of Iraq, with regard to the marriage between King Faisal and Hanzade Sultan's sixteen-year-old daughter Princess Fazile.

Namık Efendi had gone to Baghdad on 12 July 1958, both for business and to clarify some of the arrangements for the impending royal wedding, on behalf of his cousin Hanzade.

When the şehzade arrived in Baghdad he stayed at the Hotel El Mansour, the most luxurious establishment in the city, and almost immediately began to make the necessary contacts. But just two days later the coup took place, and he was dragged into the turmoil.

It was known that Namık Efendi disliked Gamal Abd al-Nasser, and there were rumors that while in Europe he had taken part in certain activities against him, so he could no longer return to Cairo. The revolutionary soldiers in Baghdad, right from the start, were chanting slogans in favor of Nasser in the streets and broadcasting them on the radio, expressing their wish to join the union between Egypt and Syria.

When Namık Efendi saw what was happening, clearly reminding him that he was disliked by the regime in Cairo, he was rather worried. A curfew was declared in the city, but he managed to leave the hotel and find a way to take refuge at the Swiss Embassy. He was the holder of a French passport, on which his nationality appeared as "Ottoman" and his name as "Prince Mahmud Namık."

The Swiss, who were familiar with the şehzade, accepted his request for protection and gave him a new passport, on which the title of prince was not mentioned. They also told him that he could stay at the embassy as long as he wished, promising that when things calmed down, they would find a way for him to leave Baghdad.

Having spent a few hours at the Swiss Embassy, the şehzade did something he should not have done. Thinking, "Since my new passport bears no mention of my title as a prince, the revolutionaries will not recognize me or bother me," he left the embassy and went back to his hotel, despite the warnings of the Swiss diplomats.

This fatal mistake would cost Namık Efendi his life, which ended in an Egyptian prison cell. That evening the military went around the hotels, one by one, making a list of the foreigners staying there. When they came to the El Mansour, their attention was caught by the name of a Muslim with a Swiss passport. After a short investigation, they realized that in the ongoing conspiracy case in Cairo, which Baghdad was following closely, this name came up frequently, and there was an arrest warrant for him in absentia.

The Iraqi revolutionaries, wanting to make a friendly gesture to Nasser in Egypt, cabled Cairo asking, "Is this man of any use to you?" The reply came back: "Yes indeed! Send him immediately!" And the şehzade was put on a military plane and sent to Egypt.

Locking him up in the Cairo Citadel, the military now decided to reopen the conspiracy case from which Neslishah and Prince Abdel Moneim had only recently been acquitted. Most of the accused had already left the country, so they could not be arrested and tried again, but now one of the main characters of the scenario was in their hands, and he could easily be put on trial.

They accused Şehzade Namık Efendi of conspiring against the regime, of attempting a coup d'état, and of aiming to restore the monarchy. According to the rumors that were circulating at the time, Gamal Abd al-Nasser had personally ordered that Namık Efendi should be found guilty. The attorney general, who regretted his previous decision to drop the charges, added two more names to the file of the accused in the new trial: Neslishah and Prince Abdel Moneim. But this time they were to appear in court not as defendants but as "witnesses to the plot prepared by Mahmud Namık."

According to Egyptian law, a person under arrest must have a male relative appointed as his guardian. The Ottomans living in Cairo, being exiles, were mostly afraid of angering Nasser. So only one person volunteered to be the guardian of Namık Efendi: Mehmed Nazım Efendi, another grandson of Sultan Reşad. The members of the Ottoman family living in Cairo collected money to prepare the food that their cousin liked, and twice a week they would send it to him. Meanwhile, a lawyer had to be engaged to defend Namık Efendi. This task was given to Neslishah. She recalled:

> No lawyer wanted to defend Namık. Some agreed at first, but a few days later they would change their mind, saying, "Please forgive me, but if I were to defend him against the government I might get into trouble."
>
> The best lawyer in Egypt at the time was Ahmed Hussein, and right from the beginning I had him in mind. I had heard that he was interested in the case and that he would be prepared to defend Namık.
>
> One day Bahija, the daughter-in-law of the Bakri family, came to me saying, "Ahmed Hussein sends you word that he wishes to be Namık's defense lawyer."
>
> I was very happy, since he was the only person who could handle this case, but there was one main drawback: he was the most notorious leftist in Egypt, and at one point he had even established a militant youth organization.[59] So I hesitated for a while to get in touch with him, and continued to contact other lawyers. But it was always the same thing: first they accepted, and then a few days later they would ask to be excused: "We can't, it's too dangerous!"
>
> While I was helplessly looking for a lawyer, the day of the trial was approaching. Not finding a defendant for Namık meant that the court would appoint someone to represent his case, who would also be scared of the government, and God knows what trouble he would cause us!
>
> Eventually, having lost all hope and having no other choice, I decided to see Ahmed Hussein. I called Bahija al-Bakri saying, "I wanted Ahmed Hussein right from the very beginning, but I am afraid of his political views. Please talk to him, and if he is still interested in taking the case, we can meet."
>
> Bahija talked to him, and a couple of days later I met Ahmed Hussein.
>
> I spoke very frankly: "You are an excellent and fearless lawyer, the best in Egypt, but your political convictions worry me. Yet there is no one else!"
>
> "A good lawyer has no political identity," he replied. "I know what Prince Namık has been accused of and how unfounded the accusations against him are. For me, from a professional point of view, this case is a

matter of prestige and principles. Therefore I shall not request any payment, and you can rest assured that I will do the very best I can. Trust me!"

As the day of the trial approached, Neslishah was summoned again by the attorney general's office, where she had previously been taken during her earlier investigation. This time she was to be confronted with Şehzade Namık Efendi. She recalled:

Although we had been acquitted, we were still under surveillance, and this situation increased further after Namık was brought to Cairo.

They summoned me again to the same place, that is, to the building of the attorney general and the intelligence office in Prince Farouk Street. After the revolution the names of all the streets were changed, including this one, but I didn't know the new name, and I still don't.[60]

The building was terrible. Thieves, murderers, prostitutes were all there. They made me wait among them for two and a half hours, just to upset me. They did not even give me a policeman to accompany me. I had to wait surrounded by thieves and prostitutes.

Then someone came and said, "You have to go upstairs." They took me upstairs to a long room. It was the office of the prosecutor in charge of the new lawsuit. He was sitting at a desk at the far end of the room; there was someone else standing beside him with his back turned to the door. I walked toward the desk. My legs were rather shaky, but I quickly pulled myself together and went on walking. As I reached the middle of the room, the man standing there turned around: it was Namık!

I felt faint, but I tried not to show it and continued to the desk, where first I shook hands with the prosecutor, and then I embraced and kissed Namık.

That large man had lost weight and become thin. I looked at the prosecutor as if to say, "Why is he in such a state, have you tortured him?" And I asked Namık in Turkish how he was. The prosecutor, in impeccable French, interrupted me saying, "Please speak only in French. You have been invited here to confront him. You are forbidden to speak in a language that I do not understand. Only French!"

Then I turned to Namık and in French I said something like, "I am happy to see you, you look well."

Namık was a kind and sweet man who had helped me immensely in the past. He was lively and funny, but incapable of keeping a secret. He would tell everything to everyone with the greatest ease. At times, he would come up with such things that you were never sure whether he was joking or telling the truth.

I openly told the prosecutor about this trait of his character. "There is no conspiracy," I said, "But even if there were, the conspirators would not take such a man among themselves."

The prosecutor was a civilized person, who did not look at me with disdain like the attorney general in my previous trial. In fact, he did not ask me to go back to that building, but he came to take my deposition at our house. I repeated the same things I had told him before and refuted all the allegations that were put forward.

A few days later I was taken to the military court again!

Ahmed Hussein defended Namık brilliantly, and he disproved all the accusations put forward by the prosecutor, one by one. In the years to come his defense was taught in law schools, but unfortunately the judges had received orders from Nasser: "You must condemn this man." As a result, in spite of all our efforts we could not save Namık from prison.

Şehzade Mahmud Namık Efendi, Sultan Reşad's grandson, was condemned to fifteen years of hard labor. He was immediately transferred to Tora Prison, a name that Egyptians mentioned with fear.

At a late hour on 10 November 1963 the warden of the prison called Şehzade Nazım Efendi, Namık's official guardian: "The inmate Mahmud Namık is unwell. Please come and bring a doctor with you." Nazım Efendi rushed to Tora Prison with a Turkish doctor living in Cairo named Saffet. Namık Efendi had had a stroke and was unconscious. Doctor Saffet said only a miracle could save him, and he suggested that his relatives should be prepared for the worst. Three days later, at five in the morning on 13 November, news arrived that he had passed away. He was barely fifty years old.

The funeral prayer took place in the garden of the prison. Some of Namık's relatives and a few Turkish citizens living in Cairo attended the funeral. He was wrapped in a shroud with seven layers of cloth, a tradition in Egypt reserved for the elite, and was buried in the private tomb of the family of his former wife, Shahrazad Rateb.

When in 1977 Neslishah transferred the mortal remains of her father Şehzade Ömer Faruk Efendi, who had passed away in Cairo in 1969, to Istanbul, she did the same for her cousin Namık Efendi, and the two şehzades were buried together in the shrine of Sultan Mahmud in the Divanyolu of Istanbul.

In the spring of 1959 the court cases that had gone on for months came to an end. Neslishah and Prince Abdel Moneim were acquitted of all the charges, but the prince's health was failing as a result of the events of the past few years, and Neslishah was also affected by what they had endured. They no longer wished to stay in Egypt, yet they knew that if they left the country, they would never be able to return.

Neslishah was first exiled in 1924 when she was three years old, hiding behind the curtains of the train station crying, "I want to go home." It was her destiny to be exiled once more. This time from Egypt.

Part Four

Turkey
Was the Caliph a Muslim?

11

The Duke of Windsor's Conga

Neslishah Sultan and Prince Abdel Moneim were both exhausted, and their health had suffered. During the hearings, Neslishah had been taking tranquilizers every day, as well as phosphorous supplements to keep herself going, and even though her troubles now seemed to be over, her nerves were shattered. The prince had developed diabetes and he had heart problems. The Greek doctor, Athanasiadis, who had been taking care of them for years was worried about their health. And of course there was always a possibility that some new tribulation would arise to disturb the peace.

They wanted to get away from the place that had caused them so much suffering and forget all that had happened. They longed to go somewhere peaceful, where they could regain their health. Then there were the children—Prince Abdel Moneim had not seen his son and daughter for five years, and missed them terribly. The letters they wrote compensated a little, but it was no longer enough, and the prince kept saying, "Let's get out of here."

Their closest friends and relatives had left Egypt, and Neslishah's mother Sabiha Sultan had been living in Istanbul for some years now. After her divorce in 1948 she had left her home in Maadi on the other side of Cairo to be closer to Neslishah, and taking a few things with her she moved to a small apartment in Heliopolis. She sent her furniture to her daughter Hanzade's house in Cairo while Hanzade was living in

Paris, but after the 1952 revolution all she owned there was confiscated along with all the belongings of her daughter and her son-in-law.

Later, Sabiha Sultan went to Paris for a while, to live with Hanzade Sultan, but as soon as the female members of the Ottoman family were allowed to return to Turkey in 1952 she moved to Istanbul. She rented a small flat in Kuyulu Bostan Street in the district of Nişantaşı, and the few things she still had in Egypt were sent to Istanbul, after which she had no further connection with Egypt.

Neslishah's two sisters had left Egypt well before the revolution and were living in Europe. Hanzade Sultan's husband, Prince Mohamed Ali Ibrahim, had asthma, and the climate in Cairo was not suitable for him, so together with his wife and children, Princess Fazile and Prince Ahmed, they moved to Paris. Necla Sultan and her husband Prince Amr Ibrahim lived in Switzerland. Necla Sultan gave birth to her son there in 1951, and they never returned to Egypt.

In 1953, when the monarchy was abolished, Prince Mohamed Ali Tewfik, the uncle of Prince Abdel Moneim and the lifelong heir to the throne of Egypt, left the country on a ship from Alexandria with his French lady companion. He had enough money to live in Europe, but he was to live only two years in Switzerland, passing away in 1955.

It was politically impossible to bring him to Egypt for burial, so he was temporarily buried in Lausanne. And as things had still not improved by 1964, Prince Abdel Moneim had his uncle's body moved to the cemetery of Karacaahmet in Istanbul, hoping one day to bring him to Cairo. Only after Nasser's death in 1970, when Anwar Sadat came to power, did the situation change. Prince Abdel Moneim was now able to return to Cairo, and during one of his visits he brought the body of Prince Mohamed Ali Tewfik with him and had him buried in the tomb of the khedives Tewfik and Abbas Hilmi, situated in the area of Afifi, in the Northern Cemetery.

Some years before the revolution, when Prince Mohamed Ali was in Paris with his nephew Prince Abdel Moneim, they went together to Lalique, the most reputable crystal maker in France, where he ordered a magnificent crystal headstone with the word 'Allah' inscribed on it, which he paid a fortune for. When it was ready it was sent to Cairo, and Prince Mohamed Ali personally placed it in the burial chamber of his father Khedive Tewfik in Afifi, where his own tomb had already been prepared. But since he died in exile, and he could not immediately be buried in Egypt, the headstone ironically ended up elsewhere. When Gamal Abd al-Nasser died in September 1970 he was buried in a new mosque built a year earlier in the district of Manshiyat al-Bakri. A headstone worthy of the revolutionary leader was required, and somebody remembered the beautiful crystal one in Prince Mohamed Ali Tewfik's empty tomb: it was removed from its original location and placed in Nasser's mausoleum. The prince probably never imagined that the headstone he had made for himself was one day to adorn the grave of the leader of the revolution who abolished the monarchy.

Youssef Kamal was one of Egypt's richest princes, and one of the most generous members of the Mohamed Ali dynasty. Every year he would go to Austria to spend the summer in Salzburg, and he was there when the revolution took place in 1952. He never returned to Egypt. But once his properties were confiscated and the revolutionary government issued the law ordering its citizens to bring their assets back from abroad he transferred all his money from Europe to Cairo and was thus left penniless. He had given a chalet in the Alps as a present to an Austrian butler who had been in his service for a number of years. The butler, hearing about his former master's precarious financial situation, and out of tremendous loyalty offered to return the chalet. The prince said, "I will not take back a gift that I have given," upon which the servant invited the prince to his chalet as a guest, and together with his sister they looked after him until his death.

Tahir Pasha, a grandson of Khedive Ismail, was one of the most intellectual princes of the family, and one of the few close friends of Neslishah and her husband while they were living in Egypt. He was also a very wealthy man and, like many members of the Mohamed Ali family, he thought of Egypt as a family corporation and he spared no expense to improve the company. He was the initiator of a specially trained police force. He was the founder or the chairman of various clubs and associations such as the Royal Historical Society, the Equestrian Club, the Aviation Club, the Fencing Club, the Automobile Club, the Agricultural Club, the Egyptian Sports Committee, and the Egyptian Olympic Committee. His most notable achievement, however, was the creation of the Mediterranean Games, which are still going strong today. The first Mediterranean Games took place in Alexandria in 1951, paid for by Tahir Pasha. He would also invite the most famous European orchestras, like the Berlin Philharmonic and its legendary conductor Wilhelm Furtwängler, to Cairo to perform at his expense.

During the 1952 revolution Tahir Pasha was in Europe, and like some of his relatives he never went back to Egypt. After the confiscation of all his assets in the country he went to Turkey, where he lived under the protection of his cousin Princess Emine Tugay, the wife of Ambassador Fuad Hulusi Tugay, who had played the leading role in the 1954 diplomatic crisis between Cairo and Ankara. But though they were both in their seventies, Princess Emine did not allow her cousin to live with her under the same roof. When Neslishah asked her, "Are you still afraid of gossip, even at this age?" she said, "You don't know this country, better safe than sorry." Tahir Pasha died at the age of seventy-three in January 1970.

Neslishah Sultan and Prince Abdel Moneim were now almost alone in Cairo, as most of their relatives had left the country, and the prince's health was declining day by day. One day, Doctor Athanasiadis visited an administrator close to Gamal Abd al-Nasser and said, "If this man remains here, he will soon be dead. What's more, you will be held responsible for his death, and it will be difficult for you to wriggle out of this accusation." The doctor's warning served its purpose: the government sent word to the prince that if he wished to leave Egypt they would be prepared to grant him an exit visa.

Neslishah's second exile began on the morning of 29 May 1959, when she left Egypt with her husband. The prince, who since early childhood had seen so much of politics and of life—from days of prosperity to days in courtrooms—knew as he boarded the plane for Paris that a significant chapter of his life was coming to an end, and that he might never see Egypt again. Neslishah recalled:

Abbas was studying in England; İkbal was attending a school in Paris. To be close to my daughter we went to Paris, and settled in a small hotel on one of the avenues in Passy. It was a simple hotel but a decent one.

Every day we would walk to Hanzade's house, have lunch there, and sit in the living room until evening. I was such a nervous wreck that I did not want to go anywhere or see anyone. Moneim would go out to meet his friends. He would often visit Prince Omar Halim and spend time with him. In the evening, we would usually stay in our hotel.

We spent about a year and a half in this hotel room in Paris.

Europe eventually became expensive, and we did not have that much money, so we decided to sell the house that Moneim had inherited from his father in Illiers.

In the days when we traveled to Europe from Egypt, we would always spend a few days in Illiers, at the beginning or the end of the summer. During the time when we were not allowed to leave Egypt, Hanzade had taken my children on holiday there on a couple of occasions, as it was their home, and also because she thought it would boost their morale. There was a large wood surrounding the house with animals wandering around, where the children used to have a great time.

We finally found a buyer for the house after a year and a half, and sold it immediately. So at last we had some money. Then İkbal went to a school in Switzerland, and in order to be with her we also moved there and settled in a hotel in Montreux. My youngest sister Necla lived in a villa nearby. We would have lunch at the hotel and in the evening we would walk to my sister's house for dinner.

The Montreux Palace Hotel had restored its old wing into apartments, which were rented both furnished and unfurnished. As we wanted to have a home again, we rented an unfurnished flat, which was one of the nicest ones they had. It was on the first floor, with a large terrace, and very quiet.

We furnished the flat with the furniture from the house that we had just sold in Illiers. The furniture had belonged to the khedive and was nice. Whatever else we needed we bought in Montreux.

Life was comfortable at the Montreux Palace. The hotel provided the cleaning and the laundry. They would bring us towels or kitchen utensils if needed, and even breakfast if we so desired.

In Switzerland, we came across several of our friends whom we knew from Egypt: Peter Ustinov, Tahir Pasha (the son of King Fuad's sister), members of prominent families from the time of the Ottoman Empire, and many others. We would spend our evenings visiting them, or they would come to us.

One day Moneim said, "We should buy you a car," so we bought a large Opel. We would go back and forth to Lausanne, while in winter after İkbal had gone to school in the morning, I would go skiing and when there was no snow left, I would go riding at the riding club.

We had been going to the Salzburg Music Festival since 1946. Many times I listened to Wilhelm Furtwängler, the conductor of the Berlin Philharmonic Orchestra, and the pianist Arthur Schnabel. While we lived in Switzerland, we never missed a festival in Salzburg.

The first time we attended the festival, Furtwängler conducted the opening concert. Years later Karajan came to the festival, and Clemens Krauss, the conductor of the Vienna orchestra, also gave excellent concerts there. We also listened to Arturo Benedetti Michelangeli, who was still a young man at the time.

In 1948, I broke my leg badly while skiing, and I had to spend months in the hospital. The doctors had said, "We have to amputate her leg if we are to save her," but Moneim would not allow it, saying, "If you amputate the leg of a woman at this young age, she will not live." After several operations my leg began to heal, but I was bored to tears. The doctors told me, "Don't move around too much, go somewhere close." So we went to the festival in Lucerne.

The most famous artists in the world were performing that year in Lucerne. Now and then we would also go to the Bayreuth music festival. We had become friends with Furtwängler when he came to conduct concerts in Cairo. At times when I could not find a seat for a concert, he would have a chair placed for me behind the orchestra, close to the backstage, from where I would listen to the music practically in the middle of the orchestra.

Beethoven's Ninth Symphony, which Furtwängler conducted in Bayreuth in July 1951, was certainly the best performance ever executed until then. The chorale was magnificently sung by the soprano Elizabeth Schwarzkopf. I went to that concert with my mother, and it was one of the finest performances I had ever attended in my life.

During the years that followed, Moneim had had enough of concerts in Salzburg, joining me only if Furtwängler was conducting. So it was either Tahir Pasha or Lászlo Almásy, the famous 'English Patient,' who would accompany me. Almásy loved music and knew how to appreciate it, but he was not well off and could not afford the concert ticket, so he was very happy to escort me.

Life in Europe helped them forget the difficult times they had lived through in Egypt. Neslishah recalled:

When we used to go to Europe before the revolution we were often invited to receptions, especially to the ones given by the aristocracy. We did not attend all of them, but if the invitations came from friends or if we thought we would see some interesting people we would go. The same happened when we moved to Europe.

The Aga Khan had a fabulous villa surrounded by a large garden near Cannes, which he had named Yakymour. The house itself was nothing special, it looked more like a bungalow than anything else, but the garden was priceless. It was built as a terrace garden with a pool that extended all the way from the the top to the entrance. During some of his receptions he had candles placed in walnut shells floating in the pool, as they used to do in Iran.

His receptions were rather strange, or at least surprising. On one occasion my husband and I were sitting in a corner chatting with Otto (Otto von Habsburg, last heir to the throne of the Austro-Hungarian Empire). The Duke of Windsor, the former King Edward VIII of Britain who had abdicated, and his wife the Duchess were amongst the guests. A new dance was very popular at that time, in which the men and women would hold each other by the waist and form a kind of queue like a snake, going round the garden or running from one end of the house to the other in a long chain. Otto told us that a prominent female member of the British royal family loved this dance and said that he had seen her doing it at a reception. "I don't believe you!" I said. "How could such a distinguished lady take part in such a ridiculous thing?"

Then all of a sudden pandemonium broke loose in the garden! Clifton Webb, the actor who played the title role in the Mr. Belvedere films, got up and said, "Come on let's dance," taking the Duke and Duchess of Windsor behind him in a line, and other guests joined in. Clifton Webb was leading what looked like a chain, and they were all running around the house and the garden like madmen. Some of the society ladies had also joined the dance.

I was both astounded and horrified at the sight of this line of people shouting their heads off. The former king of Great Britain, the woman for whom he had renounced to the throne, and the most renowned names of European high society were all running around.

"Do you believe me now?" asked Otto. It was impossible not to believe him: if even the former king danced as if he were part of a train, who knows what the royal lady mentioned by Otto would do!

But Switzerland was expensive, and the money they had obtained from the sale of Illiers was starting to run out. When İkbal graduated from school in 1964 they began to think about settling down somewhere else. Prince Abdel Moneim wanted to move to Istanbul, where he had enjoyed life as a young man, but the question was how they would live there and how they would cover their expenses. He decided to go to Istanbul to see what things would be like, and leaving Neslishah and İkbal in Switzerland, he went to Istanbul on his own—driving all the way in his tiny three-wheeled Messerschmitt car.

Willy Messerschmitt, the manufacturer of the combat aircraft used by Germany during the Second World War, had been imprisoned by the Allies after the war for two years, and after his release was forbidden from producing arms and aircraft. So the great aeronautical inventor spent years manufacturing sewing machines, prefabricated houses, and a small three-wheeled car that bore his name, with a door that opened from the top. Prince Abdel Moneim, who was mad about cars, had seen this odd masterpiece of technology named the Messerschmitt Kabinenroller and liked it. He bought the KR200 model, and drove from Switzerland to Istanbul in it.

He filled the car with a couple of suits and a few things he might need on the trip. He first went to Italy, crossed the Adriatic Sea on a car ferry, and drove through the mountains of Greece to Istanbul. He went to stay with his older sister Princess Atiya in Kızıltoprak, on the Asian side of the city, and began to look into how, where, and on what they would be able to live.

A few weeks later Neslishah, waiting in Montreux, received a telegram from her husband saying, "You can come now." She recalled:

> We did not have much money left, so we needed to live somewhere cheaper. When Moneim said, "Let's move to Istanbul," I agreed immediately. It was my homeland, and at the time life was not expensive there.
>
> There was another reason for wanting to move to Turkey: our children were growing up, and if they remained in Europe they might have been likely to marry non-Muslims. We wanted our future daughter-in-law and son-in-law to be Muslims. When we lived in Nice my parents told us that they had had the same anxieties about my sisters and me. Now I fully understood their concerns.
>
> I remember every moment of my return to my beloved country. Abbas was at school in England, and I left with İkbal in my car. From Montreux, we arrived at the Italian border and stopped in Milan, where Prince Amr, my sister's husband, had arranged for someone to reserve us a room in a hotel.
>
> We spent the night in Milan, and the following day we went to an excellent restaurant, then we took care of the formalities needed to ship

our belongings from Montreux to Istanbul. I thought, "While we are in Italy I want to show Pompeii to İkbal," so we drove there, and then we took a ferry from Naples to Istanbul.

While living in exile I grew up longing for my country. My mother had friends coming back and forth from Istanbul, whom I had asked to bring me a handful of Turkish soil—unfortunately they forgot, and no one ever fulfilled my wish. But now I had finally landed in Istanbul, and I was very happy to be here. I felt as if I were part of the city, and that I belonged there.

Neslishah had been just three years old when she had left Istanbul in 1924, and she returned for the first time in 1947, as an Egyptian princess with a diplomatic visa. Later, she applied for Turkish nationality, and in the spring of 1957 she obtained the citizenship that had been stripped from her thirty-three years before. She was never to forget an upsetting incident that occurred at the police department during the procedures to establish her identity. She recalled:

One day they took me to the police department to complete the formalities for my citizenship. They made me sit, they took my fingerprints as if I were a criminal, and fired questions at me as if it were the last judgment.

They asked: "Who was your mother, who was your father, what was their religion?" Then they wanted to know about my grandparents and asked even stranger questions: "What was Sultan Vahideddin's religion? And your other grandfather, Abdülmecid Efendi, was he a Muslim?" At which point I just exploded: "Shame on you! Both were caliphs. One of my grandfathers was both sultan and caliph; the other was caliph. How dare you!" I shouted. "What can we do, Madam, these are the instructions we have been given," they replied, "We are obliged to ask you these questions; we have been ordered to do so." "You should know the answer," I told them. "Can a Christian or a Jew become caliph? You should be ashamed of yourself for asking! If this is the order you have received, don't question me, write the answer yourself."

In spite of fielding such bizarre questions, she was glad to become a Turkish citizen again, and now she was glad to be back in Istanbul. There was a problem, though: they had to find a place to stay until they found a house to live in. Neslishah recalled:

We did not have a place where the family could live all together. Moneim was staying in Kızıltoprak at his sister Princess Atiya's house. He told me, "You will not be comfortable here, we have to find you a place on the European side." So I stayed with my friends Princess Tita[61] and her husband Mürsel in Yeniköy. İkbal moved in with Princess Wijdan, my mother's friend. My husband and I went house-hunting from morning to night.

We looked around for a house for weeks, but nothing was suitable. Just as I was thinking we were homeless, one day we found a place to rent on the Bosphorus in Baltalimanı. The house was large enough for all of us, but there was a problem: there were no cupboards in the house! I said to the owner, "Where am I going to put the stuff that is in the cardboard boxes; there are no cupboards here!" "Keep them in your trunks," the man suggested. I told him that there was not even room to store the luggage. "Put them under the beds," he replied, "We always do that."

We rented the house and tried to make it livable. First, we ordered several cupboards. There were windows everywhere but no rods or rails to hold the curtains, so then we had to care of that as well, and after quite a long time we finally settled in.

Prince Mohamed Ali Tewfik, my husband's uncle, had passed away a few years before. He had left us some money, but somehow we had not been able to settle the inheritance, which took years to resolve, and we received our share only after we moved to Istanbul. It was only then that we became more comfortable financially, so we decided to buy a place of our own, and once more we started looking for a house.

My husband found an old wooden *yalı* that he wanted to buy. The house was not dilapidated, on the contrary it was quite well kept, but I have always been afraid that something might happen to a wooden building. Moneim was saying, "Let's buy it," while I kept repeating, "I don't want it." This conversation went on for weeks, until the argument ended of its own accord when the *yalı* burned down!

Then we found a new *yalı* that was being built by the well-known architect Sedat Hakkı Eldem. We both liked the house, so we bought it and moved in.

That is how I returned to my country, and I am very pleased to have done so.

While Prince Abdel Moneim and Neslishah Sultan moved to Turkey with their daughter İkbal, their son Abbas stayed in Europe to continue his studies. He attended a Jesuit school in France, before going to Millfield in Somerset, England, where after graduating he went to Oxford to study economics. He married Mediha, from the Mumtaz family of Cairo, and worked in finance. He joined Grieveson Grant, a well-known company of stockbrokers in England, then moved to other similar firms. At one point he established his own business, and eventually in 1989 he became the head of Concorde Group, managing investments in Egypt.

In 1960, before moving to Turkey with her parents, Princess İkbal received a marriage proposal from Crown Prince Hassan, the son of King Muhammad V of Morocco. The king held the title of 'caliph,' but this caliphate was recognized only in Morocco, so he wanted his son to marry someone who was a direct descendent of the real caliph, the one who had been accepted as such by the entire Sunni world, so as to give his dynasty a long-lasting religious foundation.

The proposal was discussed at length in the family (with the sad events lived by Hanzade Sultan's daughter Princess Fazile in 1958 in mind), and eventually it was decided that Princess İkbal was not to become the future queen of Morocco.

But unforeseen circumstances anyway intervened: in February 1961 King Muhammad passed away during surgery. Rumors immediately spread that the king had been killed by the French, and there were even suggestions that his son had planned the murder. While the European press agonized over "Who Killed the King?" the crown prince ascended the throne as Hasan II.

A few days later a high-level Moroccan delegation paid a visit to Prince Abdel Moneim and Neslishah, saying that the very much desired marriage proposal they had made had to be withdrawn, due to the political situation in Morocco: after the death of the king a power struggle had begun among the tribes, and the new king was compelled to marry the daughter of a clan leader to put an end to the conflict.

So Princess İkbal did not become queen, and during the same year the young king of Morocco married Leila Latifa Hammu, a member of a prominent Moroccan tribe.

12
All That Is Beautiful Has Been Made by My Grandfathers

Neslishah lived in Istanbul from 1964 until her death in 2012. Nearly all the friends she had from her childhood and from her youth, or relatives and acquaintances who had had an impact on her life, had been scattered to the four corners of the globe. Some were no longer alive—of those, some had passed away peacefully, but many had died after much yearning, suffering, and hardship. Some did not even have a tomb to mark their passing.

The first in the family to pass away was Şehzade Ömer Faruk Efendi, on 28 March 1969 in Egypt, never having seen again the country that had expelled him in 1924. His last dream had been to return to Turkey and die in Istanbul. A few of his friends tried to bend the legal system for his return, but to no avail. He was buried in Cairo, next to his cousin Şehzade Namık Efendi, who died in Tora Prison. In 1977 Neslishah requested permission from Ankara to bring their bodies back to Istanbul for burial. Permission was granted, on condition that "it is done quietly and nobody hears about it."

The two şehzades were buried in the shrine of Sultan Mahmud in the district of Cağaloğlu. Sheikh Nazmi Efendi, who was in charge of the burial procedures, declared that the body of Faruk Efendi had remained intact in spite of the passing of the years.

Neslishah's mother, Sabiha Sultan, even though divorced from the man who was the great love of her life, never forgot him, and she passed away two years after him, in Istanbul in 1971.

"Don't bury me in the tomb of a sultan, bury me in the Aşiyan cemetery," Sabiha Sultan told her children and her friends. So long as her father Sultan Vahideddin was buried in the courtyard of a mosque in Damascus, instead of the shrine of one of the sultans in Istanbul, she did not want to be buried in an imperial tomb. She was buried in the Aşiyan cemetery as she requested, where she is not alone, as her daughters Hanzade Sultan, who passed away in Paris in 1998, Necla Sultan, who died in Lisbon in 2006, and finally Neslishah Sultan, who died in Istanbul in 2012, rest by her side.

Neslishah's husband, Prince Mohamed Abdel Moneim, died in Istanbul in December 1979. His body was taken to Egypt—the country he had been obliged to leave twenty-one years earlier—and he was buried in Cairo with a state funeral. Throughout their married life, Prince Abdel Moneim always referred to his wife as his *shirika*—his partner.

The prince had witnessed many important events in the Middle East, and was part of several of them. He was born as heir to the throne of Egypt, and his last duty was as prince regent. He lived through many kinds of trouble, but he never spoke about them.

He witnessed the downfall of the Ottoman Empire and the Kingdom of Egypt, and his destiny was to be part of that downfall. Sometimes he would be asked, "Which country do you feel you belong to? Turkey or Egypt?" To which he would reply, "You wouldn't understand. I am Ottoman! This concept is difficult to explain, and difficult to understand. I am just an Ottoman, that's all!"

In the mid-1970s, the prince began to miss Cairo, and wished to see the city again. Nasser was dead, Anwar Sadat had replaced him, and the hard-line politics of Egypt were slowly mellowing. When President Sadat said on the radio, addressing Egyptians living abroad, "Forget the old animosity and come back," Prince Abdel Moneim wrote to him, "I also wish to return to Egypt." Sadat replied, "Welcome!"

He went to the Egyptian Consulate in Istanbul with his daughter İkbal. The *yalı* that housed the consulate had belonged to the prince's grandmother, Emine Tewfik. As a child he had played in its large reception rooms, and as a young man he had lived there for some time. He knew every room, every corner of that building. He asked to see the consul, and handed him his passport, which had been canceled years before, saying, "Please renew my passport, I want to see my country."

He received his new passport and for the first time in years was able to return to Cairo. He went for a few weeks, on his own, and stayed in his house in Heliopolis, which was in a terrible state—some of the furniture was missing, and the rest was falling apart. After the prince's departure from Egypt, one of the Free Officers had come to the house with a large truck and taken away whatever took his fancy. The truck was so loaded that even the tax inspectors, who were well used to the officers' looting, said, "You have taken too much, we could get into trouble—please sign this list." And the officer who was emptying Neslishah's house was made to sign for what he took.

Later, the house became a state guesthouse, to host visiting African heads of state. Patrice Lumumba, the Congolese prime minister, stayed there for some time and, wishing to leave a memento of his visit, carved his name with a knife on the beautiful English dining table in the reception room.

Prince Abdel Moneim returned to Istanbul after his visit, and went back to Cairo a couple of times during the following years, but always alone. Neslishah, who was still trying to forget what she had gone through in Egypt, was too afraid to return.

In 1979, following the death of the prince, the consul general of Egypt in Istanbul paid Neslishah a visit, expressing his condolences on behalf of President Anwar Sadat, and informing her that the Egyptian government would like to take the prince's body to Cairo to give him a state funeral. So it was that Neslishah, with her son and daughter, went to Cairo for the first time since their departure in the 1950s. The president put a chauffeur-driven Mercedes and an aide-de-camp at their disposal. The house in Heliopolis was opened for their stay, all their meals were provided by the presidential palace, and they were even told that they could live in the house whenever they wanted to come back to Egypt. Prince Abdel Moneim's funeral took place in the Rifai Mosque, and he was buried in the family shrine of the khedive in the Afifi section of the Northern Cemetery.

As the prince was being interred in the large family mausoleum, and Neslishah waited outside, shouts were suddenly heard from the burial chamber, and an old man emerged, tears streaming down his face as he walked toward Neslishah. He stopped in front of her and greeted her, then continued his shouting: "Ah, Efendina! You were the only honest man in the country, but I betrayed you, and you left the country to the thieves. Please forgive me!" He went on to curse the makers of the 1952 revolution at length, then he kissed Neslishah's hand and embraced her, still in tears.

Neslishah thought his face was familiar. She had the impression of having seen him before, and then she remembered—and froze: this old man shouting at the top of his voice at her husband's funeral was none other than the original figurehead of the revolution and Egypt's first president, General Mohamed Naguib.

Gamal Abd al-Nasser had forced Naguib to resign in November 1954. He was sent to prison for some time and then kept under house arrest in what had been the villa of a daughter of Princess Nimet Muhtar, close to al-Marg in the north of Cairo. He had been living there in one room for years, with just a bathtub and a toilet. When he heard of the death of Prince Abdel Moneim he said, "I worked with the prince, he was good to me; I must attend his funeral," and he was granted permission to attend, though he was not in good health. He wanted to shout out his errors and regrets, and felt the need to apologize to the prince, at least on his grave.

Once the burial was over, Neslishah had to make thank-you calls: it was an old tradition in Egypt to visit those who had attended the funeral. She first went to see the woman who held the same position that she had once held in the past, that is Jihan Sadat, Egypt's first lady, and thank her husband Anwar Sadat for his help. Then she visited all the others she needed to thank. The visit to thank General Naguib was done by Neslishah's son, Abbas. He went to al-Marg in the car that the president's office had put at their disposal, and saw for himself the miserable conditions that the former president was living in. Since old habits were still in play in Egypt, and in case some intelligence officer was following and reporting on the movements of the family of the deposed regent, to avoid any misunderstanding or suspicions Prince Abbas took with him the aide-de-camp who had been assigned to them by the office of the president, and made sure the man was present during his conversation with the general.

After moving to Turkey in 1964, Neslishah spoke to the press on only two occasions, in the form of two statements to the media.

In 1966 the Turkish government was discussing the possibility of bringing Sultan Vahideddin's mortal remains from Damascus to Istanbul, as had been done for the poet Nazım Hikmet, who had been buried in Moscow but had wished to be buried, as in his poem, "in Anatolia under a walnut tree." Ankara thought this gesture could bring social stability to the country. Neslishah issued a press release to the newspapers on behalf of her sisters Hanzade Sultan and Necla Sultan, her cousin Hümeyra Hanımsultan, and herself, stating that they did not wish Sultan Vahideddin's remains to be moved to Istanbul:

> 1. We have always wanted for the family burials to be brought to Turkey, but this event should not create problems in the country. The life of the sultan was a troubled one, so he should be left to rest in peace in his grave.
>
> 2. Damascus, where Sultan Vahideddin is now buried in his eternal sleep, is both a Muslim land and the center of the largest province of the Ottoman Empire. Therefore, our grandfather's grave is not in a foreign land, but within the boundaries of the empire he used to rule. Furthermore, he is in a mosque built for his forefathers Sultan Süleyman the Magnificent and Sultan Selim II, where twenty-six other members of our family have been buried.
>
> 3. All Turkish graves abroad should be brought back to Turkey, but the comparisons that have been made in some circles with regard to these two burials are unacceptable. To equate the mortal remains of poets with those of the sultans, saying, "If the grave of such a person is brought back, then that of Vahideddin should also come back" is not a pleasant thing.

Neslishah's second and last statement to the press was given after the death of her ninety-seven-year-old cousin Şehzade Osman Ertuğrul Efendi, the grandson of Sultan Abdülhamid II and the head of the Ottoman dynasty, on 23 September 2009. He had been the last şehzade born during the time of the empire. Neslishah declared that after the death of her cousin, there was no other şehzade born during the time of the empire and raised with the essential knowledge of the rules of the imperial protocol, so the concept of 'dynasty' and of 'head of the dynasty' should now become history, and she stressed that "from now on the Ottomans will remain just a family."

Two years later a similar announcement was made by the Habsburg dynasty, one of the oldest families of Europe, which had ruled the Austro-Hungarian Empire for centuries. Archduke Otto von Habsburg, the head of the Habsburgs and the last heir to the throne born during their empire, passed away in Germany in July 2011. He had been a close friend of Neslishah. He was buried in Vienna in the imperial crypt of the Capuchin Church, but following a Habsburg tradition his heart was removed and buried in Hungary, in the Pannonhalma Abbey. After the funeral the Habsburg family released a statement to the press saying, "As there are no other princes or princesses born during the reign of the empire, there will be no other funeral ceremony like that of Archduke Otto. The members of the family will no longer be buried in the Capuchin Church but in ordinary cemeteries."

A life that began in palaces, celebrated at birth with the firing of cannons and commemorated with gold coins . . . twice exiled . . . days of high living and majestic splendor, magnificent jewels, and designer clothes . . . days when there was only one dress to wear, which became so tattered that it was unwearable to go to school . . . the first lady of a foreign country . . . long-lasting friendships with kings, politicians, and artists mentioned in history books, encyclopedias, and movies . . . dangerous and fearful days spent in military courts in front of menacing judges . . . glorious parties with the most elite members of European high society . . . multiple raids

on houses, with the confiscation of possessions, including children's toys
. . . and so much more . . . .

Neslishah lived all of the above. Forty years of her life were spent in
exile, and her last fifty years in her country of birth. In her eighties, alone
at home, she would reminisce about the sadness, the disappointments,
the anxieties, and the happiness she had experienced during her life . . . a
life so intensely lived that it could fill several lifetimes. She alone could
say whether her life was filled more with sorrow or with joy. Many were
the things she wished to forget, to erase from her memory, remembering
only the good times.

Alone in her house, her mind would take her to her grandfather the
caliph's painting studio in Dolmabahçe Palace, where she would watch
him paint. Lightly touching the tip of her nose with his brush he would
whisper, "Look my pretty one, how this red freckle suits you!"

Then to the Palace of Yıldız, to her other grandfather, Sultan Vahideddin, where she would see herself breathing the smoke of her Şahbaba's
cigarette, hanging on the tip of an ivory cigarette holder, as he smiled
affectionately at her behind his pince-nez.

She would hear her mother Sabiha Sultan playing Chopin at the
piano and ending the piece as all the pianists at the palace did, with an
oriental melody. As Neslishah attentively followed her mother's fingers
on the keyboard, she would feel the delicate rustle of her grandmother
Nazikeda Kadınefendi's long gown brushing past her and slipping away,
far away into thin air.

Looking out of the window she would glance at the slender minarets
of Istanbul rising toward the sky, the graceful domes, and the palaces,
and even though the city had changed a great deal she was quite aware
that the elegance of the skyline could be still perceived, and would say,
"All that is beautiful has been made by my grandfathers!"

Epilogue

After a long and eventful life, Neslishah passed away in the early hours of 2 April 2012, at her home in Istanbul, a few minutes away from her grandfather's Dolmabahçe Palace on the shores of the Bosphorus. She was ninety-one years old.

During the last years of her life, burdened with ailments, she rarely left the house. She described her daily life:

> I am resting, I am living the life of the old. I am past eighty-five, I am taking it easy. I don't go out much. After getting up in the morning, I go downstairs and organize the house; then I arrange my flowers. I have always listened to music while doing housework. I still do. Mozart is my favorite composer. Then I watch the news, but what I do most is read. It doesn't matter whether what I read is in Turkish, French, or English, but I prefer not to read in German, as it has been so long since I last spoke German that I have somewhat forgotten the language and have become lazy. When I have had enough of reading I play patience, and while doing all this, I try to forget the unpleasant things that happened to me in the past.

When the republic was declared, and for several decades following, Turkey rejected her Ottoman past. But toward her final years the narrative changed, and there was a new acceptance at government level of the Ottoman legacy. From the beginning the policy of the Turkish republic toward the Ottomans was one of denigration. Even in primary school textbooks the Ottoman dynasty was described as corrupt, as having no further relevance to Turkey or the Turks, and as having brought evil upon the country's people. Only a few sultans—those who had achieved significant victories in the fifteenth and sixteenth centuries—were spared from this rhetoric. The decline of the empire and the loss of territories were attributed to the sultans' lack of vision. The later rulers were persistently discredited, and Sultan Vahideddin was declared a traitor.

The Turkish people, however, had never denied their Ottoman heritage, in spite of the regime's ideology of vituperation. Today, there is still a small minority that believes the Turks only entered the arena of history after the advent of the republic in 1923, but the majority of the population is at peace with the past: they look at the Ottoman era as part of a history to be proud of.

When Neslishah moved back to Turkey in 1964, the attitude of the government was still to discredit the Ottoman legacy, which led to political fear, and so the words "Ottoman dynasty" were used with caution. Toward the end of the 1980s, with the rise of the conservatives in Turkey, the state mitigated its political discourse. Schoolbooks still mentioned Sultan Vahideddin as a "traitor," but officially a rapprochement with the Ottomans had begun. The media called it "reconciliation with history." In 1999 this went a step further when the then president of the Turkish republic, Süleyman Demirel, attended the celebrations for the 700th anniversary of the Ottoman Empire. An Ottoman exhibition was organized in Paris at the Palace of Versailles, which President Demirel, accompanied by an Ottoman Janissary band, opened alongside President Chirac of France.

Neslishah was officially invited to take part in these commemorations as the representative of the Ottoman dynasty. Unfortunately she was recovering from surgery at the time and could not attend any of the events, but she was surprised and pleased to receive the letter of invitation from the Presidency. She told her close friends:

I can't believe how things have changed! When we first arrived thirty years ago, some people would not even say hello, calling us 'the grandchildren of the traitor,' while now I am being invited by the state to represent the family.

Neslishah Sultan became something of a symbol of the country's reconciliation with the Ottoman past. Whenever the empire was mentioned, or Ottoman culture, or even "the good old days," the member of the Ottoman family that came to everyone's mind was Neslishah. For those interested in the past, when they thought about Ottoman nobility, she was the sole reference. And she was a role model for the ladies of the republican bourgeoisie in search of an Ottoman identity.

Toward the end of her life, Neslishah was preoccupied by an issue she thought needed her attention, and she believed that this was her last duty to her family. With the growing interest in the House of Osman, some members of the Ottoman family in Turkey, in particular the younger generation, were eager to be known and seen by the public. Neslishah was very much against what she called seeking undeserved recognition.

Sabiha Sultan, the daughter of the last Ottoman emperor Sultan Vahideddin, wrote in her unpublished memoirs:

> Today is the day of the foundation of the republic. Our family has done its duty and passed on. The Ottoman history is a legacy that can make our people proud. The empire was a different era, but it belonged to the Turks, just as today's republic belongs to the Turks.

Sabiha Sultan knew a great deal about the last years of the empire, yet she never spoke to a journalist, and she always remained a very private person.

Neslishah, following her mother's example, very rarely gave interviews. She believed that the Ottoman dynasty was now part of history and that the Ottomans living in Turkey were ordinary citizens who should not become involved in politics or be in the limelight of the media—she saw this kind of attitude as both undignified and not in conformity with the Ottoman tradition.

For these reasons, and until her last breath, she encouraged the younger members of the family to live a quiet life, away from the public sphere, while she tried to stop those who would not do so, and she pretty much succeeded. But she worried and used to say:

> I am the last person in the family who has lived during the time of the empire. This is the way I was brought up, this is how we should behave, yet I shudder when I think of what the younger generation might do when I am gone.

Around midday on 2 April 2012 the television channels announced the death of Neslishah Sultan as headline news, and the following day it made the front page of all the newspapers.

When she passed away she was the oldest member of the Ottoman family to have been born in the days of the empire. For the first time in the eighty-nine years of the Turkish republic, the president, the prime minister, the speaker of the parliament, and several members of the cabinet publicly expressed their condolences on the passing of a member of the Ottoman family. In his message, President Abdullah Gül, declared:

> I am deeply saddened by the death of Neslishah Osmanoğlu, the oldest member of the Ottoman dynasty, whose founders established the Ottoman State, a state that became an empire that left its mark on the history of the world. My deepest condolences go to her family and to all those who loved her. May God rest her soul.

Neslishah Sultan's funeral took place the following day, on 3 April 2012, at the Yıldız Mosque adjacent to the Yıldız Palace, which for years had been the official residence of Sultan Abdülhamid, then of Sultan Vahideddin, and the central office of their respective governments.

Abdülhamid, who reigned for thirty-three years, made his weekly Friday appearances on the way to this mosque for the noon prayer. A procession in grand style known as the *Cuma Selâmlığı* ('the Friday salutation') followed him, and extensive security measures were taken on these occasions. The processions were highly regarded by the foreigners in the city, who applied days in advance to obtain permission to attend them. The last imperial *Cuma Selâmlığı* was held for Sultan Vahideddin, Neslishah's grandfather, on 10 November 1922. Ninety years later, Neslishah Sultan was the first member of the Ottoman family to have a funeral service in this Yıldız Mosque.

The funeral was attended by Neslishah's immediate family, members of the Ottoman family living in Istanbul, the deputy prime minister, several cabinet ministers and members of parliament, and members of the public. It was the deputy prime minister who conveyed his condolences to the family on behalf of the government.

The coffin was adorned according to family tradition, covered with part of an eighteenth-century Kaaba drape. After the funerary prayers the coffin was taken to the cemetery in Aşiyan overlooking the Bosphorus, where she was buried next to her mother Sabiha Sultan and her sisters Hanzade Sultan and Necla Sultan.

Turkish laws require a government resolution, approved by the President, in order to be buried in the shrines of the sultans. While Neslishah was still alive her friends had taken care of all the necessary formalities, and had even chosen for her to be buried in the courtyard of the Yavuz Selim Mosque, where Sultan Selim I, the ruler who annexed Egypt to the Ottoman Empire in 1517, is enshrined. But Neslishah, during the last years of her life, declared that she wished to be buried next to her mother and sisters in the cemetery of Aşiyan— Sabiha Sultan had requested in her will to be buried in the Aşiyan cemetery, refusing to be buried in the shrine of the sultans as long as her father Sultan Vahideddin's body remained in Damascus; her two daughters were buried next to her, and now Neslishah Sultan was also laid to rest with them.

After the funeral, and for the first time ever, the government put at the disposal of Neslishah's family the large mansion at the Yıldız Palace, used by Sultan Abdülhamid as his office during his reign, to receive the condolences of state ministers, members of parliament, and hundreds of ordinary people.

Neslishah Sultan now rests close to her mother and sisters in the Aşiyan cemetery in Rumelihisarı, the village where she spent the first years of her childhood, just a hundred meters from the fortress built by her ancestor Mehmed II during the conquest of Istanbul in 1453.

Notes

1   Sultan Vahideddin's life before his succession to the throne from Murat
    Bardakçı, *Şahbaba*, Istanbul: Everest Publication, 2015, 35–77.
2   Several reports given to Abdülhamid regarding Vahideddin Efendi and the
    other şehzades are today preserved in the Ottoman Archives of the Prime
    Ministry. For example: "The arrival and departure of Doctor Arif Paşa and a
    lady at the palace of Vahideddin," Y.PRK. File 28, Folder 121; "Mecid Efendi
    visits Vahideddin's Palace in Çengelkoy and returns after midnight," Y.PRK.
    ZB. File 11, Folder 118; "Some individuals in the employ of Vahideddin
    Efendi in Çengelkoy fought and were wounded because of a woman," Y.PRK.
    ZB. File 22, Folder 91; "Report on the movements and events concerning
    Yusuf İzzeddin Efendi, Vahideddin Efendi, and Tevfik Efendi," Y.PRK.SGE
    File10, Folder 77; "Report on the whereabouts of Seyfeddin Efendi, Vahided-
    din Efendi, and the imperial son-in-law Ahmed Paşa as well as the people that
    visited them," Y.PRK.ZB. File 10, Folder 104.
3   Sultan Vahideddin had four more wives after Nazikeda Kadınefendi: İnşirah,
    Şadiye Meveddet, Nevvare, and Nevzad Hanım. Şadiye Meveddet Hanım gave
    birth to his son Ertuğrul Efendi. He divorced İnşirah and Nevvare years before
    leaving Turkey.
4   Tevfik Paşa descended from a princely family of Crimea. He was born in
    Istanbul in 1845. He attended the Military Academy and graduated as a cavalry
    lieutenant. When he heard the rumor about him that he had been promoted
    because he had paid a visit to a general during a religious festivity, he resigned
    from the army and first joined the Sublime Porte then the Department of For-
    eign Affairs. He started as a clerk and in time became ambassador, moving from
    one embassy to the other. During the Second Constitutionalist Period, he was
    chosen to be minister of foreign affairs in the government of Said Paşa. At the

time of the 31 March 1909 military uprising, he was appointed grand vizier, and at the outbreak of the Great War he was ambassador in London. Sultan Vahideddin appointed him three times as grand vizier. He formed his last government on 21 October 1920, with the task of cleaning up the mess left by Damad Ferid Paşa, and remained in this position until the sultanate was abolished in November 1922. He will be known as the last grand vizier of the Ottoman Empire, and in his words, he was "the one that had to bury the empire."

5   Ottoman Archives of the Prime Ministry, HR. IM. File 21, Folder 81.

6   For the full text of Sabiha Sultan's memoirs, see *Şahbaba*, pp. 491–97.

7   For the testimonials of Sultan Vahideddin and his daughter on the subject, see *Şahbaba*, pp. 424, 514.

8   Abdülmecid Efendi had four wives: Şehsuvar the head wife, Mehisti, Hayrünisa, and Behruze, who was thirty-two years his junior and whom he married in 1921.

9   Emine Dürriye Fuad Tugay (1897–1975) was the daughter of Mahmud Muhtar Paşa and the Egyptian Princess Nimetullah, the granddaughter of Gazi Ahmed Muhtar Paşa on her father's side and of Ismail Pasha, the khedive of Egypt, on her mother's side. Egypt's first king, Fuad, was her uncle and King Farouk her cousin. As a member of the royal family, she was wealthy and had personal assets in Egypt. She married the diplomat Fuad Hulûsi Tugay (d. 1967), the star of the January 1954 crisis that occurred between Turkey and Egypt and the son of Field Marshal Deli Fuad Paşa. In 1963, Emine Tugay wrote a book on the Egyptian royal family, *Three Centuries: Family Chronicles of Turkey and Egypt* (Oxford University Press), still considered one of the main reference books on the subject.

10   Upon his return to Istanbul, Şehzade Ömer Faruk Efendi became the president of the Fenerbahçe Football Club and remained so until March 1924, when the Ottoman family had to leave the country. He presided over the historic match known as "The Harrington Cup." Istanbul was under occupation, and the English, French, and Italian occupation troops had each formed their own football teams and played several matches against the Turkish teams, to whom they lost most of the time. The inhabitants of Istanbul, depressed by the occupation, found some solace in these victories.

But after losing so many matches, the English brought four professional players from their colonies and made a silver cup nearly a meter high, naming it after the English commander of the occupying forces, General Harrington. They played against Fenerbahçe in Taksim on 29 June 1923. The players were Şekip, Hasan, Kamil, Cafer, Kadri, İsmet, Fahir, Sabih, Alaaddin, Zeki, Ömer, and Bedri, and they defeated the English by two goals to one.

This victory brought joy not only to the inhabitants of Istanbul but also to the Turkish delegation that was then in Lausanne discussing the conditions for peace. The discussions were fierce, and the delegates tense, but the news from the match put them in a good mood, even if only for a while.

During his years in exile, Ömer Faruk Efendi always had both the Turkish flag and the Fenerbahçe flag on his table. Forty-one years after Faruk had left the presidency of the club, on 20 July 1966, he wrote in a letter to his friend the historian İsmail Hami Danişmend: "The other day, when again I was busy writing letters, the postman brought in a large envelope, which to my surprise had the emblem of Fenerbahçe on it. When I read the letter, I was even more astonished. The present director of the club wanted a picture of all the past presidents, to decorate the walls of the club. During forty-odd years, no one had shown me such interest. I was therefore amazed, moved, and touched, and tears streamed down my face. I sent them an old and a new photo of myself, as well as a picture taken in the past with members of the club, and thanked them for the attention they had bestowed upon me. The current president is also called Faruk, which might be the reason for his sympathy toward me! They even sent me a photo of the club with its insignia and an inscription at the back, which was quite moving: 'The members of the board send their respects to the past presidents of the club.' Now the photo is framed and stands by my side."

11   *Şahbaba*, pp. 519–20.

12   *Hanedan-ı saltanat azasının hal ve mevkileri ve vezaifini tayin eden nizamname*

13   Suade Hümeyra Hanımsultan (Özbaş) was the only child of Ulviye Sultan and the son of the last grand vizier Tevfik Paşa, İsmail Hakkı Bey (Okday), born in 1917 at her mother's mansion in Nişantaşı. In 1924, she was exiled along with the rest of her family. In 1939 a special law was passed for the return to Turkey of the three children of Enver Paşa, and the daughter of his wife Naciye Sultan from her second marriage. As Hümeyra's father had taken part in the War of Independence, she was also allowed to return to her country under the same law. She married Halil Özbaş, who came from a well-known family from Söke, and they had two children. She was also one of the founders of the Kismet Hotel in Kuşadası, İzmir. She died in Kuşadası on 17 May 2000.

14   Mehmed Ataker; "How Şehzade Faruk Efendi Went to Anatolia and Returned during the War of Independence" [in Turkish], *Resimli Tarih Mecmuası*, Volume 3, Nos. 29/30, May/June 1952.

15   In 1980 Neslishah Sultan donated the original telegram to the Research Centre for Islamic History, Art and Culture (IRCICA) in Istanbul, which is part of the Organization of Islamic Cooperation.

16   The text of the resolution of 1 November reads: Article 1. According to the Constitution, with this Act of Law, the Sovereign will of the Turkish people is wholly and undisputedly represented and enacted by the Turkish Grand National Assembly, and no other power or assembly that does not stem from the national will shall be recognized. Therefore, as of 16 March 1920, the Turkish Nation considers the Government in Istanbul, which is based on personal power, to be relegated forever to the annals of history. Article 2: While the Caliphate belongs to the Ottoman Dynasty, the Turkish Grand National Assembly will choose the Caliph among the most knowledgeable and appropriate candidates of this family. The Turkish State is the foundation of the seat of the Caliphate.

17   For the original text see *Şahbaba*, pp. 418–20.

18   Abdülmecid Efendi, *Green Book: Documents Concerning the Caliphate Published to Elucidate the Subject to the Islamic Public Opinion* [in Turkish], 1924, p. 1.

19   *Tanin*, November 20, 1338 (1922).

20   Tarık Mümtaz Göztepe, *The Last Ottoman Emperor Sultan Vahideddin and His Infernal Exile* [in Turkish], Sebil, Istanbul, 1978, p. 34.

21   Mustafa Sabri Efendi, *Caliphate and Kemalism* [in Turkish], edited by Sadik Albayrak, Istanbul Research Publications, 1992, p. 172.

22   *Green Book*, p. 3.

23   For the full text of the letter see *Şahbaba*, pp. 332–33.

24   Damad Şerif Paşa was born in 1874 in Istanbul. He was married to Emine Sultan, the daughter of Sultan Abdülaziz. He graduated from the Mülkiye vocational school of political sciences. Member and later president of the Council of State, he became governor of Istanbul, minister of education, minister of public works, and minister of the interior. He was one of the most learned persons of his time, and had translated Ibn Battuta's *Travels* and Machiavelli's *The Prince* into Turkish. Together with Abdülhamid's son-in-law Arif Hikmet Paşa, he convinced Sultan Abdülhamid, who had been deposed in 1909 and exiled to Salonika, to return to Istanbul at the start of the Balkan War, as the empire was threatened with losing Salonika. He was also on board the *Lorelei*, which Kaiser Wilhelm II had assigned to bring the deposed sultan back. Since his wife Emine Sultan had died in 1920, that is four years before the family was exiled, Şerif Paşa was not obliged to leave the country, yet he preferred to join the Ottoman family and live with them in exile. In his old age, he returned to Turkey and lived his last years in his mansion in Kızıltoprak. He took the surname Çavdaroğlu and died in 1958.

25   Salih Keramet Nigar, *How the Caliph Abdülmecid II Was Sent Away, Where He Lived When in Exile, When and Where He Passed Away, and When and Where He was Buried* [in Turkish], Istanbul: Inkilap & Aka, 1964, pp. 8–10.

26   After the battle of Ankara in 1402 between Timur and Sultan Bayezit, the
     Ottoman Empire went through an eleven-year period of chaos known as the
     Ottoman Interregnum. Dürrüşehvar Sultan means here that the expulsion of
     the Ottoman family from Turkey would give rise to a second interregnum,
     and that with the return of the family chaos would come to an end.

27   Dürrüşehvar Sultan, *Doğan*, Hyderabad: Matbaa-i Amire, 1948, pp. 79–93.

28   Salih Keramet Nigar, *How the Caliph Abdülmecid II Was Sent Away*, p. 10.

29   Dürrüşehvar Sultan, *Doğan*, pp. 94–95.

30   One of the yachts of the family bought during the reign of Sultan Abdülha-
     mid. Also used by Mustafa Kemal during the first years of the republic.

31   Dürrüşehvar Sultan, *Doğan*, pp. 95–97.

32   Abdülmecid Efendi, *Green Book*, p. 4.

33   Dürrüşehvar Sultan, *Doğan*, pp. 97–98.

34   Tarık Mümtaz Göztepe, *The Last Ottoman Emperor*, p. 186.

35   For details of the transportation of Sultan Vahideddin's coffin from Italy to
     Syria, see Bardakçı, *Şahbaba*, pp. 387–413.

36   Refia Sultan was born on 15 June 1891 at the Yıldız Palace in Istanbul and
     died in 1938 in Beirut. She was married to Fuad Bey and had two daughters,
     Rabia (1911–88) and Ayşe Hamide (1918–34), who died in Nice when she was
     sixteen years old from gas poisoning from the boiler while taking a bath. It
     was believed that the name Hamide was unlucky and that it was the cause of
     the young hanımsultan's death.

37   Seyfeddin Efendi (Istanbul 1874–1927 Nice) had four children: His eldest
     son Mehmed Abdülaziz Efendi (Istanbul 1901–77 Nice) was like his father a
     composer and played the tambur (a kind of lute); he made his living as a radi-
     onics practitioner. His second son Mahmud Şevket Efendi (Istanbul 1903–73
     Bagnols-sur-Cèze) died in mysterious circumstances in his house. His last
     two children, Ahmed Tevhid Efendi (Istanbul 1904–66 Beirut) and Fatma
     Gevheri Osmanoğlu (Istanbul 1904–80) were twins. Seyfeddin Efendi's wives,
     Neş'efelek and Nervaliter, both died in Nice.

38   In the Ottoman archives of the Prime Ministry are documents referring
     to Seyfeddin Efendi's financial difficulties and to his failure in some of his
     business ventures. "Şehzade Seyfeddin Efendi has been taken to court by Mr.
     Marten, a Belgian car dealer because of the money he was owed. This debt is
     to be paid by the Treasury" (Fund Y.MTV File 76 Folder 106). "On how the
     money owed by Şehzade Seyfeddin Efendi to the French tailor Mirkotoro is
     to be repaid" (Fund Y.PRK.HR File 15 Folder 23). "Means of payment for the
     debts of His Highness Seyfeddin Efendi" (Fund BEO File 3011178 Folder
     4016). "Request for payment from Şehzade Seyfeddin Efendi to the Ministry

of Public Works for money owed to Yano Gürci Efendi, director of the con-
cession of the Anatolian Railways" (Fund MV File 50 Folder 128).

39 Ayşe Osmanoğlu, *My Father, Sultan Abdülhamid* [in Turkish], Istanbul, 1984,
    p. 49.

40 The son of Şehzade Selahaddin Efendi and grandson of Sultan Murad V, born
    in Istanbul in 1895. He was the head of the Ottoman family between 1954 and
    his death in Paris in 1973. In 1920, he married Princess Karima, the daughter
    of Abbas Halim Pasha of the Egyptian royal family, and divorced her in 1932.

41 After being sent away by her uncle, Gevheri Sultan (Fatma Gevheri Osmanoğlu)
    attempted to live on her own: she left France and moved to Egypt, where for
    years she lived in cheap hotels in great financial difficulty. In 1952, when the
    female members of the Ottoman family were allowed to return to Istanbul, she
    went to live with her cousin Mihrişah Sultan (Mihriban Mihrişah Osmanoğlu,
    Istanbul 1916–87), who was the daughter of the heir to the throne Yusuf
    İzzeddin Efendi. Gevheri Sultan was an accomplished musician; she played the
    tambur (a long-necked lute), the *kemence* (a short-necked fiddle), and the *latva*
    (lute). She was also a composer like her father, Seyfeddin Efendi.

42 Kamil Killigil (1898–1962).

43 The children of Enver Paşa and Naciye Sultan were Mahpeyker Ürgüp
    (1917–2000), Türkan Mayatepek (1919–89), and Ali Enver (1921-1971). The
    daughter of Kamil Bey and Naciye Sultan was Rana Eldem (1926–2008).

44 French physicist George Claude (1870–1960), the inventor of neon light.

45 Empress Zita (1892–1989) was a Bourbon-Parma princess before marrying
    Charles I, the emperor of Austria-Hungary. She struggled her entire life for the
    return of the family to the throne, but only her mortal remains were allowed
    to return to Austria. Otto von Habsburg (1912–2011), the son of Empress Zita,
    who was the head of the Habsburg family, relinquished his claim to the Aus-
    trian throne in 1961, but he never gave up his rights to the Hungarian throne.
    On 15 July 2011 he was buried in a special ceremony for the members of the
    House of Habsburg at the Capuchin Church in Vienna. The president and the
    prime minister of Austria, as well as many members of European royal families
    and heads of state, attended his funeral. According to the Habsburg burial tra-
    dition for the head of the family, his heart was removed and taken to Hungary,
    where it was buried in the Pannonhalma Archabbey.

46 For the family disagreements and the court cases, see my book *Son Osmanlılar*,
    Istanbul: Inkilap, 2008, pp. 232–55.

47 Ahmed Shafiq (1911–76), another son of Ahmed Shafiq Pasha and Aziza
    Shafiq, married Princess Ashraf, the sister of the last shah of Iran, Reza
    Pahlavi, in 1944. They were divorced in 1959. Their only son, Prince Shariyar

Shafiq, born in 1945, was murdered in Paris on 7 December 1979, just after the Iranian Islamic revolution.

48   Jacob E. Smart (1909–2006) was an American Air Force general in charge of critical missions during the Second World War. He became famous when his plane was shot down and taken prisoner by the Germans in 1944. He was released a year later, and he then joined the war in Korea. In 1964, he became the deputy commander of the American forces in Europe. General Smart retired in 1966 and worked for NASA.

49   The Stuka was a dive-bomber built by Junkers and used by the Germans during the Second World War.

50   "Billy" Neil McLean (1918–86) was one of the main directors of the Special Operations Executive, which was set up during the war personally by Prime Minister Winston Churchill to coordinate the resistance and guerrilla movements in countries occupied by the Germans. His first post was Palestine, and from there he was sent to Ethiopia, where he organized the resistance against the Italian occupiers. After working in Cairo and in Istanbul he went to Albania, where after the war, he struggled to overthrow the Communist regime of Enver Hodja, but to no avail. After retiring from the army as a lieutenant colonel, he took part in the elections of 1954 and became an MP in the House of Commons, at the same time acting as an advisor to the Foreign Office, making contacts in various countries on their behalf. After the Egyptian revolution of 1952 he said that everything must be tried to overthrow Nasser, and during the 1956 Suez Crisis he played a significant role in the decision by Britain to send paratroopers to the Canal. He left politics in 1964, but continued to work in the Middle East on behalf of the Foreign Office.

51   Princess Shiwikar, the eldest daughter of Fahmi Pasha, who was the son of Ahmed Rifaat Pasha, one of the grandsons of Mohamed Ali Pasha and Nevcivan Hanım, was born in İstanbul in 1877 and died in Egypt in 1946. She married five times and had numerous lovers, and led an eventful life. Her first husband was Fuad, who later became king of Egypt, and her third husband was Mehmed Selim Bey, the son of Halil Paşa, one of the most prominent Turkish painters, and sixteen years her junior. Her last husband, İlhami Hüseyin Bey, was a young employee of a bank in Istanbul. She liked this young man, married him, and took him back to Egypt, where she managed to obtain the title of pasha for him from King Fuad. Princess Shiwikar kept her position in the palace protocol even after the advent of King Farouk. She remained close to the young king and maintained her title of Princess until she died. Her tomb, in accordance with her will, was made of marble in the shape of a large, untidy bed.

52   Princess Fawzia, known for her beauty and grace, was the eldest daughter of King Fuad and Queen Nazli. Born in 1921, she married Mohamed Reza Pahlavi in 1939 when he was the heir to the throne of Iran. She gave birth to her only child and the shah's eldest daughter, Princess Shahnaz, in 1940, and became Empress of Iran on 16 September 1941, when her husband ascended to the throne. She had a difficult life at the palace in Tehran due to constant tensions with the queen mother, Taj al-Muluk. In 1944, she traveled to Egypt to see her brother King Farouk and her family, and never returned to Tehran. She was divorced from the shah in 1945, and for years afterward the shah did not allow Fawzia to see their daughter Princess Shahnaz. In March 1949 Fawzia married İsmail Shirin (1919–74), an officer in the Egyptian army and son of an Egyptian princess. She had two children from this marriage. After Fawzia, the shah married Soraya Esfandiary, and then Farah Diba. Princess Fawzia died in Alexandria on 2 July 2013.

53   "The visa requested by Neslishah, the wife of the second-in-line to the throne of Egypt Prince Abdel Moneim and a member of the Ottoman family, can be extended to three months after her fifteen-day visa has been issued." Archives of the Prime Ministry of the Republic, 3 April 1947, File no. 24331, Folder code: 30..10.0.0, Place 203.391..25.

54   Sabahaddin Bey was Seniha Sultan's eldest son; he was not a prince but a sultanzade, yet he used the title of Prince.

55   Fahriye Hanım was a member of the Circassian Brav family and the foster sister of Ulviye Sultan, Sultan Vahideddin's eldest daughter and Neslishah's aunt. She grew up in Sultan Vahideddin's mansion in Çengelköy, and was Sabiha Sultan's closest friend. Later she moved to Egypt with her family, where she married Abd al-Hamid bin Mohamed Abdul Aziz, a *sherif* (a descendent of the Prophet). In 1929 she had a daughter named Dina. Dina studied English literature at Cambridge, and in 1955 married King Hussein of Jordan. Their marriage lasted only two years, and she was divorced in 1957. Later she married Salah Tamari a leading member of the PLO. When he was taken prisoner by the Israelis she struggled to have him released, and she wrote a book about the experience called *Duet for Freedom*, which was published in 1988.

56   A few days after her return to Istanbul, Sabiha Sultan wrote in her diary under the title "My first arrival in Istanbul":

26 August 1952: We flew from Orly at 9 in the morning. We arrived in Milan at 11:30. At 7:25 in the evening (French time), 6:25 Turkish time, we arrived in Istanbul. Several of my friends who went to the airport arrived late because of the time difference, and after going all the way to the airport and asking around they finally came to the apartment where I was staying.

Princess Wijdan [Egyptian princess], Hümeyra [Hümeyra Özbaş, daughter of her older sister Ulviye Sultan], Mahpeyker [eldest daughter of Enver Paşa and Naciye Sultan], Keramet Bey [secretary of the caliph in Istanbul], Ali Bey [Ali Haydar Germiyanoğlu, second husband of Ulviye Sultan], Fahri Şirin [cousin of İsmail Şirin, the second husband of Princess Fawzia of Egypt], Belkıs Hanım [Belkıs Ratib], Fevziye Hanım [wife of Fahreddin Rumbeyoğlu, one of the "List of 150"], Zehra Altınız [the *kalfa* to whom she had entrusted the deed of Vahideddin's mansion in Çengelköy], and others were waiting for me at the airport. No one recognized me at customs, and as they began the usual formalities they asked for my passport. When they saw my name, they just said, "Welcome," and let me go without opening my suitcases.

Ceyda [Ceyda Ratib] was waiting for me, but somehow we did not meet, and Mahpeyker invited me to stay in her apartment in Beyoğlu. We spent the night together with Princess Wijdan. The following day Naime [Naime Sultan, granddaughter of Cemile Sultan the daughter of Sultan Abdülmecid] came to see me and invited me to lunch. There I saw Mevhibe Hanım [granddaughter of Cemile Sultan] and Şerif Muhiddin Bey [well-known lute player, son of Sherif of Mecca Ali Haydar Pasha and husband of Turkish singer Safiye Ayla]. I had called them from Naime's house, and they came immediately. At five o'clock in the afternoon, I went to Ceyda together with Hümeyra.

Ali Bey, İsmail Ratib, and Fahreddin Bey [Fahreddin Rumbeyoğlu] were there waiting for me. Ekrem Rüşdü, who had previously asked me for an appointment, also came. Poor Ekrem, he also came late to the airport to welcome me like the others and not finding me he spent the whole evening going from house to house looking for me. Eventually, he called Mahpeyker and found me there. As I was exhausted that night, I asked him to meet me at Ceyda's house at five o'clock of the following day.

29 August. This morning Ekrem Rüşdü Bey came to drive me in his car to town. Last night Ziya Bey called. He will be coming today at seven.

31 August: Today is a religious holiday [Eid al-Adha]. I was not feeling well at lunchtime. Several people came to see me in the afternoon.

1 September: I spent the whole day in bed. Naciye Sultan, her mother, Kamil [Enver Paşa's younger brother and Naciya Sultan's second husband], Belkıs Ratib, and Hüseyin Siret came to see me.

57   The Cairo crisis was in the Turkish papers for weeks. One of the most read journalists of the time, Ref'î Cevad Ulunay, wrote an article on 7 January 1954 in the daily *Milliyet* under the title "Intellectual Clumsiness," in which he strongly criticizes Fuad Tugay for causing a diplomatic incident.

58   Princess Fazile later married Hayri Ürgüplü, in Paris on 10 December 1965.
      He was the son of Suad Hayri Ürgüplü (1903–81), Turkey's prime minister for
      seven months, and the grandson of Hayri Efendi, who was Shaykh al-Islam
      during the time of the Union and Progress Party. They had two sons, Ali Suad
      (b. 1967) and Selim (b. 1968).

      Thirty-six years after the Baghdad revolution of 1958, a strange claim
      was made. An Iraqi by the name of Sataa al-Jibury came to Turkey in August
      1993 and went around the newspapers claiming to be the son of King Faisal II
      and Princess Fazile, and therefore the heir to the throne of Iraq.

      The members of the family and friends who were still alive and had been
      close to the king and the princess when they were engaged declared that this
      assertion had no foundation.

      Al-Jibury's claim made the front page of a weekly magazine, and various
      newspapers reported the article from the magazine. In response, a "Mutual
      Declaration of the Ottoman Family and of Prince Mohamed Ali Ibrahim of
      the Royal Egyptian Dynasty" was released, refuting the claim as a pack of lies:

      "The information that appeared on the front page of a magazine issued
      on 15 August 1993 with the headline 'The Tragic Story of the Prince of
      Baghdad' is the product of the imagination. The Ottoman family and Prince
      Mohamed Ali of the royal Egyptian dynasty are compelled to make a joint
      declaration:

      "The article mentioned that Sataa al-Jibury, an Iraqi citizen claiming to
      be the son of the last king of Iraq Faisal II and Princess Fazile İbrahim of the
      Ottoman and Egyptian royal families, states that he was born when the king
      and the princess were engaged before the 1958 revolution.

      "Princess Fazile İbrahim, who the aforementioned Iraqi citizen pretends
      to be his mother, is the great-granddaughter of the last Ottoman sultan Vahid-
      eddin and the last caliph Abdülmecid on her maternal side of the family and
      the daughter of Prince Mohamed Ali Ibrahim, a member of the Egyptian royal
      family. In 1957, when the princess was only sixteen years old, she was officially
      engaged, and this engagement continued according to the rules of protocol
      until the assassination of the king during the Iraqi revolution of 1958.

      "Throughout their engagement the king and the princess met once in
      Paris at the family residence, twice in Cannes, once in Istanbul at the *yalı* of
      Abu Bakr, and twice when Princess Fazile went to Baghdad for the wedding
      preparations. During all these encounters, members of the family and ladies-
      in-waiting were at all time present, as per the customs and traditions of the
      two noble families. Therefore, the defamatory statements and the allegation
      that appeared in the papers are totally unfounded.

"After the murder of King Faisal II, Princess Fazile İbrahim married on 10 December 1965 Hayri Ürgüplü, the son of Suad Hayri Ürgüplü, a respected statesman, prime minister and president of the Turkish Senate. Princess Fazile had two sons, Ali Suad Ürgüplü and Selim Ürgüplü from this marriage and no other children whatsoever."

59   Ahmed Hussein, born in Cairo in 1911, was the most famous and influential lawyer of his time in Egypt, acting as the defense in some important political trials. He was also one of the most controversial names in Egyptian politics. As a student under the British occupation he became known for the slogan "Egypt is above everyone and everything." He believed that no language but Arabic should be spoken, that everything foreign should be hated, and that everyone should be ultranationalistic.

In October 1933 he established an organization named Masr al-Fatah ('Young Egypt'), which he then turned into a political party, and inside the party he created a group of young paramilitaries: they wore green shirts, and they were the first paramilitary group of a political party in Egypt. At one point he visited Germany, and he wrote a letter to Adolf Hitler, inviting him to become a Muslim.

What he embraced of Germany's National Socialist party was not nationalism but socialism. In articles and books he wrote he noted that he was against communism because of its rejection of religion, but he believed that Islam and socialism had much in common.

It is said that Gamal Abdel Nasser, Anwar Sadat, and some of the Free Officers of 1952 embraced the thoughts of Ahmed Hussein when they were young and joined Masr al-Fatah. After the 1952 revolution, his party and his group were disbanded, and in his old age he gave up his old beliefs and came closer to political Islam. He died in Cairo on 26 September 1982.

60   The name of Prince Farouk Street was changed to Sharia al-Geish (Army Street) in 1954.

61   Princess Marie-Louise Elvira Victoria Olga Saviç von Hessen, who friends called Tita, was a member of the Hesse dynasty that went back to the twelfth century. Born in Paris in 1921, she married Mürsel Saviç, a Turkish doctor, and moved to Turkey in 1953. She was a member of the Turkish national riding team and won several cups. She died on 14 January 1999 and was cremated in Switzerland according to her wish, her ashes scattered in the sea in Nice. After her death her husband, Dr Mürsel Saviç (1927–2009), married Neslishah's daughter İkbal.

Index